The econocracy

The *Manchester Capitalism* book series

General Editor

MICK MORAN

Manchester Capitalism is a series of short, accessible books that reframe the big issues of economic renewal, financial reform and political mobilisation in present-day capitalism. The books do so by directly tackling major policy issues and the assumptions that underpin the policy agenda of an unlearning state. The aim is to contribute towards the reframing of political choices that is necessary before we can ensure security in a responsible capitalism.

The first three books in the series cover the policy bias towards competition and markets, the British state's persistence with outsourcing and the development of public private partnership as an export product for the global south. Altogether these books make the argument that post-1979 structural reform promised the market and delivered an extractive, financialised capitalism that benefits elites while ordinary citizens suffer growing problems about the supply of foundational goods and services necessary to everyday welfare.

In parallel, the researchers at the Centre for Research on Socio Cultural Change have produced a series of public interest reports on mundane sectors which are freely downloadable from their website at cresc.ac.uk. These reports cover meat supply, railways, textiles and apparel and adult care. The Manchester Capitalism website gives an overview of the latest activity by the interdisciplinary team of researchers who have authored these books and reports.

The Manchester Capitalism title reflects our conviction that there is much distributed intelligence in our economy and society outside the metropolitan centres of elite decision making. We write to inform and empower that force which Victorian Britain recognised as agenda-setting, provincial radicalism and which we can promote in the twenty-first century through an informed citizenry. As *The econocracy* argues, citizens need knowledge and cannot delegate decisions to experts.

Previous titles:
Licensed larceny: Infrastructure, financial extraction and the Global South Nicholas Hildyard
The end of the experiment? Bowman et al.
What a waste: Outsourcing and how it goes wrong Bowman et al.

Praise for *The econocracy*

Economics has become the organising principle, the reigning ideology, and even the new religion of our time. And this body of knowledge is controlled by a selective priesthood trained in a very particular type of economics – that is, neoclassical economics. In this penetrating analysis, based on very sophisticated theoretical reflections and highly original empirical work, the authors show how the rule by this priesthood and its disciples is strangling our economies and societies and how we can change this situation. It is a damning indictment for the economics profession that it has taken young people barely out of university to provide this analysis. Utterly compelling and sobering.
Ha-Joon Chang, Reader in Political Economy of Development at the University of Cambridge and author of *Economics: The User's Guide*

A rousing wake-up call to the economics profession to re-think its mission in society, from a collective of dissident graduate students. Their double argument is that the 'econocracy' of economists and economic institutions which has taken charge of our future is not fit for purpose, and, in any case, it contradicts the idea of democratic control. So the problem has to be tackled at both ends: creating a different kind of economics, and restoring the accountability of the experts to the citizens. The huge nature of the challenge does not daunt this enterprising group, whose technically assured, well-argued, and informative book must be read as a manifesto of what they hope will grow into a new social reform movement.
Lord Robert Skidelsky, Professor Emeritus of Political Economy at Warwick University and Fellow of the British Academy in History and Economics

If war is too important to be left to the generals, so is the economy too important to be left to narrowly trained economists. Yet, as this book shows, such economists are precisely what we are getting from our leading universities. Given the role economists play in our society, we need them to be much more than adepts in manipulating equations based on unrealistic assumptions. This book demonstrates just why that matters and offers thought-provoking ideas on how to go about it.
Martin Wolf, Associate Editor and Chief Economics Commentator at the *Financial Times*

An interesting and highly pertinent book.
Noam Chomsky

Economics, as practised in university economics departments, regurgitated by policy makers, and summarised in the mainstream media, has become a form of propaganda. This superb book explains how dangerous ideology is hidden inside a mathematical wrapper; controversial policies are presented as 'proven' by the models of economic 'science'. This book is essential reading for anyone who wants to know about the con – that includes everyone concerned with the future of democracy.
Jonathan Aldred, Director of Studies in Economics at Emmanuel College, Cambridge and author of *The Sceptical Economist*

The econocracy explains, supported by excellent research, how one branch of economics has captured the academy and excluded the public from debate about how the economy is organised, leaving this branch almost the only source of policy advice. It is written by British members of Rethinking Economics, the international organisation of students and recent graduates dissatisfied with their curriculum. They have produced a work of high quality and national importance. Read this book.
Victoria Chick, economist and founder of the Post Keynesian Economics Study Group

This book is for the many students who want to study economics because they want to help society solve its problems: a critical introduction to contemporary economics, written by a new, post-2008 generation of economists. Aspiring economists will need to read this book early, in time to protect themselves from indoctrination into a neoclassical economics firmly associated with an economistic political-ideological worldview. To understand the real world, and not just what standard economics calls 'the economy', future economists must learn to see through and escape from a conceptual construction destined to replace democracy with 'econocracy', turning government over to a publicly unaccountable technocratic elite. There is no better vaccination against the economistic disease than this immensely readable book.
Wolfgang Streeck, Emeritus Director at the Max Planck Institute for the Study of Societies and author of *Buying Time: The Delayed Crisis of Democratic Capitalism*

The economics profession has failed disastrously in recent decades, first by failing to warn of the dangers of a bloated and poorly regulated financial sector and then through an obsession with mathematically refined, but practically useless, modelling exercises. Yet neither the confidence with which economists make pronouncements about 'the economy', nor the way in which economics is taught in universities has undergone any significant change. This book addresses these questions with a call for an economics addressed to citizens and a pluralist approach to economics education. It should be read not only by those seeking to understand how policies driven by the alleged needs of 'the economy' have failed, but also by economists who want to understand why their pronouncements are increasingly regarded with distrust and disdain.
John Quiggin, Australian Laureate Fellow in Economics at the University of Queensland

In this challenging new book, Joe Earle, Cahal Moran and Zach Ward-Perkins argue, not against expertise as such, but in favour of a new kind of economic expert: one who is better able to engage both with real problems and with 'economic citizens'. As befits members of the international economics student movement Rethinking Economics, they set out an agenda for improved education of economics students, but also of economic citizens. Their arguments are backed up by new evidence of the current situation for economics students as well as by historical analysis of the discipline. The book itself is an exemplar of the kind of expertise they advocate, being problem-oriented and accessible to a wide audience, and drawing on careful informed argument. The book should be required reading for anyone concerned about the future of economics.
Sheila Dow, Emeritus Professor of Economics at the University of Stirling

According to Sir Nicholas Macpherson, outgoing Permanent Secretary of the UK Treasury, economists were guilty of a 'monumental collective intellectual error' in failing to predict, or prevent the Great Financial Crisis of 2007–09 (*FT* 15 April 2016). The profession's repeated failures contrasts with the achievements of e.g. aerospace engineers and scientists, who have on the whole managed to protect society from aircraft failure. For the sake of our future economic security, it is vital to open up the economics profession to both new, but also old, untried economic theories and policies. That is why this book is so welcome. It will play a vital part in expanding pluralism in economics in our universities, and hopefully regenerate the profession from within.

Ann Pettifor, economist and Director of Policy Research in Macroeconomics (PRIME)

Is economics too important to be left to the economists? The authors marshal a powerful case against economics as it often is, and set out a positive vision of economics as it might be, a public interest economics which enables citizens to understand the economy better and participate more fully in the decisions which affect all our futures. An important and timely book.

Andrew Gamble, Professor of Politics at the University of Cambridge and Joint Editor of *New Political Economy* **and the** *Political Quarterly*

Economics is a subject of importance to all citizens, yet many economists have been unwilling to engage in the public debate made essential by the financial crisis and its consequences. This book is a provocative but welcome contribution to the democratic conversation that has to take place about the role of economics in public policy, and the need for the subject to be accessible to everyone. Many economists will not agree with all of the book's analysis but they certainly should not ignore it.

Diane Coyle, Visiting Professor at the University of Manchester's Institute for Political and Economic Governance and Managing Director of Enlightenment Economics

It is a scandal that the enormously important subject of economics is usually taught in British universities around a rigid, narrow, orthodox syllabus which excludes counter-cultural thinking. The 2008 financial crisis was a wake-up call for the profession, which has been dismally slow to respond. This book is badly needed, looking at academic economics afresh: clear, well-written, well-researched, non-doctrinaire. It makes the case for 'pluralistic' economics to address such questions as financial instability and climate change. Every economist and citizen should get a copy.

Vince Cable, former Secretary of State for Business, Innovation and Skills

Historians, one day, will study the mesmeric capacity of economic doctrine to override the public's faculty of rational judgement in favour of an unquestioning faith in the experts, in the face of the overwhelming evidence that they have got absolutely everything completely wrong. This research will engender the same sense of disbelief, I am convinced, that we feel today for the high mediaeval dogma that the sun must go around the earth because God ordained it so. This book will then be recognised as a turning point.

It is an eloquent, quietly passionate, but above all knowledgeable statement of the simple fact that the emperor is naked, rounded off by a remarkably clear prescription for doing without tailors. Do not miss it.
Alan Freeman, Visiting Professor at London Metropolitan University and Research Fellow of Queensland University of Technology, Australia

The econocracy offers an antidote to a tragic state of affairs in social science. Over the last century, economics has increasingly abandoned its roots as a rich science of human action in order to become an esoteric discipline with little relevance to the real world. The global financial crisis of 2008 revealed this deeper crisis in the economics profession, which is especially evident in economics teaching. Yet while understanding economics has never been more important, in some ways the barriers to economics education have never been higher. This book provides students with an accessible discussion of the problems that face economics teaching, and the perils of allowing economics to be transformed from a vital source of knowledge about human society into an obscure, technocratic field reserved for a select few. It not only calls for a reassessment of contemporary economics education, but also for a fresh look at the relationship between economists and the public. It is thus a valuable first step towards encouraging a more realistic and relevant economics. Students and professors alike will find much to discuss and debate here.
Matthew McCaffrey, Lecturer in Enterprise at the University of Manchester and recipient of the 2010 Lawrence W. Fertig Prize in Austrian Economics

This superbly written and scholarly work makes a strong case for wresting control of economic and political dialogue back from the pseudo-profession of academic economists and returning it to the body politic. Its authors are student economists who, writing after the financial crisis that mainstream economists didn't see coming, have approached their topic with refreshing scepticism, and a wisdom far beyond their years. This is an excellent read that I strongly recommend.
Steve Keen, Head of the School Of Economics, History & Politics at Kingston University, London and author of *Debunking Economics*

Since the financial crisis of 2007–08, there has been an extraordinary amount of soul-searching by the economics profession. Many macroeconomists admit that their view of the world was flawed, that ignoring the financial sector was a fatal error and that the profession has become over-reliant on certain types of mathematical model. But too often, their solutions amount to tweaking the existing paradigm in the hopes that this will somehow make it work. In this book, an enterprising group of students expose the deep flaws in mainstream economic theory that have brought us to this pass. They show how the teaching of economics in universities reinforces the existing paradigm, discouraging challenge and innovation. And they propose a new approach to the teaching and learning of economics which would encourage independence of thought and be accessible to a wider group of people. From the current chaos and confusion, a new economic paradigm will eventually emerge. The young people now studying economics, or about to do so, will determine the shape of this new paradigm. Their studies need to equip them to develop the economics of the future, rather than reinforcing the ideas of the past. This book should be required reading for teachers and students of economics, and for anyone contemplating a career in economic policymaking.
Frances Coppola, finance, banking and economics commentator

The economics profession is in crisis, as crucial flaws in its core ideas have been exposed by the financial crisis of 2008, and by the deep economic malaise which has followed. While most economists remain in denial about the need for change, a global movement among graduate students has taken up the challenge of making economics relevant again for the real world. Importantly, these students aren't just complaining, but actively developing better ideas, collaborating widely with scientists in other fields, and engaging with politicians, business leaders and ordinary citizens to make economics less esoteric and ideological, and more practically useful in building a better society. *The econocracy* is their call to arms. Beautifully written and packed with wisdom, it is a book for anyone who cares about the future of our societies, beginning, I hope, with professional economists themselves. This may be the most important economics book of the decade.
Mark Buchanan, physicist, former editor of *Nature* and *New Scientist* and author of *Forecast: What Physics, Meteorology, and the Natural Sciences Can Teach Us about Economics*

The econocracy

The perils of leaving economics to the experts

Joe Earle, Cahal Moran and Zach Ward-Perkins

Manchester University Press

Published by Manchester University Press
Altrincham Street, Manchester M1 7JA
www.manchesteruniversitypress.co.uk

British Library Cataloguing-in-Publication Data
A catalogue record for this book is available from the British Library

Library of Congress Cataloging-in-Publication Data applied for

The publication of this book has been supported by the Friends Provident Charitable Foundation

Friends Provident Foundation is an independent grant-making charity working to support greater economic resilience through building knowledge and taking action at the strategic and local levels. It is particularly interested in supporting the development of economic and financial systems that are designed to include those who are most vulnerable to market failure.

FRIENDS
PROVIDENT
Foundation

Rethinking Economics

Rethinking Economics is an international network of students, citizens and professionals building a better economics in society and the classroom. Visit rethinkeconomics.org

ISBN 978 1526 11013 8   paperback

First published 2017

Typeset by Servis Filmsetting Ltd, Stockport, Cheshire
Printed in Great Britain by Bell and Bain Ltd, Glasgow

Contents

List of exhibits

Foreword

I am writing this Foreword in the immediate aftermath of the referendum in which the UK voted to leave the European Union. That vote by the general public came against the advice of professional economists, the vast majority of whom believed that the economic costs of exit would be high. If ever there were a battle between 'econocracy' and 'democracy', this was it. It is also pretty clear who won. Time alone will tell whether there was greater wisdom among crowds than among experts. But if nothing else, this episode lays bare the distance the economics profession needs to travel if it is to win heads, to say nothing of hearts.

Perhaps that should come as no surprise. The past few years have witnessed an economic and financial crisis as great as any in anyone's lifetime. It is a crisis whose aftershocks are still being felt, whose wounds are still weeping. Some of the enormous collateral damage from that crisis has been felt, not unreasonably, by the economics profession. Indeed, it would not be too much of an exaggeration to say that the financial crisis has spawned a crisis in economics and finance. At root, this was every bit as much an analytical crisis as an economic and financial one.

And this is not the first time. Much the same occurred after the Great Depression of the 1930s. Back then, catastrophic intellectual error gave rise to catastrophic policy error, with catastrophic economic consequences. This time's crisis may not have torn the economic and social fabric quite as violently as the one in the 1930s. But it was sourced in intellectual and policy errors every bit as great. It took Keynes's leadership to diagnose and remedy those mistakes after the Great Depression, establishing him as the most influential economist of the twentieth century. Crisis offered the opportunity of a great leap forward. Thus far at least, the present crisis has yet to spawn a Keynes for the twenty-first century. And nor have we witnessed any great leap forward analytically. Perhaps it is simply early days. Revolutions, especially analytical ones, take time to build and grow. Indeed, they tend to proceed obituary by obituary. New brooms are needed to sweep clean. That means that salvation for the economics profession probably lies not among existing academic and policymaking dinosaurs, like me, but among the new generation of students of the discipline.

That makes this book – written by students drawn to the economics profession by the crisis and then frustrated by the failings of that same profession to make sense of this very crisis – poignant and relevant. It is telling that the number of students applying to study economics has shot up over recent years. For them, crisis appears to have spelled opportunity every bit as much as threat: the opportunity for another great intellectual leap forward, to reshape twenty-first-century economic thinking as Keynes did in the twentieth. This is one of the silver linings from the dark cloud of the crisis. And no profession could ask for a better endowment.

But this endowment, if it is to renew and refresh the profession, needs to be invested wisely. That goes to the very heart of this book's critique. This critique goes beyond the narrowly technical – that the workhorse neoclassical model of the economy was found to be lame when it came to running a real crisis race. The deeper critique is that these models, and the technical language that accompanies them, have played a role in policy and in society that has been disproportionate in two senses. First, disproportionate relative to our state of knowledge. Existing economic frameworks have shouldered a policy weight that is simply too great for them to bear, given the degree of uncertainty and fragility that surrounds them. Second, disproportionate because these frameworks placed an excessive degree of policy power in the hands of the technocrats wielding them. This is what the authors call 'econocracy'. Their contention is that this econocracy has been both too *narrow* in its technical focus and too *broad* in its societal impact.

When assessing the potency of this critique, it is important to prise apart its trace elements. Part of the critique is technical. Mainstream economic models have sacrificed too much realism at the altar of mathematical purity. Their various simplifying assumptions have served aesthetic rather than practical ends. As a profession, economics has become too much of a methodological monoculture. And that lack of intellectual diversity cost the profession dear when the single crop failed spectacularly during the crisis. This monoculture, it is argued, has also narrowed the economics curriculum in universities. This has generated an ever greater focus on the mathematical gymnastics of optimising models and too little focus on the everyday aerobics of how the economy functions. Accompanying this has been neglect of disciplines that abut and illuminate economics: economic history, moral philosophy, money and banking, radical uncertainty, non-rational expectations. In short, neglect of the very things that make economics interesting and economies important.

My personal view is that this is a fair cop. Indeed, I think this particular element of the critique is no longer a source of great controversy, except within some academic cliques. And since the crisis, although progress has not been rapid, plenty has been made. Some of the impetus for change has come from a global network of universities, gathered together under the umbrella of Rethinking Economics. I have myself been a supporter of student efforts to widen and deepen the curriculum and wrote (another!) foreword for the 2014 report on curriculum reform by students at the University of Manchester. But there is progress, too, within academe. Notable here have been the efforts of Wendy Carlin at University College London and colleagues, who together have drawn up a new interactive economics curriculum called CORE. This is an attempt to adapt and augment the existing macro-economic toolkit to better match real-world features, features all-too-apparent during the financial crisis. It is a notable achievement, one that appears to be gathering momentum and that deserves support.

A second element of the critique in this book, one which really flows from the first, is that the language used by economists has served as a barrier to entry, certainly for members of the general public. Indeed, it could be argued this has been a deliberately erected barrier. If so, economics and finance are hardly exceptions in this respect. Every profession has its own lexicon, in part at least intended as a barrier to entry. Language is one way in which experts can preserve the rents associated with their subject-specific human capital. So, if every subject is guilty as charged, why pick on economics? The argument is that economics is, in a way, a victim of its own success. Economic principles and frameworks have found their way into every nook and cranny of public debate and discourse. They are the frame through which virtually all public policy debates are viewed these days. If economics is affecting so many in society in so many different ways, it may have a particular and peculiar responsibility to be clear and intelligible to all those it serves.

I believe this critique has considerable force. As one example, I have looked at the linguistic complexity of the Bank of England's own communications, including my own speeches. These rank well above the levels of a broadsheet newspaper, and way beyond the levels of a tabloid. In other words, the vast majority of the Bank's communications are lost on the vast majority of the public. The various reports into the economic costs of the UK leaving the EU most likely fell at the same hurdle. They are written, in the main, by the elite for the elite. Yet there is no inherent tension between technical prowess and simple communication. There are few activities more technically complex than weather forecasting. This involves taking huge volumes of data and processing it via highly complex models using heavy-duty information technology in close to real time. Yet the outputs from this process need to be readily accessible to everyone, using simple words and graphics. Meteorologists ensure they are. Economists often at present lack those same skills.

It would be easy to suggest that redemption lies in improved programmes of public understanding of economics. And doubtless they have their part to play. But just as important will be programmes that improve *economists'* understanding of the *public*. That may include, for example, seeking ways to involve the profession in practical projects within companies or charities, putting their skills to work in the front line in real-world situations. As one example, the charity I helped co-found, *Pro Bono Economics*, does just that.

The third and final element of the critique is the link from economics to politics, from the technical to the social. The contention here is that unelected technocrats, armed only with an economics degree and an ability to differentiate quadratics, are being left to make what are essentially social choices. In other words, political choices are being handed over inadvertently to faceless technocrats, thereby giving rise to a democratic deficit. One example often quoted, one close to my own heart, is Quantitative Easing or QE by central banks. This is intended, by design, to inflate asset prices. Yet these wealth gains do not accrue equally. They are skewed towards the already wealthy. QE is thus a distributional act, albeit an inadvertent one, yet carried out by unelected technocrats. Some of the same critique could be aimed at low levels of interest rates, which cause a distributional skew towards borrowers and away from savers.

We need to place these arguments in context here. The fact is that pretty much every public policy act, central bank or otherwise, has distributional consequences. By definition, public policy shifts resources between people at a point in time or between generations over time. As monetary policy shifts resources between savers and borrowers, fiscal policy shifts them between rich and poor, between this generation and the next. They all aim to lift as many boats as possible. But rarely, if ever, are they able to lift all boats by the same amount.

The inability to do this does not, however, imply that all policy decisions should lie in the hands of politicians or that they should be delegated to the public through referenda. Expertise, exercised at arms-length from the political process, has for me a key role to play in making decisions that are in the long-term interests of society, unconstrained by political cycles and populist surges. That is why operational independence in the setting of interest rates is seen, pretty much universally, as best practice among central banks.

Technocratic institutions have an important role in the policy infrastructure. That is why they have been found historically to be a key, sometimes the key, ingredient for national success. When these acts of delegated policy authority do occur, however, they come with a heavy responsibility for the unelected technocrats put in charge. These technocrats, including myself, are there by the grace of God – or, failing that, a Parliamentary Committee. This means that technocratic institutions require the continuous consent, not just of Parliament, but of the wider public. Big steps forward have been take on that front over the past couple of decades at public institutions, including at the Bank of England. Those institutions have been subject to degrees of public scrutiny previously unimaginable, through reports, minutes, transcripts, speeches, parliamentary appearances and the like. This is little short of a revolution in transparency and accountability. And it has been essential.

But could and should more be done to improve accountability and transparency, in particular to the general public? It must. Public trust in public institutions has been dented, in some cases significantly, by the crisis. Repairing that dent will take more than a quick respray of the bodywork. It will require those institutions to seek new and wider ways of engaging, explaining and educating about their actions and intentions. As importantly, it will require new and wider means of listening to, and learning from, societal stakeholders.

I do not know whether we live in an econocracy, much less whether this is good or bad news for society. What I do know is that society is likely to be the loser if technical expertise and knowledge somehow become distrusted or ignored. Great humility about that expertise, and a desire to make it accessible to a wider set of societal stakeholders than ever previously, would be useful steps towards avoiding that outcome. This book encourages us to take those steps. For economists, they would be giant ones.

Andrew Haldane
Chief Economist at the Bank of England
July 2016

Acknowledgements

This book is an attempt to express the arguments of a movement of economics students around the world; we would therefore first like to thank members of that student movement and to recognise all the hard work done by students around the world in campaigning for better economics education. We have attempted here to articulate their worries and frustrations about the current state of modern economics; the hard part was building the movement that allowed that message to be expressed in the first place.

We would also like to thank some people in particular for input into this process. Special thanks goes to Louis James for invaluable help in some of the research for this project and to Cleo Chevalier for helping us to present that research lucidly. The copy-editing of Gail Matthews is to be credited for what we hope is a coherent piece of writing; any problems that remain are our own fault entirely. We would also like to thank Will Horwitz, Gemma Wearing, Emma Hamilton, Yuan Yang, Rafe Martyn, Ben Glover, Andrew McGettigan, Victoria Chick, Ha-Joon Chang, Daniel Chandler, Jonathan Aldred, Claire Jones, Cameron Murray and Philip Pilkington for providing such detailed and constructive feedback. That long list is still too short to fully summarise everyone who has had input into this book and we thank everyone who has contributed to the process. Thanks also goes to Diane Coyle, Martin Wolf, Diane Elson, Pat Devine, Anne Booth and all the others who so kindly agreed to be interviewed (some will remain anonymous), and to Aashish Velkar for responding to our call for a historian's opinion in Chapter 4. We would also like to thank all the staff at Rethinking Economics for their continued fantastic work and Diana García López, Kiryl Zach, Olivia Wills, Severin Reissl, Isaac Stovell and Eleanor Baggaley Simpson for all their help with research for this book. Andy Haldane deserves huge thanks for agreeing to write the foreword for this book and for his support of the student movement more broadly. He is the kind of economist we would be proud to be.

The publication of this book would not have happened without the Friends Provident Foundation and their generous support of Rethinking Economics, and we would like to extend particular thanks to Andrew Thompson for his personal support. We would also like to thank everyone at Manchester University Press who has worked to make this book a reality, rather than a just a jumbled assortment of thoughts in our heads.

Finally we would like to extend thanks to two groups of people. Firstly to the editors of this series, Karel Williams and Mick Moran, for having belief in us and for cultivating and nurturing many of the ideas contained within the book (and also for introducing us to the work of James Scott, who deserves a mention of his own for his influence on our thinking). Lastly we would like to thank our friends and family, and in particular Andrew, Jessie, Ruby, Rachel, Richard, Ben, Bryan and Kate for their continued support and faith in us.

Introduction

The perils of leaving economics
to the experts

Each generation doubtless feels called upon to reform the world. Mine
knows that it will not reform it, but its task is perhaps even greater. It
consists in preventing the world from destroying itself.

Albert Camus[1]

The authors of this book are of the generation that came of age in
the maelstrom of the 2008 global financial crisis. It was a crisis that
came as if from nowhere, interrupting our teenage years and sending
shockwaves reverberating around the world. On the news we saw
worry and confusion about debt overhangs, credit default swaps and
sub-prime mortgages. It was a first glimpse for us into a whole new
world and a strange rite of passage.

These experiences made it increasingly clear that economics was at
the heart of the society we were growing up in: the driving instructor
who lost his house and then his marriage when interest rates spiked
following Black Wednesday; our teachers hammering home the need
to get qualifications valued by the job market; and the constant
sparring over economic credibility in politics. The economy made its
presence felt almost everywhere.

The centrality of the economy in the world sat uncomfortably
with the apparent unease many of our friends and family felt talking
about it. We can each remember numerous occasions on which
conversations have run dry when they have reached economics.
Someone asks 'Who do we owe all the money to?' or states 'We can't
do that because it will ruin the economy.' There is a silence, shrugs
all round and the conversation moves swiftly on.

A few people did not seem to have this hesitation. Economists,
politicians, journalists and policymakers regularly appeared in the
media giving opinions about the health of the economy and predicting how this event or that policy would affect it. These men (and it
is mostly men) were confident and authoritative and their opinions
were respected. They conversed with each other using jargon, graphs

and statistics which made them difficult to understand. We felt that to understand and shape the world we needed to speak their language and that's how we all ended up studying economics in the same year at the University of Manchester in 2011.

After that it felt like we had swapped sides. Now, when discussion turns to the political issues of the day and someone launches into their opinion, often they finish by looking over at us, as if to say, 'Does that all make sense, you know, *economically* speaking?' Sometimes, it's even more explicit – 'You're an economist, what do you think?' As economics students we have somehow ended up with a strange authority to judge the merits of political arguments.

These situations leave us feeling uncomfortable. Having graduated now we are all keenly aware that our economics education has not equipped us with the knowledge or skills to justify any authority we are given. In fact we were so frustrated with how little our education was helping us understand the world that midway through our second year at university we began a campaign to reform economics education. While we were memorising and regurgitating abstract economic models for multiple choice exams, the Eurozone crisis was at its peak, with Greece and Italy on the brink of disaster. This wasn't mentioned in our lectures and what we were learning didn't seem to have any relevance to understanding it. The elephant in the room was hard to ignore.

This was in early 2013. Little did we know it but other students were starting similar campaigns across the world and in time we linked up with them in a network called Rethinking Economics. Amazingly, what united us across different continents and languages was the shared feeling that there was a deep malaise at the heart of economics and that as a result we were being sold short as students and as citizens. While we were supposed to be on the road to becoming economists, we could also see economics with the eyes of outsiders. We saw the ramifications of this flawed education stretched far beyond the confines of university lecture theatres. We became aware that a degree in economics was a gateway to many important positions in society, whether it prepared you for them properly or not.

From this vantage point we can see that all those people who feel locked out of economics have an important point. When someone says 'I just don't understand economics' or 'economics is not for me' they are highlighting one of the defining features of society in the modern world. We have coined the term econocracy to describe the kind of political system that has spread across much of the world today. An econocracy has all the formal institutions of a representative democracy – like political parties and regular elections – but the goals politics seeks to achieve are defined in narrow economic terms and decisions are made without significant public oversight. Of course some areas of politics, like war and national security, aren't justified in terms of their effect on the economy, but the overall trend of reducing politics to economics is clear.

It is estimated that there are about 7,000 languages in the world. The language of economics is one of the newest and least well known, but it is rapidly becoming one of the most important. The result is that citizens increasingly live in a world that they cannot shape. Without being able to speak economics it is hard to have a meaningful voice in how the economy or political system is run. We are in a very real way disconnected from important political institutions and processes, and struggle to hold experts and politicians accountable. It seems that many people have this feeling to some extent. In a poll we did with YouGov we asked 1,696 respondents their view of how politicians and the media talk about economics – only 12 per cent said it was done in an accessible way that made it easy to understand.[2]

As the economy has become central to politics and policymaking, economics has become highly influential but it has also become highly technical. In this world economics is not for most people and little effort is made to discuss it in such a way that non-experts can join in. This leads to it being seen as a technical subject not a political one, and as a result democratic culture and debate are undermined. Such a democratic deficit leads to a system where some people have economic authority without public oversight. Every year 10,000 economics students graduate and go on to become regulators, civil servants, consultants, journalists and traditional economists. These people are society's economic experts and we rely on them to manage the economy on our behalf. Currently they are being trained (not educated) to speak a language no one else can understand and to slot in unquestioningly to a system in which they have considerable authority while citizens do not. They are imbued with a confidence that it is possible to have the knowledge and tools to understand, measure and manage the economy without input from the public.

And yet the problems of economics education mean that many of the most important issues facing the world today, such as environmental catastrophe, soaring inequality and financial crises, are either absent from most syllabuses or taught in a way that grossly oversimplifies their depth and complexity. The result of this education is that we, as the next generation of economic experts, are grossly underprepared to use effectively or responsibly the power we are given.

Economics has been labelled 'the dismal science' and has developed a jargon so dense it even confuses economists. But at its core economics is really just the story of seven billion people's individual and collective choices. We are all embedded in the economy: when we work we contribute to production and when we buy things we contribute to consumption. When we're born, educated, unemployed and ill the cost is recorded in government spending. We rely on the economy, whether through income or wealth, to survive, and the behaviour of the economy depends on our decisions.

It is during times of crisis – when individuals, families, classes and whole sections of society are torn up and reconfigured – that it becomes clear just how interconnected our individual circumstances are with events in the wider economy. Whether we want to or not, we cannot escape the power of economics. The financial crisis of 2008 is the most obvious recent example, and John Lanchester expressed it perfectly when he wrote:

> There's a huge gap between the people who understand money and economics and the rest of us. Some of the gap was created deliberately, with the use of secrecy and obfuscation; but more of it, I think, is to do with the fact that it was just easier that way, easier for both sides. The money people didn't have to explain what they were up to, and got to write their own rules, and did very well out of the arrangement; and as for the rest of us, the brilliant thing was we never had to think about economics. For a long time, that felt like a win-win. But it doesn't any longer.[3]

Economics is for everyone precisely because it affects everyone. It is therefore too important to be left to the experts.

The gap between experts and citizens has not been created on purpose. Economic experts are not part of a shadowy cabal running society behind the scenes. Instead, the state we are in is the result of a particular set of historical circumstances. In this book we show how the history of economics as a discipline, the political events of the twentieth century and reforms to higher education have combined to create a world where economic decision making is delegated to experts who are not fit for purpose. This book is not about blaming anyone; it is about recognising the situation we find ourselves in and all taking responsibility to address it.

In this book we open up the discipline of academic economics to scrutiny, criticising it strongly at times. However, we also recognise that the discipline has much to offer and is a vital part of the change we want to see. We believe that it is important for people to know more about how economic experts think about the world, how their tools do (and do not) work and where their expertise is limited. By understanding better the knowledge that underpins our societal understanding of the economy, citizens can begin to engage with experts and politicians as equals, scrutinising their economic arguments and holding them accountable.

Most importantly we set out a positive vision for how academic economics could become a bridge, not a barrier, to increasing public participation in economic discussion and decision making. At Rethinking Economics our aims are to reform economics education so that tomorrow's experts are better equipped to understand the economy and engage with society. We are also trying to democratise economics because we believe that at its core economics should be a public discussion about how to organise society. There is an important role for experts here, but this role is as a humble advisor not a detached authority figure.

Albert Camus's generation had to prevent 'the world from destroying itself' in a nuclear war. Our generation has a choice of existential threats from financial meltdown to global warming and food and energy insecurity. To prevent these catastrophes and build sustainable, stable and prosperous societies our generation must have the ability to reimagine the economy. And to be able to do that it must reclaim economics from the experts, transforming it from a technical discipline into a public dialogue.

Rethinking Economics

The authors of this book are all active members of Rethinking Economics (RE). At the time of writing RE consisted of over 40 groups in 13 countries. This book is our interpretation of the history and arguments of the student movement to reform economics and features the voices of students from all over the world. However, we could not hope to speak on behalf of the movement in its entirety. Some members of RE will feel that our arguments are too bold while others will want them to go further.

Our movement calls for more openness, diversity, engagement and reflection in economics and so it has a place for all of these views. We hope that this book reflects those principles and in doing so is part of the change we want to see. Thank you for reading this book and not leaving economics to the experts! If you want to know more about Rethinking Economics or get involved all the relevant information is available at: http://www.rethinkeconomics.org/.

Notes

1 Albert Camus, speech at the Nobel Banquet at the City Hall in Stockholm, 10 December 1957. Available at: http://www.nobelprize.org/nobel_prizes/literature/laureates/1957/camus-speech.html (accessed 16 May 2016).
2 For full poll results see: https://d25d2506sfb94s.cloudfront.net/cumulus_uploads/document/5tw8cdop65/RethinkingEconomicsResults_160229_Media&Economics_w.pdf (accessed 27 April 2016).
3 John Lanchester, *How to Speak Money*, London: Faber & Faber, 2015, xiii–xiv.

Chapter 1

Econocracy

econocracy (e·con·oc·ra·cy) *n. A society in which political goals are defined in terms of their effect on the economy, which is believed to be a distinct system with its own logic that requires experts to manage it.*

Living in an econocracy

The existence of econocracy is apparent in everyday language. It is commonplace for the media to talk about 'the economy' as an entity in itself, and how something will be 'good for the economy' or 'bad for the economy'. The economy can speed up, slow down, improve, decline, crash or recover, but no matter what it does it must remain at the centre of political attention. Politicians nowadays must construct narratives based around the importance of the economy. An iconic example of this was when the campaign team of former US President Bill Clinton pinned up a sign in their headquarters that read 'The Economy, Stupid!' to keep the campaign on message. In the UK, Prime Minister David Cameron gave a speech shortly after his election in 2010 addressing 'the first priority of this government: transforming our economy'.[1] Similarly, the Labour Shadow Chancellor, John McDonnell, made a highly publicised move to establish an Economic Advisory Committee in 2015, which included some of the world's most prominent economists, in order to establish his economic credibility.[2]

It is unheard of for a political party to win an election without being seen as economically credible. In the build-up to the UK's 2015 general election the economy was the most discussed issue in the news apart from the election itself.[3] Politicians and commentators try to dismiss their opponents' policies as being 'good politics; bad economics',[4] claiming that these policies contradict economic theory or would have unintended consequences for the economy. The label of 'economic irresponsibility' is hurled like a grenade to discredit one's political opponents.

Econocracy has its own rituals and traditions. Every quarter the Office for National Statistics publishes its official Gross Domestic Product (GDP) estimates which measure the money value of the goods and services produced in the economy over the previous quarter. GDP is the central statistic by which the economy is judged. For a few days before and after publication the national media is full of economic experts poring over productivity, growth rates, changes to trade, political events and the confidence of markets. From this they can offer their diagnosis on the economy and predictions for the future.

As a consequence of this focus, increasingly diverse areas of life now justify their existence in terms of their contribution to the economy. One famous children's charity justified a campaign to encourage fathers to read to their children on the basis that improving literacy would increase GDP by 1.5 per cent by 2020.[5] In 2014 the Organisation for Economic Co-operation and Development (OECD), a prominent economic institution, highlighted that mental health issues cost the UK around £70 billion every year – roughly 4.5 per cent of GDP – in lost productivity at work, benefit payments and healthcare expenditure.[6] Even the existence of the monarchy is often justified in terms of its beneficial effect on the economy.[7]

The Arts Council now refers to the 'arts economy' and publishes regular reports highlighting the value of the arts to the economy. The most recent report highlighted that the industry generates an increasing amount of turnover and that for every pound spent on arts and culture, an additional £1.06 is generated in the economy.[8] The British Library also feels the need to justify its activities by claiming that for every pound in public funding it receives, £4.40 is created.[9] It's surprising that no one (to our knowledge) has yet worked out the value of Shakespeare to the economy.

The econocracy extends beyond a fixation with the economy's success. It is built on a particular vision of the economy that over time has been bought into by politicians, businesspeople and the general public. Within an econocracy, economic discussion and decision making has become a technocratic rather than a political or social process. We increasingly view the economy as something separate from wider society and, in many cases, outside the sphere of democratic debate. The philosophy of econocracy is to leave decisions about the economy to those who supposedly know best.

The philosophy of econocracy

In this world economics as an academic discipline has found itself with a unique position and will be a central part of the story we tell. Academic economists in universities are responsible for training the experts who play a central role in an econocracy. Economic knowledge gives the experts who hold it claims to know how the economy works and therefore to shape our collective views about its health, design policies to improve it and pass judgement on the economic competence of businesses, political parties and whole nations. Academic economics increasingly provides a framework with which to do this.

Economic logic does not prescribe a fixed set of views – one can find economists arguing about a variety of political issues – but it defines social goals, how political decisions are made and the terms on which issues are debated. There are also a number of political issues on which nearly all economists agree.[10] We argue that this dominance in society limits collective thinking because it is based on a narrow conception of 'economics'. It also undermines political culture because it turns many political debates into purely 'economic' questions to be answered by experts.

Economists generally perceive their role in society as a technical one, providing neutral and scientific advice on policy rather than engaging in politics directly. The widespread acceptance of this belief is a key feature of an econocracy. In this section we show how the technical language and tools of economics obscure political judgements and subtly redefine the goals of political problems, in turn excluding the public and other important stakeholders from the policy process.[11] Moreover, we show how ideas from economics have actively shaped society in new and unprecedented ways.

One prominent example of how technical calculations hide political judgements is cost–benefit analysis (CBA), which weighs up policies by estimating the money gained and lost in different areas of society as a result of the policy, then calculates the impact in monetary terms, defined as benefits minus costs. If the benefits are higher than the costs then the monetary value is positive and the policy is a net gain for society; if the costs are higher than the benefits then the value is negative and the policy is a net loss. CBA is used to address a wide range of important issues ranging from environmental damage to new infrastructure projects and buying new drugs for the NHS.[12]

CBA is illuminating because it highlights two key features of an econocracy. Firstly, it takes what are often hugely complex social problems and reduces them to figures, giving policymakers an easy, digestible way of seeing the problem. The use of CBA throughout government illustrates the core assumption that the economy is knowable (to the point of precise measurement) by experts, and that everything can be assigned a monetary value that reflects its value to society. Secondly, the decision rule for CBA doesn't appear to require political judgement because it is a simple calculation: if the benefits of a policy outweigh the costs, it should be done. The implication is that economic policy can be carried out neutrally by technocrats, removing the need for messy political debate.

Economists would argue that tools like CBA are simply frame-works for trying to think rigorously about the pros and cons of a certain policy, and that they often include non-economic aspects of a problem. However, methods for attaching money valuations to such a broad range of costs and benefits always involve choices, value judge-ments and assumptions that are inherently political in nature. Buying drugs for the NHS requires assigning a monetary value to the extra years someone will live as a result of the treatment; CBA as applied to climate change requires quantifying possible future environmental disasters. We shall return to some of the problems with this approach in Chapter 3, but suffice to say that there is rarely a neutral scientific way to make these calculations. Yet under CBA this part of the process is hidden in a black box, invisible to Parliament and the public, and decided, without wider input or accountability, by the expert.

CBA is just one prominent example of how the internal logic of economic theory reshapes politics and thus entrenches its influence. As political issues are turned into economic issues, the discipline of economics gains greater influence, changing society in ways that impact everyone. One such example is from the financial sector, where economics has played a hand in constructing entirely new markets. A historically important example of this construction was the creation of the Chicago Board Options Exchange (CBOE) as a financial market in 1973.

Prior to the 1970s, options – a form of financial 'bet' on how the price of an asset will move – had been banned for certain assets on the grounds that they were effectively gambling. Economists provided the intellectual rationale for eliminating these regulations, claiming that this would improve economic efficiency and make society better off. The creation of the CBOE kicked off a massive expansion in options trading, so that 'by June 2000, the total notional amount of derivatives contracts [which include options] outstanding worldwide was $108 trillion, the equivalent of $18,000 for every human being on earth'.[13]

Economics was not only crucial in creating and rationalising the CBOE; it also provided the logic that governed the trading that took place within its walls. Over time the price of many options became increasingly determined by the 'Black-Scholes' equation, developed by several economists (some of whom later won the Nobel Prize) to attach a price to financial assets. Initially, the equation proved fairly unreliable in predicting the prices of assets, but as its use became more widespread, and as economists and lawyers lobbied for changes to the regulatory structure to make the model's assumptions more accurate, the market began to align with the model's predictions. The equation became important precisely because it was being used by so many people.[14]

The influence of economics in actively shaping the economy does not end with finance. The increasing use of economic methods in policymaking limits the aims that can be pursued, narrowing the possibilities of government by focusing on solely economic objectives. This is shown clearly in the auctions that took place in many western countries in the early 2000s to sell parts of the electromagnetic spectrum to mobile phone companies. Wishing to design auctions that would achieve their political goals, governments across the world hired economists from an area known as 'game theory', which studies how individuals react strategically to one another's behaviour. The companies in turn hired economists to lobby for auction designs which would further their own goals.[15]

The resultant auctions focused on goals that could be easily modelled by economic theory – in particular, maximisation of government revenues from the sales – which meant that considerations outside this narrow lens were ignored. In the US other political goals, such as selling to smaller companies and rural mobile coverage, fell by the wayside.[16] In the UK, the long-term health of the bidding companies was not considered, and some of the winners encountered significant difficulties, with BT having to sell off assets in order to pay for its successful bid.[17] Focusing on revenue maximisation led to the neglect of other aspects of the situation, a debatable political decision that was obscured by the remarkably complicated nature of auction theory.

Such decisions can, in isolation, seem small but their cumulative effect is to transform the political process. We have given just a few examples but the application of economic logic to political decisions is extending further and further because government is increasingly dominated by economists. Every year over ten thousand economics students graduate from UK universities. Economics graduates dominate society's most important political institutions and design our government's most important policies and laws, constructing and shaping the economy in the ways outlined above every day. The UK civil service has a Government Economic Service (GES), which has roughly trebled in size in the twenty-first century and now employs about 1,600 economists. There are twice as many economists employed in the civil service as there are other social researchers.

Economics provides a common language for policymakers to communicate with one another. Government reports are laden with economic jargon like 'efficiency', 'externalities' and 'opportunity costs'. A whole community of think tanks and research institutes has grown up, attempting to influence politics with policy analysis and recommendations based on economic logic. For example, the Institute for Fiscal Studies (IFS) regularly provides evaluations of government tax and spending policies and has helped governments design and rationalise policy changes.[18] These organisations often strive to present their analysis as objective and scientific evidence (rather than political argument), and the IFS in particular has a reputation for objectivity. This reputation has given the IFS great power and it has been called the 'umpire of British politics' because its assessment of government policy is given such authority in political circles and across the media, resulting in further deference from politicians to the authority of economic analysis.[19]

Perhaps the most significant example of how modern societies are increasingly becoming econocracies is the rise of independent Central Banks (CBs) across the world. CBs control monetary policy, which determines the interest rate charged on mortgages and savings and also influences the level of money in the economy. Both of these can have an enormous impact on individuals and on society. In Britain the decision to devolve the setting of monetary policy to a committee, known as the Monetary Policy Committee, of nine economists at the Bank of England was taken in 1997 without being mentioned in the ruling Labour Party's pre-election manifesto.[20] Moreover, the bank is tasked with overseeing commercial financial institutions and constructing regulations to ensure financial stability. These important societal functions have been outsourced to economic experts, with the bank employing two hundred economists in total.[21]

There have been similar developments elsewhere in the world. Independent CBs are present in the US, Japan, Australia and most starkly in Europe in the form of the European Central Bank, which is completely unaccountable to the democratic wishes of particular Eurozone countries. In an incredible turn of events in Italy in 2011, a coalition of technocrats headed by the economist Mario Monti was sworn into government without an election after pressure from Italy's creditors.[22] Monti had never served in government before. He then appointed a cabinet without any members from Italy's political parties and was in office for close to eighteen months before facing elections, in which time he attempted to radically reshape the economy.[23] When a general election was held, Monti was relegated to fourth place.

In Greece, also in 2011, something similar happened as the economist and former vice-president of the European Central Bank, Lucas Papademos, was installed as Prime Minister without being elected.[24] Just before Papademos was appointed a *Financial Times* article stated 'Wanted: a temporary prime minister for small eurozone country in distress. Must be an economist with international background, fluent in Greek. No political experience required.'[25] While it may have been a joke it sums up the new status quo perfectly.

The rise of economics can also be seen in international institutions such as the International Monetary Fund (IMF), World Trade Organisation (WTO), World Bank and aforementioned OECD. All of these institutions have an economic *raison d'être*, rely heavily on economic experts, and conduct their business in the language of economics. For example, the IMF acts as a lender of last resort to countries facing debt crises. In return for bailouts it requires countries to implement various reforms of their public expenditure, tax policies, labour markets, trade policies and monetary policy, all of which are influenced by economic theory and designed by economists. In 2005 nearly two-thirds of the IMF's professional staff and almost three-quarters of its new professional recruits were economists.[26] In a recent survey of IMF staff, nearly 75 per cent of respondents saw the Fund's organisational culture as 'technical' and 'economistic'.[27]

Similarly, the WTO facilitates trade rounds with the aim of removing tariffs and regulations that prevent trade. The WTO's mission is possibly most closely linked to economic theory because the case for trade liberalisation is agreed by almost all economists. Collectively these organisations illustrate the rise of econocracy as a global phenomenon. They all rest on the assumption that the economy is a distinct sphere of life with its own logic. They support and sometimes heavily pressure countries to enact policies that at the time are widely considered by economists to be desirable for the economy (although this consensus changes over time), and they place great faith in technical economic expertise.

A defining feature of econocracy is the power given to economic experts, as the accepted spokespeople for society's economic knowledge, to shape political goals and the means of achieving them. But how did economics come to occupy such a place in our society? Hasn't 'the economy' been around since time immemorial? We now turn to the history of econocracy to show its rise in the second half of the twentieth century.

The roots of econocracy

The roots of econocracy lie both in the events and ideas of the twentieth century, when innumerable economic institutions devoted to measuring, analysing and managing the economy arose.[28] It was during this time that the discipline of economics created the conception of the economy as something that needs to be understood and therefore overseen by experts. Econocracy was born when societies began to seek to improve the economy as an end in itself, detached from its relationship to other parts of life, based on the assumption that improving the economy improves all of our lives.

Many economists would argue that the economy has been important for at least as long as human societies themselves. But there is an important difference between concrete activities such as business, finance and trade, and the idea of 'the economy' as a distinct system with its own internal logic. The former have indeed been part of human life since we began to live in societies. The economy, on the other hand, is an abstract concept which is a relatively recent invention.

Our current understanding of the economy as a distinct sphere of human life – in which production, distribution and consumption occur – is an entirely modern phenomenon. In the past, economy (*oikonomia* in ancient Greek, which literally means 'household management') focused on the self-sufficiency of households. Jane Austen, writing in the early nineteenth century, could describe one of her characters as a poor 'economist' for her inability to handle the servants.[29]

Between 1900 and the end of the Second World War in the UK, the term 'economy' was used only twice in any winning party's manifesto, both times to mean frugality. It was not until the 1950 Conservative Party manifesto that it first appeared, just once, in its modern usage. In 1955 it appeared ten times. In the 2015 Conservative Party manifesto, the word 'economy' appeared 59 times (see Exhibit 1.1).[30]

An important point that emerges from the historical record is that the existence of an econocracy requires a modern,

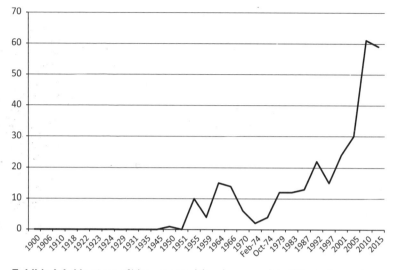

Exhibit 1.1 Mentions of 'the economy' (modern usage) in UK winning party manifesto

centralised state with advanced information-collecting abilities and the desire to actively shape the world in ambitious ways.[31] In the nineteenth century the state didn't have the capacity to collect the statistics that allow it to map the economy today.[32] Since then the combination of an increasingly centralised state and modern technology has allowed a far greater and more systematic collection of data.

Developments from within economics were also fundamental to this shift. In 1929 the economist John Maynard Keynes was one of the first to begin to refer to the economy as an abstract entity, using terms like 'economic society' and 'the economic system as a whole' to describe something more than the combined activity of individual economic units.[33] In 1936, at the request of the Dutch government, Jan Tinderberg built the first model of the economy, using maths to represent the activities of businesses, workers and governments and therefore allowing him to make predictions about the likely impact of various policy responses to the Great Depression. Later he was commissioned by the League of Nations and detailed a model of the US economy with 71 variables and 48 equations.[34] Models like this allowed economists to begin to define the core features and relationships they believed made up the economy.[35]

The Second World War gave economists the opportunity to show-case their rapidly developing technical skills. The war necessitated a mobilisation of resources that was unprecedented, and economists were hired for a broad range of tasks, from optimising shipping routes and loads to planning war manufacturing. Economics pro-vided a seemingly scientific, mathematical basis on which to make the kind of clear-cut decisions that are so vital during wartime. The war also saw the development of state control and information-gathering systems which would later form the core of econocracy.[36] National Income Accounting and what would become measurements of GDP were born.

The war raised the status of the discipline and cemented its central role in government. It also effected a shift in the centre of gravity of economics away from Britain to the US, which has dominated the profession ever since. Economics was used so extensively, and so many of the economists' tools were suited to the problem at hand, that the economist Paul Samuelson declared the Second World War the 'economists' war'.[37]

After the Second World War economic ideas increasingly influ-enced both the structure and aims of government in Britain and else-where. Successive governments were committed to full employment and 'Keynesian demand management', which was the idea that fiscal policy (the government altering levels of taxation and expenditure) could be used to provide stimulus when the economy was faltering, and to put the brakes on when it was booming. The rise of economics was symbolised in the US in 1946 by the creation of the Council of Economic Advisors inside the White House to advise the President directly. In the UK, the Government Economic Service was set up in 1964 to provide the civil service with economic expertise.

The UK Treasury began preparing qualitative assessments of economic prospects shortly after the war. Initially these forecasts were not derived from a formal model but were based on the judge-ment and intuition of Treasury economists. By 1961 these had been replaced with equations and the Treasury's projections became quantitative.[38] This shift, by hiding judgements and assumptions about the future in the technical exercise of setting up the model, made economic policymaking appear more rigorous and scientific than that which came before.

Globalisation and international economic governance after 1945 was increasingly based on managing national economies and the interconnections between them. The Bretton Woods system, which managed the exchange rates of the major industrialised nations from

1945 to 1973, was designed by prominent economists such as Keynes and Harry Dexter White.[39] Major international financial institutions arose, such as the IMF and World Bank, which were both founded in 1944; the OECD was established in 1961 and the WTO was founded in 1995 but was preceded by the General Agreement on Tariffs and Trade, which was signed directly after the Second World War. After the war the United Nations played a significant role in standardising and spreading measurements of economic performance across the world. As a result, nations could start comparing GDP growth, unemployment and inflation, and these became central indicators of development and progress.[40]

There was a corresponding gradual shift in news coverage towards an active conception of the economy. It was in the 1930s that 'the economy' appeared in British and American newspapers for the first time as a way to describe a unified and coherent national economic structure. As time went on, this structure gained the capacity to act by itself and developed needs of its own: *Time* stated that the economy 'was working at such high pressure that any additional burdens … were bound to blow price valves' (1944) [41], while *The Economist* argued that the economy needed 'room to manoeuvre' (1952).[42] In the UK a whole raft of institutions (including the Bank of England's Monetary Policy Committee, the Competition Commission and the National Audit Office) were set up to measure, manage and forecast different parts of the economy. It has been estimated that there were 99 organisations producing forecasts of the UK economy by the end of the 1970s.[43]

Econocracies evolve over time but even as they change, a number of features remain at their core. This is demonstrated by one especially striking (or disturbing) new organisation, the innocuous-sounding 'Behavioural Insights Team', also known as the 'Nudge Unit'.[44] Inspired by the relatively young field of behavioural economics, the task of this unit is to exploit psychological tendencies in order to 'nudge' us towards certain decisions, or in their words to enable people to 'make better choices for themselves'.[45] The unit boasts of such things as having doubled the application rates to join the Army Reserves.[46] The role of the economic expert has been expanded beyond simply designing policies to influencing the decisions of citizens.

The Nudge Unit illustrates that an econocracy is not simply defined by the goal of GDP, or by certain types of policies or institutions. Recently many politicians have been flirting with the idea of moving away from GDP as the central measure of economic success.[47]

However, whichever measure or measures we target, as long as we remain within the same institutional structures the core features of econocracy will persist. It is a changeable beast that evolves with economic knowledge, but that always values this knowledge above all else and always involves experts turning political problems into purely 'economic' ones.

In a little over seventy years we have gone from the idea of the economy being marginal to having national and international institutions dedicated to monitoring and improving it, and to having many areas of politics revolve around it. During that time we have begun to think of the economy as a self-contained sphere, distinct from social, cultural and political spheres of life.[48] The modern state wanted a scientific and objective way of shaping politics and economic experts offered it to them – whether through full-scale planning, policy design or 'nudging'. This has turned out to be a Faustian pact – a deal with the devil – because it has disempowered and disenfranchised citizens.

The absence of the citizen

There is a glaring absence at the heart of econocracy: the citizen. If elites and experts can make special claims to knowledge, they can carve out a sphere of life in which they are given decision-making authority. As a result the voices of those who don't have that knowledge are often devalued and disempowered because they don't have the formal credentials and they can't engage with technical language and ideas. This leaves little room for the citizen in economic discussions and decision making, since economic issues are discussed in a language few can engage with and in places few have access to. This reality makes econocracy incompatible with one of our greatest political traditions, liberal democracy.

The idea of liberal democracy is the intellectual cornerstone of British parliamentary politics and of many other administrations across the world. There are competing views of liberal democracy and the role of the citizen within it but there remain some undeniable core features. Liberal democracy aims to provide a way for societies to make collective decisions while still protecting the rights of individuals. The electorate votes for representatives at different levels of government and there is also a strong and broad private sphere which protects individuals' freedoms from infringement by the collective.

The key characteristic of liberal democracy is that involvement in public life and collective decision making is delegated to representative politicians. Citizens can choose how much they want to engage and do so by joining political parties, campaigning and protesting, and voting at the ballot box. Choice is key to this concept of liberal democracy and something our leaders preach to the rest of the world. Take, for example, David Cameron telling the Chinese that 'it is important that democracy involves real choices'.[49]

We argue that econocracy is incompatible with liberal democracy in two ways. Firstly, as we have already seen, in an econocracy political decisions are redefined as technical questions to be answered by experts and thus removed from the public arena. Secondly, as increasing areas of political and social life are colonised by economic language and logic, the vast majority of citizens face the struggle of making informed democratic choices in a language they have never been taught. Real choices require an understanding of the options available and this is difficult when they are so often obscured by the jargon of economics. We would not be comfortable with a doctor offering different treatment choices to a patient if he or she was speaking a language that the patient didn't understand; in fact, the NHS regularly pays for translators to make sure this never happens.[50]

Yet elites seem happy to conduct public discussion about economic decision making in a language that excludes the vast majority. This point is supported by a poll we took in collaboration with YouGov in January 2015 of 1,548 British adults, consisting of multiple choice questions about their knowledge of economics.[51] This poll was, to our knowledge, one of the first of its kind in the UK and provides new insights into how citizens relate to economic policy and the subject of economics more generally. Given the widespread use of economic language in public debate, it is interesting that few others are asking these questions. Whilst we are aware that our results represent only one poll, they remain deeply worrying and warrant further public discussion.

The poll showed that even though political choices are increasingly framed in economic terms, understanding of the language of economics is poor. As we have mentioned, GDP is the central number by which the health of the economy is judged. However, our poll found that only 39 per cent of respondents could define GDP and 25 per cent simply ticked 'don't know'. Political goals, from improving child literacy to reducing mental health problems, are increasingly justified in terms of their effect on GDP, but at the same time most citizens aren't clear what GDP actually is. The organisations that study GDP in meticulous detail exist in an alternative reality to everyone else. Economists, politicians and the media simply assert that changes in

GDP signify the health of the economy and the competence of the government, expecting everyone else to accept that this is true as a token of faith.

The results of the poll suggest that a lack of knowledge of economics is not due to the inability of the public to understand it, but to the tendency of elites to speak to each other in this language rather than actively trying to engage with non-experts. In the cases where economic ideas appear more frequently on the news, more people were able to answer the questions correctly, a point that is illustrated by another key economic statistic in the media: the government budget deficit.

The deficit is the amount the government has to borrow each year, given by the difference between government spending and government revenues. If spending is higher than revenues, then the government is in deficit; if revenues are higher than spending, the government is in surplus. A continued large deficit means borrowing every year, so that the country's national debt will increase significantly over time. Before the 2015 election the three main UK parties all committed to reducing the deficit by cutting public spending, but differentiated themselves over what to cut and how quickly to do it. It was the defining issue of the election campaign and indeed of the success or otherwise of the entire coalition government term. When the former Labour leader Ed Miliband forgot to mention the deficit in his 2014 party conference speech it caused an outcry among the press and rival politicians. The debates about the deficit were a proxy for a wider contest over which party could convince the electorate they were economically competent. Post-election reports into the result have repeatedly found that lack of trust over the economy was the most significant reason why Labour lost, with arguments over the deficit being crucial to this.[52]

Our polling found that in a multiple choice question, 43 per cent of the adult population were unable to define the government budget deficit. That 57 per cent of respondents were able to define it suggests that many have engaged at least to some extent with this debate. However, given its omnipresence on the news and in politics over the last five years, it might have been expected that this number would be much closer to 100 per cent. Moreover, the deficit is one issue where there has been lots of research into public understanding, and other polls which have delved more deeply suggest that people often don't engage with what the deficit really means. Another YouGov Poll found that only 31 per cent of respondents knew the correct definition of the deficit, with 51 per cent confusing it with total government debt.[53] A report by the Centre for Policy Studies found that in 2012, earlier in the Parliament, only 10 per cent of people properly understood the implications of the Conservative government's plans for the deficit, i.e. that government debt as a total was set to rise. Furthermore, it found that 61 per cent of those who voted for the Conservatives in 2010 thought that they planned to cut the total debt, even though in reality they were planning for significant increases.[54]

Knowledge of basic economic terminology is a necessary but not sufficient condition for being able to make informed political choices, and the widespread absence of greater understanding makes meaningful political engagement increasingly difficult. If we do not reverse this situation, our collective choices will feel increasingly hollow.

Our survey with YouGov highlighted a split among respondents between around 35 per cent of the population who felt happy engaging with economics, and the remainder who self-identified as disengaged. Among the 35 per cent of our sample who said they talked about economics once a week or more, people most often highlighted as the reasons for engagement the importance of knowing about economics, that their family and friends were interested in it, or that they had a personal interest in the subject.

This relatively effortless engagement with the subject is in stark contrast to the large number of people who rarely or never talk about economics. 47 per cent of our respondents stated that they talked about economics once a month or less, and a further 12 per cent only talked about it two or three times a month. Disengagement was considerably more prevalent among women and people from less privileged socio-economic backgrounds. Some of the most popular reasons given to explain this lack of engagement included 'I have no interest in economics', 'I find economics difficult to understand', and 'Economics is out of my hands so there is no point discussing it'.

In an econocracy, there are two camps that eye each other distrustfully across the barricades. Those who speak the language of economics are on the inside. They look out and see apathy and a lack of interest in economics among the masses, but rarely reflect on the causes. Those who don't speak economics are on the outside. They look in and see the dominance of the arcane language of economics as evidence that the political classes are disconnected from the reality they live in. In our view an important cause of this disconnect is the intuitive feeling among many people that the kind of economic logic that is dominant often fails to speak to them or describe their concerns. In an econocracy, economics is left to the experts and real democratic debate is stifled as a result.

Disengagement allows economic decision making to become even more technical and obscure, resulting in a vicious circle that undermines the possibility of a more democratic alternative, as political choices are increasingly made without public oversight or accountability. As we saw earlier, central banks have largely been taken out of politics and handed over to economists. Yet the primary response of the Bank of England to the recession of 2008, Quantitative Easing (QE), has had undeniably political consequences. QE is often referred to as 'printing money', and though this is oversimplified it does capture the key idea. Through the creation of electronic money out of nothing, the bank has sought to stimulate the economy by spending this money in financial markets, buying long-term government bonds and other financial assets. The bank itself innocuously labels this a 'cash injection' and argues that the majority of people have benefited from the policy.

Whether or not this is true, the consequences of QE are far from neutral, and the fact that many people would have been worse off without it does not mean that other policies would not have achieved a better outcome. By the bank's own admission, the top 5 per cent of households have benefited most from the bank creating new money to buy assets, since the richest generally own more of these assets than the poorest.[55] We therefore have an example of a supposedly depoliticised economic policy whose impact, if authorised by a government through a tax break, would have been a central part of political discussion.

The operations of a central bank are often political but our poll findings suggest that the public are unaware of this when such operations are carried out without consultation and in a manner that is disconnected from ordinary lives. On the other hand, when the Bank of England's actions affect people in clear ways, they are more likely to engage with what it does. Hence, 84 per cent of the population were able to correctly identify that the base interest rate is set by the bank – probably due to the effect that interest rates have on mortgage costs – but only 30 per cent of people were able to correctly define QE and only 37 per cent correctly defined the official rationale for using it. In both the latter questions, over 40 per cent of people simply didn't know.

The lack of public debate about the rationale behind QE and whether or not to pursue it also means that alternatives are undisclosed and undiscussed. Other means to achieve similar ends could include creating money and using it to fund public spending. Or the bank could have given one-off cash payments to households to stimulate demand.[56] Our aim is not to raise a preference for a particular route. It is to show that citizens are unaware that decisions with political consequences are being made, decisions that directly concern themselves and society, and that they have little knowledge of these decisions and no control over them.

Widespread disengagement with economics and a corresponding lack of confidence make it hard for citizens to evaluate political narratives about the economy and hold their governments accountable. GDP as the primary indicator of a government's economic success is a perfect illustration of this. In 2014 the government was obliged by European statute to add drug dealing and sex work to the audit of measurements of GDP. This added around £10 billion to the UK's annual GDP (0.7 per cent).[57] Growth in 2014 was 2.6 per cent and the media reported it as the 'fastest growth since 2007', but this picture would have looked very different without the measurement changes.[58] In a boost to UK national morale this change also saw the UK leapfrog France, which doesn't include these activities, in the World Economic League Table.[59] By also deciding to include such activities, Spain did even better, increasing its GDP by €26.2 billion or 2.5 per cent in 2013.[60]

The focus of successive governments on expanding GDP is part of a trend in which the concerns of the public are ignored. The British public as a whole has never been asked what the aims of the economy should be. Instead, the goal is simply to increase a number that may fail to capture much of social reality and that many people do not truly understand. A failure to challenge this state of affairs creates the impression that there is no alternative. The dominance of a single measure of economic success is inevitably going to shape collective perceptions about the economy and reduce important political debates to narrower technical questions of how to ensure strong and stable growth.

How to define economic success is a political rather than a technical question, and decisions about what to measure, and how, both reflect and influence collective values about what is important. For example, in the UK we don't attempt to measure the vast amounts of care work that occur in our society. As a consequence, the daily activities of millions of people (mainly women) are deemed unproductive and made invisible in economic terms.[61] This is an implicit judgement that the work families and individuals do to bring up their children and care for the sick and elderly are not important parts of a functioning social and economic system. What we choose to measure is not an innocuous choice; it frames the subsequent debate that we have as a society.

The knowledge and accountability vacuum surrounding the economy makes it difficult to evaluate the choices politicians and economists make on our behalf, or to come to a judgement about which narrative best explains the empirical evidence in public economic debates: Is the level of public and/or private debt unsustainable? If it is, what is the best way to lower it? How should we change banking after the financial crisis, if at all? Is all debt bad or is borrowing to fund infrastructure desirable? These are just some of the big questions that we as a society have had to address in the last few years. How we answer these questions should be the subject of proper democratic debate.

We are caught in an uncomfortable bind. On the one hand, the difficulty of understanding the economy on a systemic level creates an impenetrable wall of confusion between its workings and our lives. On the other hand, many aspects of our lives are embedded in and dependent upon the wider economic system. The barrier that prevents us understanding the economy and participating in economic debate doesn't shield us from its consequences.

A movement to open economics and reinvigorate democracy

The devaluation of citizenship at the heart of econocracy forms the backdrop to the recent rise in populist political movements across Europe and the US. Many of these movements have developed an explicitly anti-technocratic rhetoric which appears to be a direct reaction to the conditions of econocracy. For example, Donald Trump and Ted Cruz present themselves as anti-elites and have both stated that they want to curb the independence of the USA's central bank (the Federal Reserve). Many of these groups have developed a strong anti-free trade rhetoric. Populist movements of all political stripes from Jeremy Corbyn and Bernie Sanders to UKIP and the National Front are, we would suggest, defining their different political positions in opposition to central aspects of the world we have described.

The single largest challenge to econocracy to date came on Friday 24 June 2016 when the UK woke to find that 52 per cent of voters had decided that they wanted Britain to leave the European Union. The result was shocking because during the preceding debate almost the whole global economic and financial establishment had lined up to warn of the consequences of Brexit. Yet over 17 million people ignored the economists and supposedly voted against their own economic interest, or else decided that the economists' predictions weren't to be trusted.

From the outset the Remain campaign focused on the economic case against leaving the EU, wheeling out quantitative modelling to forecast the effects of Brexit on the economy.[62] From the Remain control room the examples of countless general elections and the referendum on Scottish independence suggested that winning the economic argument would be crucial to winning the referendum. However, they didn't count on the effectiveness of the Leave campaign strategy of discrediting the economic expertise that the Remain case relied upon. The economic forecasts of Brexit were labelled as 'Project Fear' and the Conservative politician Michael Gove claimed that the nation had 'had enough of experts', comparing those supporting the Remain campaign to the scientists who worked for the Nazis.[63] This strategy proved to be effective in an econocracy because it played on how disconnected from economic discussion and decision-making people feel.

The economics profession feels that it has been ignored and diminished by the result of the EU referendum and there has been much soul searching in its aftermath. Paul Johnson, director of the Institute for Fiscal Studies, lamented that economists had 'failed to communicate basic economic concepts to politicians, journalists and businesspeople, never mind the public'.[64] This is a positive shift and one that we hope will lead to reforms within economics that attempt to reconnect it with the general public. However, we worry that the broad message from influential economists like Johnson is still about 'presenting the facts', not about giving people the tools to engage critically and make up their own minds.

Despite the divisiveness of economics during the referendum, it is clear that economic issues were an important part of the debate. Social class and location were key determinants of how one voted, with Leave voters much more likely to have lower incomes and come from poorer areas.[65] What is striking is how unlikely most of those people are to use the language of economics to describe their views. When people lack control over their economic circumstances and the public language or spaces to air their economic grievances, they will naturally be drawn towards arguments about sovereignty which promise to take back control of the political process. Similarly, issues such as immigration seem to be closer to the lived experience of the economy for many people than the abstract models and statistics of economics. The EU referendum illustrates very clearly our argument in this chapter: we live in a nation divided between a minority who feel they own the language of economics and a majority who don't.

However, populist politics alone is no answer to the problems of econocracy and it is often simply a rhetoric that criticises elites and experts while failing to offer people more control in shaping the world they live in. Populist politicians present themselves as 'the voice of the people' but citizens will still struggle to make informed decisions or exercise citizenship positively when it comes to economic issues. Instead, power will shift to yet another group who claim to speak on behalf of the people.[66] To properly reclaim democracy we must address deeper, more structural issues.

We believe that experts are a vital part of the modern world. We no longer live in insular, small-scale communities but in an interconnected global community, and many of its most important facets are not necessarily intuitive or easily observable. The concept of climate change is a perfect example. Why do the majority of people, including these authors, believe in anthropogenic climate change? It is because we choose to have trust in the community of scientific experts who do the primary research, analyse the data and then communicate the reality as they understand it to the public. Many other aspects of society such as crossing bridges without fearing that they will collapse, or taking the medicine that our doctors prescribe without fearing it will make our ailments worse, rely on a trust in expertise.

The question then is not whether we want experts but what kind of experts we want. Our vision is of a world in which economic experts recognise that their knowledge of a complex economy is limited and that economic issues are the proper subject of collective democratic debate. The role of experts is to inform citizens of their choices rather than to make those choices for them. This in turn requires that they speak in a language the public understands, make an effort to engage the public in conversation, and have the broad knowledge and skills necessary to respond to publicly agreed economic priorities.

This kind of expert would in turn pave the way for a world in which economics was democratised, and much larger swathes of the general public were able to engage with economic discussion and hold economic decision makers to account. In this world, citizens would be able to articulate their economic needs and preferences; participate in the political system to negotiate those needs; and then have the knowledge to make informed choices between alternative economic proposals to achieve them. This in turn would change the relationship between citizens and experts so that experts became accountable to the broader public.

As we have shown in this chapter, econocracy could not be further from the world we have sketched out here. These failures aren't the result of negligence or spite on the part of experts. Economic experts can only be as good as their expertise because it shapes their understanding of the world and their role within it. In this book we argue that academic economics is in urgent need of reform. We show how economics has become dominated by a particular, narrow way of thinking about the economy. We outline the history of economics as a discipline and how it has over time gone from a broad, diverse subject closely linked to politics, philosophy and ethics to a disconnected and closed system of knowledge. The result of this is that economic experts who have only been trained in this way of thinking do not have the knowledge or skills to properly understand the complex, changing modern economy.

While similar states of affairs in the history of art or palaeontology might be considered niche issues best left to the academics, economics is different. Economics affects everyone, sometimes painfully so; in this book we'll show how economists and their frameworks have been unable to help societies address some of their most important problems, from financial crises to environmental degradation. Our case in this book is that economic experts have ended up with hugely influential roles in society but that the economic knowledge that forms the basis of their claim to expertise is often inadequate. If there is a crisis in economics, it means that there is also a crisis in society.

This book and its authors are part of a movement that is attempting to challenge the status quo. Growing numbers of economics students are setting up and joining student societies with names like Rethinking Economics, Post-Crash Economics and the Cambridge Society for Economic Pluralism. There are now 14 such groups at universities across the UK and they are part of a global movement to reform economics education. We believe that the status quo must be challenged if we are to build societies that are sustainable, prosperous and fair, and if we are to have meaningful democracy. Over three years we have come a long way both as individuals and a movement. We have gained confidence in our calls for change, we understand more about how important economics is to society and we have established connections with like-minded students, academics and citizens across the world.

This book is an attempt, in line with the movement's ethos, to articulate to the layperson why economics matters to them and how they can play a part in building a new kind of economics. It is part of a wider recognition that to open up economics we must go from being a student movement to being a social movement. We want to create an alliance between economists and citizens. We therefore now turn to the second part of our story, which is set in economics departments in universities across the UK. We focus on the education that economics students receive because the education of students can give us an important insight into what the discipline of economics has become. It is in the education system that the next generation of economists are created. It is these institutions that reproduce econocracy.

Notes

1 David Cameron, 'Transforming the British economy: Coalition strategy for economic growth', speech given in Shipley, 2010. Available at: http://www.britishpoliticalspeech.org/speech-archive.htm?speech=351 (accessed 24 April 2016).
2 Chris Giles, 'Team McDonnell: meet Labour's seven economic advisers', *Financial Times*, 28 September 2015. Available at: http://www.ft.com/cms/s/0/96534d2e-65c1-11e5-a28b-50226830d644.html#axzz46LyM6emQ (accessed 25 April 2016).
3 *Media Coverage of the 2015 Campaign (report 4)*, report, Loughborough University Communication Research Centre, 2015.
4 This comment is from the critique of Ed Miliband's energy price freeze by one of the leading fund managers in the UK, whose comment appeared in the *Daily Mail*. The same phrase can also be found in the *Financial Times* article, predicting significant inflation from money injections by the European Central Bank: Neil Woodford, 'Good Politics, Bad Economics', Woodford Funds, 14 January 2015. Available at: https://woodfordfunds.com/good-politics-bad-economics/ (accessed on 24 April 2016); Josef Josse, 'Merkel's Good Politics and Bad Economics', *Financial Times*, 4 September 2012. Available at: https://next.ft.com/content/89c270d6-f5ed-11e1-a6c2-00144feabdc0 (accessed 24 April 2016).
5 From Save the Children's 'Read on. Get on' campaign, cited in *Read on Get on: How reading can help children escape poverty*, report, Save the Children, 2014, 17.
6 *Mental Health and Work: United Kingdom*, report, OECD Publishing, 2014.
7 Heather Power, 'How valuable is the Queen to our economy?', *Business Life*, 31 May 2012. Available at: http://businesslife.ba.com/Ideas/Features/how-valuable-is-the-Queen-to-our-economy.html (accessed 24 April 2016).
8 *Contribution of the Arts and Culture Industry to the National Economy*, report for Arts Council England, Centre for Economics and Business Research, 2015.

9   *Measuring Our Value*, report, British Library, 2013.

10 The best-selling introductory economics textbook by Gregory Mankiw lists 14 issues on which the vast majority of economists agree. See Gregory Mankiw, *Principles of Economics*, Fort Worth, TX: Dryden Press, 1998, 35.

11 We are especially indebted to Daniel Hirschman and Elizabeth Popp Berman for the point that economists redefine political problems as technical ones. For a more detailed and academic take on this issue, see Daniel Hirschman and Elizabeth Berman, 'Do economists make policies? On the political effects of economics', *Socio-Economic Review* 12(4) (2014): 779–811.

12 *How Economics is Used in Government Decision Making*, report, New Economics Foundation, 2013; and Jonathan Aldred, *The Skeptical Economist: Revealing the Ethics Inside Economics*, London: Earthscan, 2009, 146.

13 Donald MacKenzie and Yuval Millo, 'Constructing a market-performing theory: the historical sociology of a financial derivatives exchange', *American Journal of Sociology* 109(1) (2003): 107–45.

14 Ibid.

15 Edward Nik-Khan, 'A tale of two auctions', *Journal of Institutional Economics* 4(1) (2008): 73–97.

16 Ibid.

17 Roger Backhouse, *The Puzzle of Modern Economics: Science or Ideology?* Cambridge: Cambridge University Press, 2011, 33.

18 See the IFS's 'About' page on its website: http://www.ifs.org.uk/about/ which includes several documents on the institute's history and influence (accessed 24 April 2016).

19 Simon Akam, 'The British umpire: How the IFS became the most influential voice in the economic debate', *The Guardian*, 15 March 2016. Available at: http://www.theguardian.com/business/2016/mar/15/british-umpire-how-institute-fiscal-studies-became-most-influential-voice-in-uk-economic-debate (accessed 24 April 2016).

20 Available at: http://labourmanifesto.com/1997/1997-labour-manifesto. shtml. Five of these economists are Bank of England employees and four are appointed by the Chancellor of the Exchequer.

21 Details available at: http://www.bankofengland.co.uk/research/Pages/ economists/default.aspx (accessed 24 April 2016).

22 Guy Dinmore and Guilia Segreti, 'Italy races to install Monti government', *Financial Times*, 13 November 2011. Available at: https://next. ft.com/content/f8106b1a-0e21-11e1-91e5-00144feabdc0 (accessed 25 May 2016); Guy Dinmore, Rachel Sanderson and Peter Spiegel, 'Straight-talking Monti boosts Italy's hopes', *Financial Times*, 10 November 2011. Available at: https://next.ft.com/content/48461414-0bb5-11e1-9a61-00144feabdc0 (accessed 25 April 2016).

23 Duncan McDonnell, 'The rise of governments led by technocrats in

Europe illustrates the failure of mainstream political parties', London School of Economic's European Politics and Policy blog, 11 June 2013. Available at: http://blogs.lse.ac.uk/europpblog/2013/06/11/the-rise-of-governments-led-by-technocrats-in-europe-illustrates-the-failure-of-mainstream-political-parties/ (accessed 25 April 2016). Guy Dinmore, 'Monti gets approval for labour reforms', *Financial Times*, 27 June 2012. Available at: https://next.ft.com/content/8d2cf956-c070-11e1-9372-001 44feabdc0 (accessed 25 April 2016).

24 Kerin Hope, 'Papademos named new Greek PM', *Financial Times*, 10 November 2011. Available at: https://next.ft.com/content/8fb2b3c8-0afe-11e1-ae56-00144feabdc0 (accessed 25 April 2016).

25 Kerin Hope, 'Wanted – a prime minister', *Financial Times*, 7 November 2011. Available at: https://next.ft.com/content/0cfb4bf6-08ca-11e1-9fe8-00144feabdc0 (accessed 25 April 2016).

26 Jeffrey M. Chwieroth, *Capital Ideas: The IMF and the Rise of Financial Liberalization*, Princeton, NJ: Princeton University Press, 2010, 36.

27 Ibid.

28 There are many histories of the economics profession that chart the discipline's rise to prominence. We have drawn from Michael A. Bernstein, *A Perilous Progress: Economists and Public Purpose in Twentieth-Century America*, Princeton, NJ: Princeton University Press, 2001; and Marion Fourcade, *Economists and Societies: Discipline and Profession in the United States, Britain, and France, 1890s to 1990s*, Princeton, NJ: Princeton University Press, 2009.

29 Keith Hart and Chris Hann, 'Introduction: Learning from Polanyi 1', in Chris Hann and Keith Hart (eds), *Market and Society: The Great Transformation Today*, Cambridge: Cambridge University Press, 2011, 1.

30 Manifestos are available at http://www.conservativemanifesto.com/1918/1918-conservative-manifesto.shtml; http://labourmanifesto.com; and http://www.libdemmanifesto.com (accessed 24 April 2016).

31 James C. Scott, *Seeing Like a State: How Certain Schemes to Improve the Human Condition Have Failed*, New Haven, CT: Yale University Press, 1999.

32 Mick Moran, *The Regulatory State: High Modernism and Hyper-Innovation*, Oxford: Oxford University Press, 2003.

33 Timothy Mitchell, 'Fixing the economy', *Cultural Studies* 12(1) (1998): 82–101.

34 Robert Evans, *Macroeconomic Forecasting: A Sociological Perspective*, London: Routledge, 1999, 14.

35 Mitchell, 'Fixing the economy', 86–7.

36 See Mark Guglielmo, 'The contribution of economists to military intelligence during World War II', *Journal of Economic History* 68(1) (2008): 109–50; and Michael Bernstein, 'American economics and the national security state, 1941–1953', *Radical History Review* 63 (1995): 9–26.

37 Paul Samuelson, 'Unemployment ahead: a warning to the Washington expert', *The New Republic*, 11 September 1944: 297–9.

38 Evans, *Macroeconomic Forecasting*, 13.

39 Raymond F. Mikesell, *The Bretton Woods Debates: A Memoir*, Princeton, NJ: International Finance Section, Dept. of Economics, Princeton University, 1994.

40 Marilyn Waring, *If Women Counted: A New Feminist Economics*, San Francisco: Harper & Row, 1988; and Mitchell, 'Fixing the economy'.

41 Quoted from Mike Emmison, '"The Economy": Its Emergence in Media Discourse', in Howard Davis and Paul Walton (eds), *Language, Image, Media*, Oxford: Blackwell, 1983, 149.

42 Ibid., 150.

43 Evans, *Macroeconomic Forecasting*, 14.

44 This organisation has an interesting, if strange, history: it started life as a government institution, but now describes itself as a social purpose company, jointly owned by the UK government, Nesta (the innovation charity) and its employees.

45 Behavioural Insights Team, 'Who We Are: The Behavioural Insights Team'. Available at: http://www.behaviouralinsights.co.uk/about-us/ (accessed 24 April 2016).

46 Tamsin Rutter, 'The rise of nudge – the unit helping politicians to fathom human behaviour', *The Guardian*, 23 July 2015. Available at: http://www.theguardian.com/public-leaders-network/2015/jul/23/rise-nudge-unit-politicians-human-behaviour (accessed 24 April 2016).

47 Most notably David Cameron in 2010, although these plans appear to have fallen by the wayside. Allegra Stratton, 'David Cameron aims to make happiness the new GDP', *The Guardian*, 14 November 2010. Available at: http://www.theguardian.com/politics/2010/nov/14/david-cameron-wellbeing-inquiry (accessed 25 April 2016).

48 Mitchell, 'Fixing the economy', 82–101.

49 Carlos Barria, 'PM Cameron says Britain should stand up for Hong Kong rights', *Reuters*, 15 October 2014. Available at: http://in.reuters.com/article/hongkong-china-britain-idINKCN0I41WF20141015 (accessed 24 April 2016)

50 Matthew Holehouse, 'NHS spends £23m a year on translators', *The Telegraph*, 6 February 2012. Available at: http://www.telegraph.co.uk/news/health/news/9063200/NHS-spends-23m-a-year-on-translators.html (accessed 25 April 2016).

51 The poll is available online: https://d25d2506sfb94s.cloudfront.net/cumulus_uploads/document/1h0dojy3oj/PostCrashEconomicsSociety Results_150128_economics_W.pdf

52 Of particular importance was the perception that Labour had been wrong to run a deficit in the year preceding the financial crisis: Margaret Beckett, *Learning the Lessons from Defeat: Taskforce Report*, Labour Party, 2015.

53 Results available at: https://d25d2506sfb94s.cloudfront.net/cumulus_ uploads/document/2rm33oydgm/SOS_Results_150115_Website.pdf (accessed 24 April 2016)

54 Ryan Bourne and Tim Knox, *A Distorted Debate: The Need for Clarity on Debt, Deficit and Coalition Aims*, report, Centre for Policy Studies, 2012.

55 *The Distributional Effects of Asset Purchases*, report, Bank of England, Quarterly Bulletin Q3, 2012.

56 Note that variants of this latter policy have been endorsed by people across the political spectrum, from current Labour leader Jeremy Corbyn to the *Financial Times*'s Martin Wolf to the libertarian economist Milton Friedman. Ambrose Evans-Pritchard, 'Jeremy Corbyn's QE for the people is exactly what the world may soon need', *Telegraph*, 16 September 2015. Available at: http://www.telegraph.co.uk/finance/eco nomics/11869701/Jeremy-Corbyns-QE-for-the-people-is-exactly-what-the-world-may-soon-need.html (accessed 24 April 2016); Martin Wolf, 'The case for helicopter money', *Financial Times*, 12 February 2013. Available at: http://www.ft.com/cms/s/0/9bcf0eea-6f98-11e2-b906-00144feab49a.html#axzz46V5sxFR8 (accessed 24 April 2016); Milton Friedman. *Optimum Quantity of Money*, Chicago: Aldine, 1969, 4.

57 Sarah O'Connor, 'Drugs and prostitution add £10bn to UK economy – FT.Com', 29 May 2014. Available at: http://www.ft.com/cms/s/2/65704ba0-e730-11e3-88be-00144feabdc0.html#axzz46k4tODTg (accessed 24 April 2016)

58 BBC, 'UK economy records fastest growth since 2007', 27 January 2015. Available at: http://www.bbc.co.uk/news/business-30999206 (accessed 24 April 2016).

59 Stephanie Linning, 'Who said crime doesn't pay? Counting prostitution and drugs in the GDP figure has seen the UK's economy overtake France as fifth largest in the world', *Mail Online*, 27 December 2014. Available at: http://www.dailymail.co.uk/news/article-2888416/Who-said-crime-doesn-t-pay-Counting-prostitution-drugs-GDP-figure-seen-UK-s-economy-overtake-France-fifth-largest-world.html (accessed 24 April 2016).

60 Ian Mount, 'Spain gets a questionable GDP boost, thanks to drugs and prostitution', *Fortune*, 8 October 2014. Available at: http://fortune.com/2014/10/08/spain-gdp-drugs-prostitution/ (accessed 24 April 2016).

61 Academics call this part of the economy social reproduction. Social reproduction, the processes by which humans sustain themselves and others, and by which the labour force is reproduced, encompasses not only the daily and intergenerational transmission of material necessities of life such as food, water, shelter and clothing but also the reproduction of cultural and social aspects of life such as social hierarchies, religion, and gender orders and cultures.

62 See, for example, Chris Giles, 'Treasury's Brexit analysis: what it says –
    and what it doesn't', *Financial Times*, 18 April 2016. Available at:
    https://next.ft.com/content/c15cd060-0550-11e6-96e5-f85cb08b0730
    (accessed 27 April 2016); *United Kingdom Selected Issues*, report,
    International Monetary Fund, 1 June 2016.

63 Henry Mance, 'Britain has had enough of experts, says Gove', *Financial
    Times*, 3 June 2016. Available at: http://www.ft.com/cms/s/0/3be49734-
    29cb-11e6-83e4-abc22d5d108c.html#axzz4JZbdCmwx (accessed 8
    September 2016); Ben Riley-Smith and Michael Wilkinson, 'Michael
    Gove compares experts warning against Brexit to Nazis who smeared
    Albert Einstein's work as he threatens to quit David Cameron's Cabinet',
    The Telegraph, 21 June 2016. Available at: http://www.telegraph.co.uk/
    news/2016/06/21/michael-gove-compares-experts-warning-against-
    brexit-to-nazis-wh/ (accessed 8 September 2016).

64 Paul Johnson, 'We economists must face the plain truth that the refer-
    endum showed our failings', *The Times*, 28 June 2016. Available at:
    http://www.thetimes.co.uk/article/paul-johnson-s5pnw9rn0 (accessed 8
    September).

65 Ron Johnston, Kelvyn Jones and David Manley, 'Predicting the Brexit
    vote: getting the geography right (more or less)', LSE British Politics
    and Policy blog, 2 July 2016. Available at: http://blogs.lse.ac.uk/poli
    ticsandpolicy/the-brexit-vote-getting-the-geography-more-or-less-right/
    (accessed 8 September 2016); *Brexit vote explained: poverty, low skills
    and lack of opportunities*, report, Joseph Rowntree Foundation, 31
    August 2016. Available at: https://www.jrf.org.uk/brexit-vote-explained-
    poverty-low-skills-and-lack-opportunities (accessed 8 September 2016).

66 Martin Wolf, chief economics commentator at the *Financial Times*, has
    spelled out very clearly 'the danger that the gulf between economic and
    technocratic elites on the one hand, and the mass of the people on the
    other, becomes too vast to be bridged'. Martin Wolf, 'Bring our elites
    closer to the people', *Financial Times*, 2 February 2016. Available at:
    http://www.ft.com/cms/s/0/94176826-c8fc-11e5-be0b-b7ece4e953a0.
    html#axzz46Sy5Kodx (accessed 24 April 2016).

Chapter 2

Economics as indoctrination

The ideas of economists and political philosophers, both when they are right and when they are wrong, are more powerful than is commonly understood. Indeed, the world is ruled by little else

John Maynard Keynes[1]

I don't care who writes a nation's laws, if I can write its economics textbooks

Paul Samuelson[2]

In the space of seventy or eighty years the idea of 'the economy' went from non-existent to occupying a central place in our world. As a result of this meteoric ascent, economics – the study of the economy – has gained enormous influence. Academic economics, through its widely accepted claim that it explains how the economy works, now provides a logic that shapes how to think about and make decisions in vast areas of political and social life. As we outlined in Chapter 1, this state of affairs gives economic experts a unique authority. Economics is a complex, technical language and those who can speak it can engage with politics and policy in a way others cannot. Economic experts now have important positions in some of society's most important institutions. But what makes someone an economics expert and, by extension, what gives them this authority?

As in all professions, the answer is formal education, training and – most importantly – qualifications, which are the concrete proof of their holder's expertise. The content of economics education is revealing because it reflects the dominant view within the academic discipline of the knowledge and skills economists must have and what the role of an economist should be. It was this insight that inspired Paul Samuelson, one of the most influential economists of the twentieth century, to declare: 'I don't care who writes a nation's laws, if I can write its economics textbooks.' Economic experts have the power to define the accepted economic logic and that, in a society in which the success of the economy has become central, shapes what is believed to be desirable and possible in broader political and economic life. Those who decide what they are taught have a position of great power and responsibility and Samuelson recognised this. Our argument in this chapter is that economics education currently neglects that responsibility.

'Didn't they tell you? Economics education isn't about the economy'

> indoctrinate, *v.*, *teach (a person or group) to accept a set of beliefs uncritically*[3]

Maeve Cohen, an economics student at the University of Manchester, remembers the insight that led her to want to study economics at university: 'I began to realise that those who understood economics understood power.' Maeve is from a mining town in the north-east of England and for her the influence of economics was difficult to miss. Growing up, local events such as the Miners' Gala in County Durham carried her and others back on a wave of nostalgia to celebrate the region's history as 'a once thriving hub of industry'. Equally regularly came the collective hangover and the inescapable reality that the north-east had become one of the most deprived regions in the country.

Travelling around the world in her twenties only added to her feeling that the answers to the most interesting questions lay in economics. She recalls how she was 'struck again and again by how "economic" decisions have a serious impact on the welfare of people who have very little say in these decisions'. Maeve is not alone. Speaking to students who are part of the movement to reform economics education, it is clear that many decided to study the subject for similar reasons. One talked of wanting to learn 'the language spoken in the highest spheres of power today'. Another explained how he wanted 'to understand how society as a whole functions'. With the rise of econocracy it has become increasingly apparent to many young people that to be able to follow, engage with and influence the great social debates of our time one must be able to speak the language of economics.

These aspirations end quickly. Students beginning an economics degree could be forgiven for thinking they had been transported to an alternative reality. The urge to learn about society, expressed by Maeve and many other economics students, must be suppressed as they are confronted with a series of abstract concepts and ideas that seem to have little to do with the actual economy. Students may wonder why it is necessary to detach the study of economics from reality in this way, but they must also learn to inhabit this parallel universe if they want any hope of passing their exams.

Not only must the student inhabit this world; for some unspecified reason it must be built up meticulously from first principles, which tests their ability but also has the effect of walling the students in and preventing them from thinking in any other way. A set of assumptions – typically long and obscure – is drilled into students' minds, followed by the steps required to erect the logical superstructure built on these assumptions. This is often done as a stand-alone exercise, so that any trace of the world the students actually inhabit is excluded. Sceptical students will be met with the catch-all that all theories make assumptions (more on this later), or are told that if they go on to do a PhD (which most of them won't) then the assumptions will eventually be dropped.

This economic world is said to be inhabited by 'agents', a broad term economists use to refer to any sort of economic decision-maker. Agents make supposedly perfect decisions by 'optimising', working out the kinds of mathematical problems in an instant that the students themselves may struggle to solve in a day. Whole economies are composed of individual agents whose interaction is based on these optimising rules, producing a situation which is said to be stable, known as 'equilibrium'. Any view of the economy which is not composed from this underlying view of individual agents is generally unwelcome in this universe.

For students who wish to understand the world and even shape it, being transported into this alternative reality is a great shock. In our own studies we clung to the belief that we were learning a framework that we might begin to apply to the real world in the next course or in the next year. It wasn't until halfway through our degree that we realised that we might be waiting in vain. This was the spark for us to set up the Post-Crash Economics Society and start to campaign for curriculum reform. It was not until later that we found out that this particular and narrow way of thinking about the economy was the approach taught at most universities across the world.

In this chapter we examine university economics education in the UK and argue that the next generation of economic experts are being systematically miseducated. It is clear to us – based on the research we have carried out and our own experiences of economics education – that the monopoly of a particular and narrow form of economics, and the way the subject matter is taught ('pedagogy') amount to nothing less than the dictionary definition of indoctrination. We argue this by showing two things. Firstly, that economics students only learn one particular type of economics; and secondly, that they are taught to accept this type of economics in an uncritical manner. We illustrate this by drawing on evidence from an in-depth curriculum review of seven Russell Group universities.[4] We analysed all of the course guides and examinations at these universities, for a total of 174 economics modules.[5] As far as we know, this kind of detailed curriculum review has never been undertaken before.

What are the consequences of this indoctrination in economics education? At a basic level students are being sold short and are receiving an inadequate education. We are also failing to equip the next generation of economic experts with the knowledge and skills to build healthy, resilient societies. Economics graduates leave university with a narrow, fixed understanding of what economics is and little or no empirical knowledge of how the UK economy functions or of the key economic events of the last century that have shaped our world today. Tomorrow's experts are being taught only one perspective as if there were no other way of doing economics. Critical and independent thinking is discouraged and there is little or no history, ethics or politics in economics courses.

There are also more fundamental consequences of the domination of economics by a single perspective. In the next section we outline the core features of the dominant perspective in economics and illustrate its connections with econocracy.

Reproducing econocracy

Critics of the type of economics that dominates economics education today often refer to it as 'neoclassical economics', a term that has changed its meaning over the past century. In the early twentieth century, neoclassical economics referred to the model of the market economy as a self-stabilising system that always produced the best possible outcomes, but today it is a broader and more flexible label.

Neoclassical economics, like all academic perspectives, involves certain assumptions about the object of study (in this case the economy): how to define it, what to focus on, how humans behave within it, and what research methods are appropriate for undertaking this study. It doesn't necessarily prescribe what its proponents should think but it does shape how they think, what they value and how they make decisions. There are diverse and even conflicting

Exhibit 2.1 The three prongs of neoclassical economics[6]

Individualism: Neoclassical theory focuses on the behaviour of individual agents, an 'agent' being defined as some sort of economic decision-maker. These include agents such as consumers, who must decide what to buy, but also entail modelling the production decisions of firms or even the political decisions of governments as individual decisions. Neoclassical economics therefore has an 'atomistic' view of the world, and tries to build an understanding of the economy as a whole from the decisions of individuals.

Optimisation: These agents seek to optimise explicit goals in their behaviour. The definition of 'optimise' is to 'make the best or most effective use of a situation or resource'. A consumer might want to use the money they have to buy the commodities they want the most; a firm might want to get the highest profit given the materials available and their technological prowess. The aims of agents can be wide ranging and they may even suffer from faulty decision making, but in neoclassical economics agents almost always optimise some goal.

Equilibrium: The decisions of individual agents must balance – a situation which is called 'equilibrium'. Agents make decisions about what to produce, buy, sell, and invest in, and if these decisions are correct then no agent will have an incentive to change their behaviour. Agents adjust their behaviour until they have, based on their individual judgment, achieved the outcome which is best for them, and there is no reason for anyone to alter their behaviour, resulting in a stable equilibrium.

---

theories within neoclassical economics but they all share three key theoretical 'prongs' which taken together form its core, outlined in Exhibit 2.1.

Neoclassical economics encourages a view of the economy that is characterised by two main features and is intimately linked to the three prongs. Firstly, it is based on a mechanical view of the world. Economies are composed of individual agents who interact in a way based on well-behaved, predictable mathematical rules. This behaviour tends to produce a situation that, though not necessarily ideal, is stable, and this is known as equilibrium. In this sense economies are not unlike pendulums: they may experience short-term change and volatility but they eventually return to a stable state. Economists study how changes in the economy affect agents' optimal decisions and therefore the ultimate equilibrium they settle at to come to conclusions about different aspects of the economy.

This view of the economy as characterised by *knowable, predictable forces* – underpinned by the certainty of optimisation and equilibrium – means that economic experts believe they can model a situation, often mathematically, to make a prediction of how some policy will affect the economy. This idea is reflected in econocracy in the assumption that there are fixed mechanical relationships between variables like unemployment and inflation, or taxes and investment. This is not the same as saying that everything in neoclassical economics is certain: there will almost always be probabilities and potential errors attached to any prediction. But it does mean that if policymakers want to achieve particular political goals, economists can claim to design policy scientifically to achieve those goals. We have seen this with the many examples of economists being employed in important policymaking positions and institutions in Chapter 1.

Secondly, neoclassical economics paints a picture of the economy as a stand-alone, abstract system that emerges naturally from the actions of individual agents. It remains largely silent on questions of how the modern economy came about, which institutions (accepted legal structures like property rights, as well as the social norms surrounding possession that go with them) and systems of governance are required for it to function. Neither is there a question of *why* agents behave as they do – agents simply take 'optimal' decisions which it is not for the economist to question – or whether the economic goals embedded in its models are desirable. This results in a detached, technocratic vision of the economy.

This view rests on the distinction economists make between 'positive' and 'normative' economics. They claim that much of economics is positive, which means it merely describes the world and is thus value free. Such a view was summarised by the writers of the popular book *Freakonomics*, Steven Levitt and Stephen Dubner, when they said that 'the economic approach isn't meant to describe the world as any of us might want it to be … but rather explain what it actually is'.[7] On this logic, economic experts can take the objectives set by politicians through democratic mechanisms and work out the best way to achieve them within the boundaries of how their education taught them that the economy functions.

However, by taking certain goals as a given in their models and policy prescriptions, economists often make political decisions about how to define the economy. We saw this in practice in Chapter 1, when economists designed the mobile phone spectrum auctions that neglected goals such as rural network coverage in favour of government revenue maximisation. It also applies more broadly: the emphasis on quantifiable aspects of economic well-being – what economists usually term 'welfare' – leads to a neglect of other components of well-being. In principle, economic agents can 'optimise' anything, but in practice the type of mathematics used by economists means that there is a focus on material sources of well-being such as income and consumption over less tangible issues such as human rights, job security and mental health. All of these things are clearly valued by humans, but neoclassical economics pushes the latter to one side. The choice of what models focus on represents an implicit judgement about what is important which is ultimately political in nature.

Neoclassical economics, as defined above, underpinned almost every model taught in every module in our curriculum review. Teaching this perspective as if it *is* economics allows economists to see their discipline as a complete system, and imbues them with the idea that neoclassical economics can and should be used to understand any problem that they face. Economics education is encouraging the economists of tomorrow to believe that we should delegate large parts of economic decision making to experts and that public engagement with economics discussion and decision making is not necessary or desirable.

In the next section we illustrate how this way of thinking about the economy is drilled into the next generation of economic experts in a systematic way. Widespread belief in the scientific toolkit of neoclassical economics means that the content of economics education across the seven universities we studied was remarkably uniform. Econocracy is reproducing itself. As long as this continues we will not be able to build the new relationship between economists and society that we have argued is so important in reclaiming democracy.

The monopoly of neoclassical economics

At the seven universities we studied there was a remarkable similarity in the content and structure of economics courses.[8] Economics education mass-produces graduates by teaching them a set of standardised core topics that form the heart of the neoclassical approach. The feeling for students of being transported into an alternative, neoclassical reality as described above is the process all economics students must go through to become experts.

The neoclassical toolkit is imparted to students through a series of compulsory core modules made up of macroeconomics, microeconomics (often abbreviated to macro and micro, respectively), as well as mathematics, statistics and econometrics (a branch of statistics specifically developed for answering economic questions). We identified two generic course structures, which either had the core macro and micro models squeezed into (the former) two years or spread out over all three. Our curriculum review shows that both macro and micro courses are taught in similar ways across the country.

If, as we have argued, society's collective understanding of the economy is shaped by neoclassical economics without us realising it, then it is important for citizens to understand some of the key features of this perspective. Therefore, we now briefly sketch out the core toolkit of neoclassical economics taught at all the universities we studied. We are keenly aware that despite our best efforts this section is technical and abstract, but we hope that if readers persevere they will at the end have a much better idea of how economic experts think and will as a result be better equipped to hold them to account.

Microeconomics

Microeconomics is focused on the small: it is the study of individual households, firms, industries and markets. An outsider might expect such an approach to be quite hands-on, entailing case studies of firms, visits to the stock market and interviews with people about how they spend their money. Yet economic teaching of micro-economics is almost universally abstract and mathematical. As the economist Ronald Coase once joked, 'If economists wished to study the horse, they wouldn't go and look at horses. They'd sit in their studies and say to themselves, "What would I do if I were a horse?"'[9] Students across the country are invited to solve abstract mathematical problems that they are told represent the decisions of economic agents – even though evidence for this is rarely given in class – but they are not told to go out and study these agents themselves.

Microeconomics modules at every university in our curriculum review centre on individual consumers (consumer theory) and firms (producer theory). Agents follow the type of optimising rules outlined in the previous section: for example, consumers in economic theory 'maximise utility', which means they buy the combination of products that gives them the most satisfaction compared to any other combination they could afford with their income. The most basic world in microeconomics, and one to which all students will be introduced, is a smoothly functioning world where everyone behaves rationally and has all the relevant information, and where markets

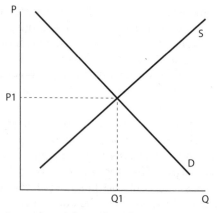

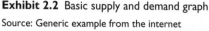

Exhibit 2.2 Basic supply and demand graph

Source: Generic example from the internet

function perfectly, resulting in a 'socially optimal' (i.e. desirable, in the language of economists) outcome.

Such a situation can be represented using the types of maths and diagrams loved by economics, as illustrated by the supply and demand graph in Exhibit 2.2, taught at every university in our curriculum review. The basic idea is that in a given market – say, the one for shoes – the S curve represents the underlying decisions of producers about how many shoes they are willing to manufacture, while the D curve represents the decisions of consumers about how many they are willing to buy. Where these two curves meet – where the decisions of consumer and producers balance – is a stable and optimal equilibrium, showing what quantity of shoes will be bought/sold (Q1) and at what price (P1).

After teaching the 'ideal' economy outlined above, microeconomics classes move on to discuss things that may prevent the economy from reaching a socially optimal outcome. It could be that consumers or firms do not have enough information about their potential choices and so make a decision that is objectively not in their best interests. A famous example that routinely pops up in economics education is the used-car market, where it is said that the risk that you might be buying a defective car will lead the market to break down, or 'market failure'. There are many types of these market imperfections, and economists study them to see how much of a problem they are and how government policy might rectify them, if at all.

Microeconomics courses show how directly economic logic influences politics. For example, the introductory textbook *Economics* by John Sloman and Alison Wride argues that 'there are two major [social] objectives that we can identify: efficiency and equity'.[10] The textbook begins by showing 'how a perfect market economy could under certain conditions lead to "social efficiency" [but] how markets in practice fail to meet social goals'. It then states that 'if the government is to replace the market and provide goods and services directly, it will need some way of establishing their costs and benefits', which can be done by using cost–benefit analysis (CBA).[11]

The Green Book, a document produced by the Treasury that sets out the framework for the appraisal and evaluation of all government policies, programmes and projects, reads remarkably like an economics textbook in places.[12] It stresses from the outset that the two main rationales for government intervention in the market are 'efficiency' and 'equity'. It then specifies the use of CBA to determine different ways of achieving this rationale.[13]

Macroeconomics

Macroeconomics deals with bigger questions such as how countries can establish and sustain long-term growth, how they can control short-term economic fluctuations (commonly known as 'boom and bust') and how they can manage unemployment and inflation. It is therefore surprising that instead of giving students a historical and empirical understanding of these issues, macroeconomics classes also focus on abstract models. These models are a little easier to relate to than microeconomic models, since they deal with ideas that we hear about in the news every day. Despite this, they are also remarkably similar in some respects. Macroeconomics can broadly be split into two different areas: models that focus on how countries can sustain long-term economic growth, and models that focus on how countries can control short-term boom and bust.

Long-term growth models are based almost entirely on a model known as the 'Solow Growth Model' – referring to its inventor Robert Solow – which is featured at every university in our review. Such models attempt to show how different factors (such as technology or natural resources) contribute to the growth of economies. They have been influential, with a modern variant called 'Endogenous Growth Theory' (which was also taught at all seven universities we reviewed) having been cited by politicians such as Gordon Brown.[14] Essentially, this theory states that long-term sustained growth can be achieved by boosting skill levels and improving technology. Such a theory is the backbone for the current focus within government policymaking on

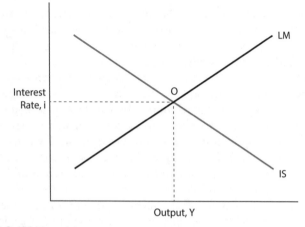

Exhibit 2.3 IS/LM model

Source: Generic example from the internet

improving education and skills, which – as we shall see in Chapter 5 – has influenced higher education policy in important ways.

Short-term macroeconomics uses two main approaches. The first, which could be described as introductory or intermediate, entails the use of simple diagrams to represent the economy as a whole, the most famous of which is the IS-LM model,[15] taught at every university in our curriculum review. This closely resembles the demand–supply diagram from microeconomics, but now the curves show how interactions between the market for goods and services (the IS curve) and the market for money (the LM curve) affect the GDP of the whole economy, rather than just how a particular market works (see Exhibit 2.3).

The second, more advanced approach in macroeconomics also resembles microeconomics, borrowing the 'optimising agent' in the form of a 'representative agent' that is supposed to represent the economy as a whole. This agent lives forever and makes optimal production and consumption decisions over its entire lifetime, predicting a path for GDP, prices and other economic variables such as unemployment over time. Recessions in this world are generally caused by 'exogenous shocks': sudden disturbances that come from nowhere, affecting the agents' decisions and therefore the economy.

One of the main pillars of econocracy, Central Bank (CB) independence – now established across the world – has roots in this type of economics. CB independence is almost universally accepted among economists at least in part due to a model known as the 'Barro–Gordon' model, a mathematical model that follows the 'optimising agent' logic outlined above and is taught at four out of seven universities in our curriculum review.[16] It concludes that politicians, if left in charge of CBs, will simply pursue short-term gain, pushing inflation above its optimal level to reduce unemployment and making everyone worse off in the long run. This reduces the management of central banks to a technical exercise to be conducted by economists, who supposedly know better.

Textbook teaching

One key indicator of how similar economics education is across the country is the central role textbooks play. A key part of other social science courses is engaging critically with the discipline's academic literature. This has many purposes, including giving the student an understanding of the debates and research agendas in their discipline, and allowing the student to engage independently and critically with academics while improving research and review skills. In economics, by contrast, textbooks play a dominant role and few modules, particularly core modules, have any required reading from economics journals. Students are rarely required to undertake independent research and, as a student so aptly stated, 'the textbook is the bible'. When students are pointed towards the literature, it remains firmly within the realms of the neoclassical perspective. Such an approach to research entrenches the view that economics is a closed, fixed body of knowledge.

The prominent use of textbooks in economics education means that the market is highly lucrative and is dominated in the UK by a few of the usual suspects. In microeconomics a textbook written by Hal Varian is used as the primary textbook by five of the seven universities, and one written by Hugh Gravelle and Ray Rees is used at some point by three of the seven. The situation is similar in macroeconomics, where Greg Mankiw's textbook is used at some point during the three years of core macro modules at all seven universities. In the second year, usually the year in which the standardised models are really pushed on students, six out of the seven either use a textbook by Mankiw or one by Stephen Williamson.

These textbooks are written with generic examples so that they can be sold in as many countries as possible, and universities often buy textbook bundles that come with lecture slides and multiple-choice questions. Academics are expected to provide standardised modules that will be similar wherever you study. They often follow a textbook closely and may even teach from lecture slides provided by the textbook publisher. Academic freedom over what is taught is severely curtailed so that teaching style, which is itself constrained by the lecture format, becomes one of the few outlets through which academics can express themselves.

That economics has become a textbook subject illustrates something important about its view of academic progress. All the knowledge that is considered to be relevant to an economist is in the textbook, and to the student of economics these works set in stone what economics is. The textbook is considered to be the crystallisation of the economic toolkit and what isn't included becomes irrelevant to the modern discipline.

Models that fall from heaven

Yuan Yang studied politics, philosophy and economics. In her philosophy classes, she recalls the teachers saying, 'You see all this furniture in this room and the mental furniture you've got lying round in your mind? We're going to take all that away from you and rebuild it from scratch.' These classes involved grappling with questions like 'What is it to *know* something?', 'What are the roots of ethics?' and 'What's the point of having a government and education provided by the state?' However, while she struggled in philosophy classes with these fundamental questions about the fabric of the world and our place in it, in her economics classes there was no questioning at all:

> It was as if we'd walked into a very specifically prepared room and we just had to accept that. And you'd think 'but this room is really clumsy and I'd like to put the table here and I'd rather rearrange it.' And the teachers would say, 'No this is how the room was when we got here and we have to keep it this way for all purposes.' The relationship between what you do [in economics] and what you think it is about is so stretched that you might imagine there would be a disclaimer saying, 'This is why we are doing this, not what you thought you were going to do.' And I just remember the feeling of it being really jarring. And thinking, 'is this really what it's all about?'

The abilities to think critically and independently are two skills that are universally agreed to be important parts of education and are qualities that all universities, without fail, claim to give to their graduates. Their complete absence was what was so jarring for Yuan.

Critical thinking is about being able to deconstruct academic arguments into their constituent parts and evaluate their strengths and weaknesses. This can include evaluation of how well theory explains empirical evidence, the quality of empirical evidence, the internal logic of the argument, or the values and assumptions underlying the theory. Independent thinking is about critically evaluating different theories and perspectives and coming to a reasoned judgement about which best fits a particular purpose in a particular situation. It is about not deferring to authority or 'group think' but about being brave enough to argue a point even if it isn't popular. While critical and independent thinking are distinct skills, they are arguably interrelated to the extent that one isn't possible without the other.

These are essential skills not only for academia but for participating in social and political life and succeeding in the working world. They are also almost completely absent from economics education across the country. In our curriculum review we went through every question of the final exams of all modules to look at what they asked students to do and to understand what skills they require for students to do well.[17] On average at the universities studied, final exams constitute 81 per cent of all assessment (with the rest being made up by midterms and coursework) and so we are analysing the vast bulk of assessment. We divided the questions into four categories: operate a model, description, multiple-choice questions and critical evaluation. We will discuss in turn the role of each of these in economics education.

All academic disciplines, to varying degrees, rely on abstraction: the process of detaching objects and processes from their specific characteristics and grouping them according to some shared characteristic so that a more general theory about them may be constructed. Economics chooses to do this mostly through modelling, expressing human behaviour mathematically. Models are often associated with economics and, as discussed in Chapter 1, they can imbue economics with a technical mystique. Economists sell models as simple, harmless devices for isolating key parts of the world and telling a story about them, and they can indeed serve this purpose. But generally speaking, the reality of economic models is far less benign.

The trouble is that in economics education, abstraction seems to be the object of interest rather than a tool to advance understanding. As one student put it, 'You learn to solve models before you even know what a model is and its purpose.' Even further from sight is the notion that there may be other ways to study economics, whether through different modelling methods or through more qualitative approaches.

It is as if students must be initiated into neoclassical economics in a way that shields them entirely from the real world, potential criticism or alternatives. The specifics and supposed context of a model may change (as we saw earlier, it might be a model that claims to represent the whole economy, or one that claims to represent an individual market such as the one for shoes), but the general methodology, underpinned by the three prongs outlined earlier, does not. By the time students leave education, they are wont to believe that any economic question must use neoclassical economics as its starting point.

What our criterion 'operate a model' tries to capture is questions where students have been asked to solve models and not comment in any way on their usefulness or evaluate their applicability. In our curriculum review we found that 55 per cent of all the macro and micro modules studied and 48 per cent of all exams consisted of operating a model.[18] Therefore, economics education is largely made up of models that are, according to one student, presented as if they 'fall from heaven in a perfect, ever-true form'.

Students are surrounded by a series of diagrammatical and mathematical models that frame economic issues as purely mechanical problems with clear right-or-wrong answers. The questions asked are often purely abstract, with students rarely or never asked to apply the model to real-world data or evaluate its applicability in particular circumstances. Exhibits 2.4 and 2.5 show a typical macroeconomic and microeconomic model, respectively. In both cases, the student is asked to solve the maths of a utility maximising representative agent and show how tweaking the model affects the results. On first glance one could be fooled by words like 'income' and 'taxes' into thinking that this exercise is related to the real world, but in fact it is a purely hypothetical exercise and reality is nowhere to be found. These exam questions are used merely as a test of technical ability and of students' capacity to think within a model, rather than as a way of critically engaging with what they have been taught.

Even though these theories all use similar techniques, their relationship to one another is not always clear: a typical exam will have a separate model for each question and no discussion of their relevance to one another. Thus, much like a worker on a production line, the student must learn only to perform particular tasks at particular times, without necessarily developing a coherent understanding of the theory, the discipline or the model's applicability.

Methods to guide students in choosing when (and when not) to use models in different situations are largely absent from core macro and micro modules; in other words, they are asked to solve mathematical

Exhibit 2.4 A typical macroeconomic 'operate a model' question

Where appropriate, make use of graphs and equations in your answers.

11. Consider a two-period economy in which the representative consumer maximizes the life-time utility function $U(C_1,C_2) = u(C_1) + (1 + t)$ $\beta u(C_2)$ subject to the life-time budget constraint $(1 + t)C_1 + \dfrac{C_2}{R} = W$, where $0 < \beta < 1$, W is the present value of after-tax life-time income, t is the VAT tax rate, and $R = 1 + r$, where r is the interest rate.

(a) [3 marks] Show that the optimality condition relating C_1 and C_2 is the following:

$$u'(C_1) = (1 + t)\beta R u'(C_2)$$

(b) [3 marks] Suppose the utility function is $u(C) = \log(C)$. Derive the optimal levels of (C_1) and (C_2).

(c) [3 marks] The consumer receives incomes Y_1 and Y_2 and pays lump-sum taxes T_1 and T_2 in periods 1 and 2. Suppose the government uses all tax revenue to finance a project that costs G in period 1. Write down the intertemporal budget constraint for the government.

(d) [5 marks] Suppose there is no VAT, i.e. $t = 0$. Use this model to explain Ricardian equivalence.

(e) [6 marks] Suppose there is VAT, i.e. $t > 0$. Show that the result you have derived in part (d) might not hold here. Explain your answer.

Source: Reproduced from a 2nd year LSE Macroeconomic Principles exam

puzzles unthinkingly. This form of training creates economic experts who view the economy as a model that can be broken down into clearly defined problems with a set number of variables and clear right-and-wrong answers. It is one of the founding assumptions of econocracy because it forms the basis of the special claim on knowledge held by economists about the way the economy works.

On the other hand, qualitative tools such as surveys, interviews, case studies, ethnographies and analysis of written documents are almost completely absent from economics curricula. While the modelling tools that are taught are designed to be operated by detached experts, these qualitative methods are often those which require engagement with the subject of analysis – whether this is the consumer, firm, government institution or citizen. As a consequence, students are taught to study the economy without ever having to study or engage with real people. This state of affairs in economics provides

Exhibit 2.5 A typical microeconomic 'operate a model' question

---

Question 7: (2+2+2 marks) A risk-averse agent with von-Neumann Morgenstern utility function $U(w,a)= -\dfrac{100,000}{w} - a$, where w denotes his wealth and a the unobservable cost of effort, could be employed by a monopolistic principal to perform a task. This task yields a profit of £7,500 when it is a success and a profit £5,000 when it is a "failure". The probability of success or failure depends on the effort put in by the agent. If the agent puts in no effort $(a = a_L = 0)$ the probability of failure is 100%. If the agent puts in high effort $(a = a_H = 0)$ the probability of failure is reduced to $0 < p < 0.5$. If the agent decides not to be employed by the principal, he receives the reservation utility $U_0 = -20$.

- In an optimal contract which induces effort, how much will the agent be paid if the project is a failure?
- In an optimal contract, which induces effort, how much will the agent be paid if the project is a success and $p = 0.5$?
- What is the highest possible failure rate p such that the project yields a non-negative profit rate when it effort is induced?

Source: Reproduced from a 2nd year Exeter Microeconomics II exam

the intellectual basis for the devaluation of the role and knowledge of the non-expert in economic discussion and decision making.

Our case that economics education involves memorising and regurgitating neoclassical economic theory uncritically is supported by the large proportion of marks available for descriptive questions. The 'describe' questions can be broken into two broad categories:

1) Describe a policy, institution, argument or event, e.g. 'What is a fully funded social security system?' 'What did Barack Obama's stimulus package consist of?'
2) Describe a theory, e.g. 'What is the Friedman rule?'

Crucially, these questions do not ask students to critically engage but to regurgitate. As with operating a model, there is no indication that evaluation is required. A further 17 per cent of the exams for core micro and macro modules and 20 per cent of the exams for all modules consist of 'describe' questions.

Multiple-choice questions are similarly prominent and problematic, since they directly frame economic questions as having one right answer. This may apply to some questions, such as the definition of

GDP, but it does not apply to questions such as how one would go about measuring GDP in practice, the advantages and drawbacks of GDP, or alternative measures of economic progress. Four of the seven universities make use of multiple-choice in the core micro and macro exams: multiple-choice accounts for 44 per cent of macro/ micro exams at Exeter and 53 per cent at Manchester. In total, 20 per cent of core macro and micro exams and 8 per cent of all modules consist of multiple-choice questions. The vast majority of these were simply another way of asking 'operate a model'-style questions, meaning that such questions actually constitute an even higher proportion of degrees than outlined earlier.

Questions that are evaluative come broadly under the umbrella of independent judgement. They ask students to take a theory, model, argument or event and critically engage with it using independent thought and drawing on appropriate empirical evidence. To take two of the examples above, if they were instead testing a student's ability to evaluate, they would become: 1) 'Was Obama's stimulus package effective?' and 2) 'How useful is the Friedman rule in design-ing policy?' A defining feature of critical evaluation is that there is more than one possible answer and therefore the student must demonstrate an ability to arrive at their own (coherent) conclusion.

We found that in the core macro and micro exams only 8 per cent of marks awarded asked for any form of critical evaluation or independent judgement. This low figure was boosted notably by the percentage of marks for evaluation at Cambridge. Exhibit 2.6 shows the overall breakdown between different types of questions for all the exams in core macro and micro modules. For all exams we examined, a staggering 76 per cent of questions entailed no form of critical or independent thinking whatsoever.[19] At the London School of Economics (LSE), the top-ranked university in our sample and one of the most prestigious places to study economics in the world, this figure stands at 83 per cent and at 97 per cent for all compulsory modules. Exhibit 2.7 lays out all the modules taught at LSE and their corresponding percentages of marks for evaluation tasks.

What all this means is that the people who are entrusted to run our economy are in almost no way taught to think about it critically. It is hardly an exaggeration to say that it is now possible to go through an economics degree without once having to venture an opinion. A striking case study of the lack of development of critical skills in economics is the total lack of focus on ethics. Economists tend to regard ethics as a subject for philosophy classes and, instead of engag-ing deeply with questions, students learn standard narrow theoretical

A: All modules

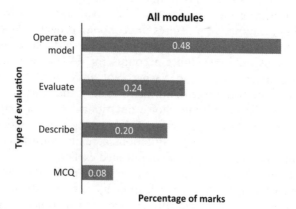

B: All modules by university

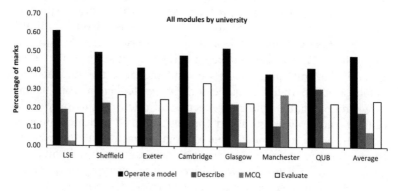

C: Core micro and macro modules

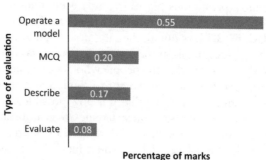

Exhibit 2.6 Curriculum review breakdown of assessment

D: Core micro and macro modules by university

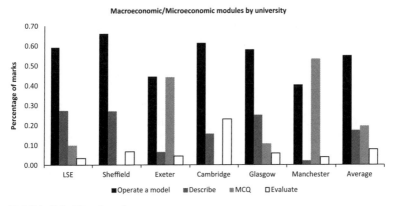

Exhibit 2.6 (Continued)

Exhibit 2.7 Percentage of marks for evaluation in all London School of Economics economics modules

Module	Percentage of marks for evaluation
History of Economic Thought	91.6
Development Economics	34.7
Economic Policy Analysis	26.7
Public Economics	25
Monetary Economics	20
International Economics	18.5
Labour Economics	18
Industrial Economics	8.4
Macroeconomic Principles	8
Political Economy	6.8
Economics B	5.8
Behavioural Economics	4.4
Advanced Economic Analysis	3.3
Economic Theory and it's applications	0
Microeconomic Principles 1	0
Microeconomic Principles 2	0

criteria for judging whether or not something is desirable. 'Ideas of the good society were generally absent,' reported one student.

As is common, this narrowness is probably a consequence of the closed-off nature of the discipline: economic theory sidesteps ethical questions by making them seem like technical questions.

Textbooks typically ask which policies are 'optimal' based on theoretical, scientific-sounding criteria such as Pareto optimality, social welfare functions and cost–benefit analysis, present throughout degree programmes, all of which we discuss in more detail in Chapter 3. Refusing to engage with other ethical theories shuts out any potential for debate and leads students to believe that there are only set ways of judging policies.

In the film *Modern Times*, Charlie Chaplin famously played the role of a production line worker who has to robotically carry out the same task over and over again at breakneck speed. Chaplin's protagonist stops to catch his breath, complaining about his current situation, but this leads him to fall behind the other workers, so that he needs to work increasingly frantically in order to keep up. In many ways, modern economics students have become like Chaplin's worker, incentivised to act in a similar way. Students are delivered set tasks, composed of models on which they must robotically perform some operation in order to to solve a problem, but are not incentivised to think about them critically. Today's syllabuses do not encourage students to step back and assess what they are being taught, but reward repeated regurgitation and conformism. This amounts to nothing less than indoctrination into the neoclassical way of thinking about the economy.

The eviction of the real world

'I could have read the *Financial Times* and the *Economist* for the past 100 hundred years and I wouldn't have got a single extra point', one student told us. One of the features of an economics degree that often irritates students is the near total absence of the real world in the classroom. For example, of the 'operate a model' questions that form such a large part of an economics degree, only 3 per cent attempt any link to the real world, for instance by asking students to show how a particular model explains the Eurozone crisis.

Where facts *are* presented in economics classes, they are often 'stylised facts' – general, widely accepted pieces of evidence about economics – and the answers can even be found in the lecture notes. While better than nothing, stylised facts are simply insufficient to give students a critical perspective on models, since by their nature they are broad and could be consistent with any number of models; one example of a 'stylised fact' about the labour market might be that unemployment rises in recessions. Students do not build an in-depth knowledge of real-world economics but instead glean only a superficial understanding of the world while devoting most of their time to abstract models.

Here are some things you might expect an economics graduate to know but which are not typically required to pass an economics degree:

- what international institutions like the IMF and World Bank do and how they are run
- what happened during key events in twentieth-century economic history, like the Great Depression, Bretton Woods, the East Asian financial crisis and end of the Gold Standard
- how multinational firms like Apple and Glencore operate in practice
- the names of any of the 20 biggest companies in the world
- the current or projected size and shape of the British economy as measured by economic indicators such as GDP, real wage trends, the Gini coefficient, poverty, unemployment, balance of trade, inflation, Government Budget Deficit and private debt
- how those statistics are measured and their strengths and weaknesses
- the different sides of current economic debates such as the effect of immigration on the economy, the effect of EU membership and the future for Greece in the Eurozone
- the causes and consequences of the 2008 financial crisis.

The eviction of the real world is perhaps directly linked to the rise of a single perspective. It symbolises a discipline that believes that if it can find the 'true' story or model in a given situation, there will be little need for extensive and wide-ranging knowledge of that world – practitioners can merely check their models if they want to make a prediction. The lack of more fundamental debate about how to think about the economy means that the models can simply be learned and regurgitated one after another.

A consequence of this state of affairs is that students who feel there is a gap between what they are taught and the real world often suffer from impostor syndrome. When we are asked what caused the financial crisis we can't explain using knowledge from our degree except by drawing an IS-LM graph, a source of deep frustration to us and many of our contemporaries. This gap in our knowledge was starkly illustrated when the Post-Crash Economics Society (PCES) hosted a lecture on what had happened during the 2008 financial crisis. Afterwards one of the authors of this book commented to another member of PCES, who was a sociology student, that the lecture had been informative. The sociology student replied that he had already had similar in-depth lectures on the financial crisis in one of his classes. When sociology students know more about financial crises than economics students, something is wrong – and not with sociology.

In a similar vein, one student who had recently started a Master's course at Oxford told us:

> If I was put into a central bank or position in economic policy-making right now, I would have almost no tools that would help me understand the situation the economy is in or to help me make decisions.

Economic experts are at the heart of econocracy. Yet their understanding of the world is often limited to a fixed set of models, taught in a manner that is almost completely disconnected from the real world. Those who do not believe in these models feel they lack the basic empirical knowledge to fall back on; those who do believe in these models will not feel that the real world is crucial for their understanding of the economy.

The failure of economics

The evidence we have presented shows conclusively that the next generation of economists, policymakers, bankers and business people are being taught that there is one way of doing economics. As a result whole generations of economists believe that there is only one legitimate way to study the economy and that everything else is either a different subject or bad economics. The methodological approach of neoclassical economics is rarely evaluated critically but instead taken as a given.

The result of teaching students only the neoclassical way of thinking is that economic experts have no critical perspective on the limitations of their expertise. Most students are not even told that there are other ways to think about the economy and as a result they do not see economics as a subject with debate and disagreement. In the words of one bemused student, 'I had always thought of economics as a lively debate. Until I started university, that is.' Students are repeatedly exposed to abstract economic concepts, ideas and models that have the same key features, which cements them in the student's mind and shapes how they think about the economy. As a result the next generation of economists will continue to hold a belief in the scientific rigour of their expertise.

We do not want to seem as if we are criticising or undermining economics students themselves. Economics students are intelligent and capable, which is one of the reasons they remain in high demand *despite* receiving the education we have detailed (more on this in Chapter 5). It is a further testament to these students if they manage to come out with a critical, broad array of knowledge about economics. However, the evidence above cannot be ignored. Receiving an education that is narrow, uncritical and disconnected from the real world will necessarily limit students' understanding and teach them to think in a particular way. These limitations are something the authors of this book have struggled to address in our own lives, and are highly damaging given that economics has become so important in modern society.

When we set out to do our curriculum review we wanted to understand how economics is taught, but our results also revealed much about the current state of academic economics. Most academic economists might recognise this picture of economics education but would argue that it was a sign of the strength of the discipline, not a shortcoming. The claim is that the uniformity of economics education is a result of progress in economic knowledge and consensus within the profession. Instead of disputing the monopoly of neoclassical economics, economists might simply deny it matters by rejecting the possibility that there is more than one legitimate economic toolkit which students should learn how to use.

Earlier in this chapter we set out the links between neoclassical economics and the particular understanding of the economy present in an econocracy. Now we have shown that economists define their subject in terms of the neoclassical way of thinking, we can see how neoclassical economics, through the influence of experts, shapes wider societal views about the economy. The exclusion of other ways of thinking about the economy limits the political choices we have in society to those which make sense within the neoclassical framework.

The aim of this chapter was to open up the academic discipline of economics to public scrutiny. If political debates are going to become dominated by economics, and if people believe that economics is only understood by economists, then it is important that the public understand the neoclassical way of thinking and its limitations. The worst thing about the status quo is that whole generations of economists now genuinely believe that neoclassical economics is the one and only way to study economics. In the next chapter we show how mistaken this belief is.

58 The econocracy

Notes

1 John, M. Keynes, *The General Theory of Employment, Interest and Money*, New York: Harcourt, Brace & World, 1936, 383–4.
2 Paul A. Samuelson, 'Foreword', in Phillip Saunders and William Walstad (eds), *The Principles of Economics Course: A Handbook for Instructors*, New York: McGraw-Hill Publishing, 1990, ix–x.
3 *Oxford Dictionaries*, 1st edn [online]. Available at: http://www.oxford dictionaries.com/definition/english/indoctrinate (accessed 22 April 2016).
4 Cambridge, Cardiff, Exeter, London School of Economics, Manchester, Queen's University Belfast and Sheffield.
5 See Appendix 2 for the methodology of the curriculum review
6 Yanis Varoufakis and Christian Arnsperger, 'What is neoclassical economics?', *Post-Autistic Economics Review* 38 (July 2006): 2–13.
7 Stephen J. Dubner and Steven D. Levitt. *Superfreakonomics: Global Cooling, Patriotic Prostitutes and Why Suicide Bombers Should Buy Life Insurance*, London: Penguin, 2010, 16.
8 The only exception was Queen's University Belfast, which does not follow the otherwise ubiquitous structure of compulsory macroeconomic and microeconomic modules. At QUB, modules focus on more specific topics, such as growth theory or game theory, and do not try and fit everything into the core. In the final year they do have advanced macro and micro courses that are similar to ones at other universities but these are non-compulsory. The advanced microeconomics course is also very pluralist. Regardless of this, overall the style of exam questions was remarkably similar.
9 Ronald Coase, 'Opening speech to ISNIE 1999'. Available at: https://coase.org/coasespeech.htm (accessed 25 April 2016).
10 John Sloman and Alison Wride, *Economics*, Harlow: Pearson, 7th edn, 2009, 10. Loosely speaking, equity is fairness or equality.
11 Sloman and Wride, *Economics*, 304.
12 HM Treasury. *The Green Book: Appraisal and Evaluation in Central Government*, Treasury Guidance, July 2011.
13 Efficiency is also defined as Pareto optimality, a very specific definition of the word used by economists that we return to discuss in more detail in Chapter 3.
14 Nick Crafts, '"Post-neoclassical Endogenous Growth Theory": what are its policy implications?', *Oxford Review of Economic Policy* 12(2) (1996): 30–47.
15 'IS' stands for Investment-Savings, while 'LM' standards for 'Liquidity Preference-Money'.
16 Robert Barro and David Gordon, 'Rules, discretion and reputation in a model of monetary policy', *Journal of Monetary Economics* 12(1) (1983): 101–21.

17 We had 174 course module guides but only 156 exams. This is because some courses are 100 per cent coursework-based, but also because others could not be obtained. We have no reason to believe that the exams that we failed to attain were significantly different from the rest of our sample.

18 QUB is not included in the core macro/micro figures for the reasons outlined in footnote 6.

19 Even the low evaluative scores we have given may well be inflated. Often questions appear to be asking for an independent judgement, but actually the answer is contained within the lecture notes. However, it was not always possible to know this, and wherever we have been uncertain whether or not a question was evaluative, we have given it the benefit of the doubt. See methodology in Appendix 2 for full details.

Chapter 3

Beyond neoclassical economics

Economics as a contested discipline

pluralism *n. a condition or system in which two or more states, groups, principles, sources of authority, etc., coexist.*[1]

Economics education shapes how its students think about the world. This makes economics powerful, as those who study it often go on to have significant authority. Economics is presented as a unified field and its association with maths and statistics makes it easy to see it as a science. However, this is not the reality. In this chapter we argue that there is a strong case for multiple perspectives in economics (pluralism), each of which provide different ways of analysing reality.

We begin by making a two-pronged theoretical case for pluralism in economics. Firstly, pluralism is a necessary feature of economics education because it teaches students to realise that there is more than one way of thinking about the economy. This is valuable educationally because students develop broader analytical skills as well as independent and critical thinking skills, and must be more reflective. Secondly, widely held standards of academic practice are undermined by the attempt to define economics as a single perspective, and pluralism is necessary to rectify these shortcomings. The status quo in economics is not legitimate from an educational or intellectual perspective.

We then go on to make the practical case for pluralism. Neoclassical economics has strengths, but it also has shortcomings and blind spots, and experts trained only in neoclassical economics are unable to address many of the most important challenges the world faces. We show this through three case studies: macroeconomic stability, the environment and climate change, and inequality. Pluralism in economics is crucial for properly understanding modern societies.

Finally, we illustrate the political implications of neoclassical economics. As we demonstrated in Chapter 1, economics has never before had such influence over politics and so it is important to understand how it has shaped politics. We argue that pluralism in economics is necessary to broaden political debate and build a political system through which to make complex political decisions democratically. Taken together, these arguments form a clear case for the urgent reform of the academic discipline of economics.

The theoretical case for pluralism in economics[2]

> Whether you can observe a thing or not depends on the theory which you use. It is the theory which decides what can be observed.
>
> Albert Einstein[3]

As we showed in Chapter 2, economics students are currently taught as if there is only one type of economics. But economics is actually much broader than most students (and academics) may realise given the education outlined in Chapter 2. Exhibit 3.1 illustrates nine different coherent economic perspectives which we argue students should be exposed to in their education.[4] These perspectives provide fundamentally different ways of thinking about the economy from the ground up. They have different assumptions about human behaviour and the role of institutions, and how the two interact. They have different focuses and priorities which represent value judgements about what is important and this means they ask different questions. They have different tools and approaches which lead them to different answers to economic questions. They are diverse and not all of equal value but they all hold valuable insights.

Our curriculum review showed that the absence of these perspectives from economics education was near universal. Of all 172 module course outlines reviewed, only 17 modules and two core modules mention non-neoclassical economic perspectives, while Cambridge University does not mention them at all. Modules that do mention other perspectives are usually pushed towards the fringes as they are non-compulsory or students are discouraged from taking them. For example, five of the seventeen modules that mention non-neoclassical theories are History of [Economic] Thought (HoT) courses. These are not taken by many students because they are essay-based and often only available in the final year of study; by this time it is too late. Essay writing is a skill that economics students often lack after years of only doing mathematical derivations, and they understandably do not want to take the course in their final year when it counts most for their degree. Without HoT a further two universities would contain no mention of alternative perspectives in their syllabus.

Exhibit 3.1 Economic perspectives

	'Old' neoclassical	'New' neoclassical	Post-Keynesian	Classical	Marxist
Humans…	optimise narrow self-interest	can optimise a variety of goals	use rules of thumb	act in their self-interest	do not have a predetermined nature
Humans act within…	a vacuum	a market context	a macro-economic context	a class context	a class and historical context
The economy is…	stable	stable in the absence of frictions and shocks	naturally volatile	largely self-stabilising	both volatile and exploitative
Economic analysis should…	start from rationality and scarce resources	be built up from individual optimisation	be descriptively realistic	be grounded in politics	recognise power relations
Implications for education	teach both models and broader social knowledge	teach mostly models	teach models with realistic assumptions	ground education in broader social knowledge	ground education in broader social knowledge
Analysis of income inequality	increased productivity of richer individuals	driven by market frictions	increased power of finance and capital	increased power of capitalists	increased power of capitalists
Views on financial crises	not possible	caused by external shocks and frictions in financial markets	generated by financial markets	ambiguous	generated by a falling rate of profit

Source: adapted from Ha-Joon Chang, *Economics: A User's Guide*, London: Penguin, 2014, 166–9

Departments steer students away from these kinds of modules in two main ways. The first is that HoT and other more critical or qualitative courses – such as those from other disciplines – are often non-compulsory, whereas compulsory courses are almost universally neoclassical. The second is that students are told they should be focusing on modules in mathematics if they want to be a 'proper economist'.[5]

This is reflected in student numbers. In 2013/14 at LSE, 57 students took the non-compulsory HoT, compared to 581 who took

Austrian	Institutional	Evolutionary	Feminist	Ecological
act according to their subjective knowledge and preferences	exhibit changeable behaviour	act 'sensibly' but not optimally	exhibit gendered behaviour	ambiguous
a market context	an institutional environment that shapes rules and social norms	an evolving complex system	a social context	a social and environmental context
volatile, but this is often a sign of health	dependent on legal and social structures	complex: both stable and volatile	ambiguous	embedded in the environment
be based on individual action	focus on the relationships between people and institutions	recognise complexity and interdependence	recognise more than just the 'economic'	recognise environmental constraint
teach economics without maths	ground education in historical context	ambiguous	ground education in broader social knowledge	ground education in environmental knowledge
caused by government intervention	changes to tax and regulatory structures	ambiguous	highly gendered	ambiguous
generated by central banks	consequence of the concentration of firms and poor financial regulation	generated by complex, interdependent phenomena	related to male domination in finance, and impact is stratified by gender	ambiguous

the second-year macro course, or 866 who took the Introduction to Economics course – both of which are compulsory. Our sample is actually atypical of standard UK economics degrees, as five of the seven universities had HoT courses, whereas within the Russell Group as a whole only 12 of 23 run such a course.[6] As a result, many students will not even have the opportunity to study HoT and yet this is one of the few modules that actually asks students to think critically about economic theory.

This compartmentalisation of alternative perspectives at British universities means that the vast majority of economics graduates will never have been exposed to the fact that there is more than one way to study economics. Pluralist economics education – introducing students to different perspectives and clearly illustrating that economics is contested – is necessary to avoid indoctrinating the next generation of economic experts.

Pluralist economics reframes the way students think about economics. It goes from being about applying one universally established way of doing economics to recognising that different perspectives can give you different valid answers. Looking back at the last chapter, it is plausible that the History of Economic Thought module at LSE had far more marks for evaluation than any other because it is the only economics course at the university that introduces students to a plurality of perspectives.

Pluralism in economics is entirely achievable: politics, philosophy, sociology and even some economics courses manage to teach students a range of different approaches to analysing their subject matter. Students are examined on their ability to argue a particular position, drawing on the appropriate empirical evidence and demonstrating a critical understanding of the issue from more than one relevant perspective. Thus, pluralism should not be confused with relativism, where 'anything goes'; critical students will not accept ideas that do not withstand logical and empirical scrutiny. Pluralism in economics would create a generation of critical thinkers who can produce innovative answers to society's most pressing problems. This is the educational case for pluralism in undergraduate economics.

There is also a strong intellectual case for rejecting the status quo in economics. When we ask to be taught about other ways of thinking about the economy, we are often told that it wouldn't make sense for medical students to learn about alternative medicine, or for engineers to be taught alternative theories of bridge building.[6] In defining economics only in terms of the neoclassical way of thinking, the discipline reveals a widespread belief in the intellectual authority of neoclassical economics that simply cannot be justified.

From the standpoint of the scientific method, it is clear that economists cannot rely on controlled experiments in the same way that natural scientists can. Unlike the physical world, the social world is changeable and so empirical evidence from one setting does not necessarily apply to another. As a result, no economic theory or set of theories can be shown to be empirically robust enough to warrant complete dominance. Consequently, it is not surprising that economics has failed to provide definitive answers to major economic questions such as 'How do countries get rich?', 'What causes recessions?' and 'How do financial markets work?'[8] Without a strong set of answers to these questions, neoclassical economics cannot justify excluding economic perspectives that answer them using a different set of tools. Post-Keynesians, for example, would emphasise private debt as a cause of financial crises, while Austrians would emphasise the role of central banks. Economics students are currently introduced to neither of these perspectives and are not given reasons why they should be considered wrong compared to neoclassical models.

The lack of clear answers to these questions is a symptom of the fact that the social world is complex. This means that approaching it from only one perspective can miss vital insights. For example, a central area of feminist economics is the importance of work done in the home – largely by women – in feeding, resting and raising the workers who produce the goods and services that we all consume. Neoclassical economics has historically failed to recognise this insight, probably because in its models agents act through exchanging commodities in markets, which are absent from homes (and also, perhaps, because economics more broadly since its inception has been dominated almost entirely by men).[9] Feminist economists have proposed time-use surveys, which measure how people spend their time in the home and hence could track economic activity in a way that neoclassical economists would not have considered.[10] Many other such insights that are easily missed by neoclassical economics should be apparent from Exhibit 2.7, particularly in the last two rows.

As with social systems, knowledge is complex and multifaceted, and a lack of pluralism silences certain viewpoints, blocking potential advances. Even if one school of thought *is* justified in its dominance at a given point in time, major developments often occur at the margins of disciplines where people are more willing to take risks. This extends beyond economics: when the famous physicist Max Planck first discovered quantum physics – now widely accepted – his colleagues' reluctance to accept it led him to declare morbidly that 'science advances one funeral at a time'.

Similarly, non-neoclassical economists have been pointing out for a long time that money is created by private banks in the process of making loans (a theory called 'endogenous money'), rather than originating from central banks.[11] Neoclassical economics is only just catching up with this insight that is now deemed fundamental by important economic institutions.[12]

Hence there are many cases where neoclassical economics cannot claim to have a comprehensive understanding of how the economy works (or doesn't). But even when a particular idea concurrently has significant academic support behind it, students must be made aware that facts and theories are subject to change and that other perspectives exist. This is the approach that is currently taken in other social sciences when a particular theory is thought to be dominant.

Moreover, understanding in social sciences is not only based on scientific criteria but is wedded to value judgements and political views, even if only implicitly. Conventional economics takes growth, efficiency and individual utility as focal points of analysis, implying that these things are the appropriate criteria by which to judge economic performance. Alternative criteria might be stability, sustainability and innovation, which are usually absent as explicit goals in economic models, even if they are mentioned in classes. It's not that economics professors are consciously instilling certain views in their students, but students are likely to be influenced by the ideas they are presented with – something that becomes more obvious when you consider what you would think if models focused on goals you disagreed with.

One example of the role played by different values and perspectives comes from comparing neoclassical economics to Marxist economics. The former has a theory known as the 'Non Accelerating Inflation Rate of Unemployment', or NAIRU, known to every economist around the world.[13] This argues that if unemployment is below the NAIRU, workers will increase their wage demands since they are less easy to replace. Firms will then increase prices to pay for their higher wage costs, resulting in further wage demands from workers to compensate for the increase in prices, which creates a spiral of accelerating inflation. Unemployment should be no lower than the NAIRU if inflation is to be kept stable.

It is interesting that Marx expressed the same basic idea but called it the 'reserve army' of the unemployed, and his interpretation was that, under capitalism, workers must be disciplined by keeping a certain number of them unemployed.[14] Despite using different language and coming to very different conclusions, the two approaches arrived at the same insight. A plurality of perspectives would help students appreciate that there are different criteria by which to judge the same insight, shining a light on their own preconceptions about which policies or systems are desirable.

Here we have set out the case for pluralism on educational, intellectual and philosophical grounds. As long as economics education continues to indoctrinate experts into a single perspective, the result will be the continued limitation of the scope of enquiry and overconfident, uncritical economic experts. In the next section we show how inadequate the neoclassical perspective is for addressing many of the most important challenges the world faces.

The limits of neoclassical economics

As we outlined in the last chapter, neoclassical economics has a view of the economy as a distinct system that follows a particular, often mechanical logic, and that can be managed using scientific criteria. Consequently, applications of neoclassical economics can claim most success in situations where institutions and goals are narrow, clearly defined and often separated from the rest of the economy. One such example is in designing algorithms for matching children to schools, or organ donors to patients, where economic theory has had notable success.[15]

Our argument is, therefore, not that neoclassical economics is without use. However, because it is the dominant approach, here we only focus on its flaws. Like any grand vision of the world, neoclassical economics has shortcomings and blind spots that severely limit the ability of economists to address many important issues. To illustrate this, we use the examples of macroeconomic stability, the environment and inequality. Each example will detail some of the main limitations of the neoclassical approach, before we discuss how other economic perspectives can improve our understanding of the problem.

Macroeconomics

The financial crisis of 2008 had devastating global effects and changed the course of history. Yet virtually no neoclassical macroeconomists saw the crisis coming and their models also proved inadequate in understanding it as it unfurled. Macroeconomists were convinced that consumer inflation, GDP and unemployment were the relevant ways to measure economic stability, blinding them to the housing bubble and the instability brewing in the financial sector. A supposedly straightforward, inverse relationship between interest rates and inflation[16] made macroeconomics seem like a set of technical problems with technical solutions, to be solved by those who had a formal economics education.

As a consequence, macroeconomists demonstrated extreme levels of hubris prior to the crisis. Ben Bernanke, the head of the Federal Reserve, praised economists for bringing about the 'Great Moderation' (a period of low inflation and high growth);[17] the Nobel Prize-winning Robert Lucas declared that macroeconomics' 'central problem of depression prevention has been solved';[18] and even as the crisis began to unfold, Olivier Blanchard, the head of the IMF at the time, declared that 'the state of macro is good'.[19] This complacent 'group think' was made possible by the dominance of the neoclassical way of thinking among experts in prominent institutions.

The mechanics of the crisis have been described in great depth and with great eloquence by many other authors, and it is not our purpose to provide another in-depth description.[20] Suffice to say that in 2008 a stock market crash and a wave of bankruptcies and defaults on mortgages triggered the worst financial crisis the world has seen since the 1930s. And although banks, politicians and individuals all undoubtedly hold some responsibility for what happened, we believe that at a fundamental level the crisis represented a failure of economic ideas.

By drawing the boundaries of the economy in the wrong places, the economists in positions of power failed to anticipate how different aspects of the economy – the housing market, the financial sector,[21] and government and central bank policy – would combine to create a bubble that had huge consequences for the rest of the economy when it burst. The false precision offered by models used to manage central banks, price financial instruments 'scientifically',[22] and make macroeconomic forecasts proved to be a mirage as the instability of the real world became apparent.

These models not only failed to foresee the possibility of such an event, but they were unable to explain it after it happened. Macroeconomic models are complicated but ultimately rest on the neoclassical view of the economy as a series of predictable relationships that tend towards a stable state. Macroeconomics has therefore resorted to labelling the crisis as the type of 'exogenous shock' we saw in the previous chapter, which means that it came from *outside* the system. This leaves no scope for understanding what causes such a shock or how it might be prevented. As Andrew Haldane, the Chief Economist at the Bank of England, has argued in the wake of the crisis: 'These models have failed to make sense of the sorts of extreme macro-economic event ... which matter most to society.'[23]

Through both commission and omission, economics had failed to fulfil its duties. The collective dismay at the failure of these experts to do their job was famously crystallised when the Queen asked a group of LSE economists why none of them had seen it coming. Illustrating the difficulty of getting an unqualified apology from economists, the response to the Queen by Tim Besley and Peter Hennessy concluded that the crisis had been 'a failure of the collective imagination of many bright people [by which they meant themselves] … to understand the risks to the system as a whole'.[24] Similar admissions of failure can be found from prominent economists such as Robert Solow and Paul Krugman.[25]

Had macroeconomists been more aware of other economic perspectives, they might have been more prepared for the crisis. One such perspective is Hyman Minsky's Financial Instability Hypothesis (FIH), written long before the crisis, whose central idea is that 'stability is destabilising': tranquil economic times sow the seeds of their own demise.[26] When the economy is calm and growing, investors, firms and consumers find that their investments tend to pay off. They therefore extend themselves a little further the next time round – borrowing more and taking on riskier investments – then extend further still the time after that, and so forth. When investors become reliant on asset price rises to fund their borrowing, this fuels bubbles that have far-reaching consequences when they burst.

Minsky adhered to the post-Keynesian economic perspective and his FIH was largely unrecognised by neoclassical economists until the 2008 crash, but the crash fitted his description so well that his ideas quickly became popular in the media and gained some recognition among economists such as Paul Krugman.[27] Tellingly, the complacency Minsky thought was engendered by the good times was supposed to apply not only to investors, but to politicians, regulators and even to academics as well. One can't help but feel that if economists had been more aware of the FIH, they might have been more humble, and blithe pronouncements about the 'end of boom and bust' might have been treated with more scepticism, as they were by those economists who followed in Minsky's tradition.[28]

More broadly, post-Keynesian economists tend to emphasise the importance of the financial system and the general instability of capitalism, believing that crises happen 'endogenously'; that is, they come from within the system itself. As the name implies, post-Keynesians believe they are following in the tradition of the famous economist John Maynard Keynes, who was one of the first economists to model the economy as a whole. He introduced the idea of the 'animal spirits' of investors driving booms and busts in financial markets; economists like Minsky built on and developed these ideas while neoclassical economists largely ignored the financial sector.

Unfortunately, as the crisis has receded from memory the economics profession has been quick to reassert its authority. One of the more surprising responses has been to invoke a theory called the Efficient Markets Hypothesis (EMH) to excuse economists for not predicting the crisis. The idea is that financial markets process new information faster than any one individual, government or institution could, and so for most people they may seem to behave unpredictably. However, even economists cannot be expected to understand these sudden movements better than anyone else, so expecting them to foresee market crashes is mistaken. While it is certainly convenient to have a theory that relieves you of responsibility for understanding how financial markets behave, economist Stephen Kinsella has aptly suggested that not realising the crisis was unfolding is more akin to a doctor failing to realise their patient was bleeding. Even if economists cannot predict crises in their entirety, they should know the warning signs.

Another approach has been simply to deny that macroeconomists failed to foresee the crisis, which seems to us a bizarre attempt to rewrite history. For example, Nobel Laureate Thomas Sargent claimed in 2010 that 'it is just wrong to say that this financial crisis caught modern macroeconomists by surprise'.[29] Yet Sargent didn't seem to anticipate the crisis in his 2008 paper arguing that investors were not taking as much risk as they could due to their memories of the Great Depression, stating in his model that 'the consumer *over-estimates* the likelihood of another Depression'.[30] Economists should not be allowed to excuse themselves like this with the benefit of hindsight.

It would be unfair to blame every macroeconomic problem faced by society solely on economists. But the failure of the discipline to come up with answers to these problems leads us to question the authority it currently has over policy and in debate. We would not employ engineers if the bridges they designed fell down so frequently; similarly, for as long as macroeconomists demonstrate that they have failed to understand fully the system that they study, they cannot be trusted to manage it without input from other economic perspectives and broader democratic accountability.

The environment

The environment is perhaps the defining issue of our generation. From existential threats like climate change to natural resource depletion and increasing pollution and waste, it seems man-made environmental change could pose a fundamental threat to the sustainability of human life on earth.[31] Responsibility for environmental destruction cannot and should not be attributed to economic experts in the same way as failures of macroeconomic management. Nevertheless, since the environmental challenges we face are fundamentally linked to our current economic system, economists have a duty to call attention to this and provide solutions. Yet neoclassical economics has proven incapable of incorporating the links between the environmental and economic systems.

The environment represents a fundamental challenge to neoclassical economics. As a complex system whose components are not necessarily quantifiable, it does not lend itself to the simple, mechanical relationships that are so often used in economic models. In particular, the fact that neoclassical economic analysis focuses on prices and output as the key aspects of the economy means that it neglects the role of the broader ecosystem. Indeed, one of the key ways in which the environment is pushed to one side in an econocracy is in how the economy is defined, since statistics such as GDP and inflation do not take the environment into account, often ignoring the environmental consequences of economic policies.

The environment is virtually absent from basic economic analysis. Worryingly, of the 23 Russell Group universities that have economics departments, only nine have separate 'environmental economics' modules. This suggests that these universities either do not see environmental issues as a major concern, or believe they can be dealt with using standard economic tools in other classes. The majority of students will therefore graduate without even attempting to gain a systemic, in-depth understanding of how economics is linked to the environment. The environment must form a much more central part of economics education if future policymakers, business people and civil servants are to be aware of the challenges it poses.

Even when the environment is treated explicitly, the neoclassical way of thinking about the economy prevents us from understanding many important aspects of the issue. Environmental economics incorporates the environment into neoclassical economic analysis, which justifies policy intervention on the basis that the market is failing to value the environment. Technical methods are used to determine what the value of the environment should be, and therefore the level of resources worth investing through taxes, subsidies, regulations or other schemes to protect it.

According to environmental economics, the market fails to value the environment in two main ways. On the one hand, the environment provides free economic benefits such as natural resources, or ecosystems like the ozone layer, rainforests and coral reefs, which will be overexploited. On the other hand, the environment is undervalued because private agents do not take into account the costs of environmental degradation, as they are borne by someone else. These costs are sometimes known as spillover effects or externalities. Pollution is the go-to example of a negative spillover: a factory may pollute a nearby river, which damages farmers' crops downstream and even the health of citizens. The factory does not take these costs into account; since it would produce less if it had to pay these costs, it overproduces from society's point of view.

Proposed interventions all involve attaching money values to the environment, and cost–benefit analysis plays a central role in weighing up the various benefits of the environment and the costs of associated interventions. Economic institutions also use specially built models with names like DICE (Dynamic Integrated Model of Climate and the Economy) and FUND (The Climate Framework for Uncertainty, Negotiation and Distribution)[32] to predict how much monetary damage the rise in temperature from climate change will cause the global economy. The limitations of these approaches stem from the practice of trying to assign a monetary value to something as broad and multifaceted as the environment and to climate change.[33] Possibly the most commonly used tool is 'revealed preference', which assigns monetary values to the environment by studying peoples' economic decisions. Travel costs to get to a natural landmark may be used to value that landmark; more bizarrely, the wage difference between a dangerous and non-dangerous job may be used to attach a value to the risk of deaths from climate change on the grounds that the worker is 'revealing' their preference for a greater chance of death.[34]

Revealed preference can lead to some strange and unpalatable conclusions, such as the idea that lives in poor countries are worth less than those in rich countries, and has been criticised on the basis that it extrapolates from trivial individual behaviour to life-or-death political issues.[35] It is especially problematic when dealing with the impact of environmental damage in the far future, since it relies on the decisions of people who are alive today. It therefore cannot take into account the interests of future generations simply because they are not born yet.

More generally, the future – central to debates over climate change – throws up major challenges for environmental economics.[36] Economic analysis approaches the environment from a cost–benefit framework, which has the effect of turning debatable ethical propositions about the environment into technical questions about how to measure the costs and benefits. One key example is the 'discount rate', a method economists use for reducing – or 'discounting' – costs from environmental damage in the future.

Let us explain with a simple if unrealistic example. Say economists believe that something will cause £1,000 of damage; then we should want to pay up to £1,000 to avoid this damage by the logic of cost–benefit analysis. Now imagine further that climate change will cause £1,000 of damage *every year*. Such a scenario is easy to envision (though the real numbers are much higher): changing weather patterns may lead to more parts of the earth becoming dry and arid, meaning they can no longer produce agricultural goods. There will be £1,000 worth of damage in 2017, followed by £1,000 worth of damage in 2018 and so on, a repeated cost that stretches out forever. This implies that we should sacrifice anything and everything to prevent climate change because if you keep adding on £1,000 every year, you approach infinity. Infinity aside, you get to a high number very quickly when you replace £1,000 with the actual estimated costs of climate change (i.e. billions or trillions of pounds every year).

However, discounting these costs means that £1,000 of damage is worth less and less the further into the future you go. For example, if economists choose a discount rate of 3 per cent, that means reducing the value by 3 per cent for every year that goes by: £1,000 of damage is worth only £970 one year into the future, and £941 two years into the future. This value keeps winding down and within two hundred years £1,000 worth of damage is valued at only £2.26! The rationale economists give for this is that people value the present more than the future, so environmental damage in the future must be reduced to find the equivalent cost today. Or they argue that an asteroid may wipe out the human race tomorrow, meaning that there will be no humans around to enjoy the benefits of not incurring such costs, so discounting adjusts for the chance that future generations may not even exist. The bottom line, however, is that the application of the discount rate signifies a contentious ethical choice obscured by technical language. While economists may need to discount the future to make their calculations feasible, this also implies that future generations are not valued as highly as the current one.

Beyond the discount rate, economic models struggle because the effects of climate change are too complex and uncertain to be captured by neoclassical models, which rely on knowing the costs of future environmental catastrophes, the chances of them happening, and how all of these components will interact. In contrast, climate models from the natural sciences typically emphasise the fundamental unknowability of the climate system and the possibility for absolute catastrophe, neither of which can meaningfully be assigned probabilities or economic values without the kind of arbitrary leaps discussed above, and both of which in practice involve a lot of judgements. The result of all of these difficulties is that climate scientists recommend a 'precautionary' approach over cost–benefit trade-offs, setting physical targets such as preventing a rise in global temperatures above 2°C. This approach is an attempt to guard against worst-case scenarios so that the planet is habitable for future generations.

The tension created by a concern for the environment coupled with an attachment to the framework of neoclassical economics is perhaps best summed up by two influential economists, Nicholas Stern and Richard Tol, who come to opposing conclusions about climate change. In 2005 Stern was commissioned by the UK government to outline the economic consequences of climate change and to explore solutions. The resulting 'Stern Review' is a flagship example of the political sphere turning to the guidance of economists in order to deal with a major issue. Tol is also influential, having designed the aforementioned FUND model, and is on the Intergovernmental Panel on Climate Change as well as having worked with the UN and the EU.

The Stern Review uses economic models to estimate the benefits of preventing climate change and the costs of preventative interventions, and concludes that action must be taken, since 'climate change is a serious global threat, and it demands an urgent global response'.[37] In contrast, Tol has drawn on his FUND model to argue that 'the idea that climate change poses an existential threat to humankind is laughable' and 'half a century of climate change is about as bad as losing one year of economic growth'.[38] How could two economists who are using similar frameworks come to such differing conclusions?

The answer is that Tol takes his models literally, whereas Stern's recommendations are tempered and informed by scientific and ethical judgements from outside his models. A telling example of this was Stern's choice of an unusually low discount rate (implying that future generations should be highly valued), which Stern justified not by using economics, but by arguing that future generations are *morally* equal to the current generation. This caused outcry from Tol and other economists, who pointed out that a discount rate more in line with economists' usual, theoretical values would greatly reduce the estimated costs of damage from climate change.

These technical debates are a symptom of a broader problem. Environmental economics is a natural conclusion of economic logic, where there is a 'price for everything': even the most important parts of the ecosystem can be assigned a value, and then traded off against some economic benefit. To believe these models in full is to believe that the only real challenge of climate change is to decide the technical details of such a valuation exercise.

In contrast, scientists warn that global warming may lead to large numbers of coastal cities being under water and weather systems becoming much more volatile and unpredictable, exactly the kind of tipping point the models do not account for.[39] Stern himself has argued that his report probably *understates* the risks from climate change, and that the kinds of models used by environmental economists are fundamentally unsuitable for modelling the environment.[40]

The perspective known as 'ecological economics' argues that environmental economics misses important aspects of what makes the environment unique. In particular, the major tools in environmental economics fail to acknowledge that the economy – and human society – is embedded in the ecosystem: all resources must come from the environment, and all waste must exit back into it. The environment is not an exception to the norm of functioning markets; it must form a core part of any understanding of the economy.

Ecological economists dispute that economic costs can be compared to ecological costs because the ozone layer and the rainforest have functions in ecosystems that cannot be replaced. It therefore takes into account the limitations on the resources that can be extracted and the waste that can be emitted, while maintaining ecological stability. This approach implies that there may be physical limits to economic growth and has led ecological economists to explore how no-growth economies could work.[41] The idea that growth might not be possible or even desirable is anathema to most neoclassical economists because it is a foundational principle of their framework.

The ecological economist Herman Daly has outlined the philosophical difference between the ecological and the neoclassical vision of the economy. He argues that the vision underpinning neoclassical economics is of an individualistic world with no limits, where natural resources are just one of many available inputs to production, wants are endless, welfare is primarily a function of material consumption, and growth in the size of the economy is the primary objective.[42] In contrast, the vision underpinning ecological economics is of a world in which the economy is a subsystem of the ecosystem (and the social system) and where well-being is determined by a range of factors, only some of which are quantifiable. Philosophically, the neoclassical framework only judges the environment to be valuable if it impacts on humans (with impact judged by the assignment of a monetary value) whereas the ecological framework sees the environment as valuable in and of itself.

Ecological economics provides an important critique of neoclassical environmental economics that helps us to understand its shortcomings, and it has also developed a different framework for understanding the economy. Unfortunately, the next generation of economic experts are not being made aware of this and so their understanding of the environment remains necessarily limited. An illustrative example is the climate change module at the University of Manchester, which states that students are to 'discuss climate change *from the perspective of an economist*' (emphasis ours). There is a single perspective to learn and it is the neoclassical one. The theories in the lecture notes are based entirely on neoclassical economics: the course teaches efficiency, cost–benefit analysis and utility maximisation, and then applies them to environmental issues. Only 6 per cent of the available exam marks are for evaluating a theory, while the rest are merely for describing or operating a theory or policy. There is no mention of ecological economics or any other alternative perspectives.

An econocracy, in resting solely upon a neoclassical understanding of the economy, cannot incorporate insights from other perspectives which could help to address the myriad of environmental problems faced by society. It rules out many possible responses to climate change, resource depletion and environmental degradation. This is particularly damaging as neoclassical environmental economics has fostered a narrow, technical approach that is blind to the possibility or necessity of the kind of deep individual and structural changes that might be necessary to prevent environmental collapse.

Inequality

The financial crisis refocused public attention on inequality. During the boom years, inequality seemed like a side issue compared to the general prosperity experienced across all levels of the income distribution. But a big recession tends to change public perceptions of fairness as some face economic hardship while others do not. It is at this point that investigating inequality becomes of greater public concern.

People differ on whether they see inequality as good or bad, but in order to have the debate the ideas must first be defined and empirically investigated. Questions arise over which types of inequality exist and what they look like; whether they are justified and why; and what, if anything, should be done to change them. For example, virtually everyone would agree that inequality of height is *not* something that should be changed, while the type of racial inequality that was in place in apartheid South Africa *is* something that should be changed. Contemporary political debate covers a wide variety of inequalities such as income and wealth, race and gender and even between generations.

Income inequality is probably what most people have in mind when they think about inequality. In the UK income inequality increased in the 1980s and has remained at historic highs ever since.[43] Globally, the past few decades have seen stagnation in the incomes of the Western middle classes and the very poorest (in regions such as sub-Saharan Africa), while the incomes of the very richest in the West and the middle classes of fast-growing developing countries such as China have gained.[44] The story of income inequality over this period is a result of the interplay of complex global and national forces.

Unfortunately, a lack of conceptual, geographic, political and historical analysis means that the neoclassical framework often fails to conceptualise income and wealth inequality (hereafter simply 'inequality') in a satisfactory way. Neoclassical economics takes an abstract, almost 'hands-off' approach to inequality, which makes it easy to miss entirely. This means that economic experts are not trained to develop a comprehensive understanding of inequality, and as such debate is stifled.

In basic neoclassical economics, the distribution of income is simply a natural outcome of the market forces of supply and demand, and any interventions are deemed to disrupt these market forces. More sophisticated models justify some interventions, but these still focus on the purely 'economic' forces that may alter the basic model and therefore distribution. Questions of institutions, power and politics are rarely addressed, and when they are discussed they are not modelled but come as incidental addenda to the core theory. Economics as practised promotes an understanding of distribution that is purely technical and separate from broader historical questions about how inequality has arisen.

The principles economists use to evaluate the desirability of policies – known as welfare analysis – are also silent on questions of distribution. One key idea from welfare economics is 'Pareto optimality'. A situation is Pareto optimal if nobody can be made better off without making at least one person worse off; any one person's gains must effectively be taken from another person. In other words, there are no unused resources available.

But in reality a broad range of situations can be Pareto optimal. Consider three people dividing a pie: whichever way they decide to do it, the outcome will be Pareto optimal as long as all of the pie is used. Whether they divide the pie equally or one person has the entire pie and the others have none, 'redistributing' the pie will involve taking it from one person and making them worse off. Hence the Pareto criterion often has nothing to say on questions of distribution.

Another tool of welfare analysis is the social welfare function (SWF). This tries to transplant the individual utility function we saw earlier on to society as a whole: in other words, it asks which policy outcome 'we' would collectively prefer. The economist Amartya Sen has argued that since the SWF is concerned with maximising the total utility in a society, it is 'supremely unconcerned with the interpersonal distribution of that sum' and as a result is highly unsuitable for measuring or judging inequality.[45] SWFs are obscure and technical and all too often simply invite economists to solve more elaborate mathematical puzzles, rather than to consider why inequality matters and how it came about.[46]

As well as broad inequalities of income and wealth, neoclassical economics struggles with more specific types of inequality such as regional inequality. This is hard to model using neoclassical economics, since everything essentially takes place in a geographical vacuum, but statistics show how much the framework can miss. The UK is the ninth-richest country in the world, but nine out of ten of the poorest regions in north-western Europe are in the UK, even though London itself is the single richest region in north-western Europe.[47] Central banks, governments and economic models generally focus on aggregate inflation, GDP and unemployment, making these regional disparities invisible.

Similarly, feminist economics has long argued that the dominance of the neoclassical framework entrenches unequal gender relations. We have already pointed out how GDP, by defining productive activity in a certain way, does not take into account unpaid care, which across the globe is mostly carried out by women. Economic models also tend to ignore social norms and power relations, such as the expectation that women should take care of children, passing off such decisions as free choices and therefore potentially hiding social inequalities between men and women.[48]

As a result of these shortcomings many economists dispute the relevance of inequality to economics. The Nobel Laureate Robert Lucas went so far as to say that 'of the tendencies that are harmful to sound economics, the most seductive, and in my opinion the most poisonous, is to focus on questions of distribution'.[49] Martin Feldstein, who was the chair of Ronald Reagan's Council of Economic Advisers, expressed similar sentiments: 'If you ask me whether we should worry about the fact that some people on Wall Street and basketball players are making a lot of money, I say no.'[50] The monopoly of a single perspective is so ingrained that these economists were not willing to even *consider* distribution as an important economic problem.

Not all economists follow this logic, but in a similar vein to those who take climate change seriously, economists who *do* discuss inequality often do so for reasons outside of their models. It has been suggested by Paul Krugman that economists have partly avoided the problem because inequality is hard to model mathematically in the style of neoclassical economics.[51] The dominant framework in economics is that of the 'representative agent' discussed in Chapter 2, which clearly cannot model inequality effectively as each model contains only one type of person. As with Stern and environmental economics, we are relying on economists to go beyond their framework to address such issues, which is especially worrying when our curriculum review suggests that new economists are being taught to accept this framework uncritically.

Questions of distribution should not be avoided just because they are hard to model. Any economic system will create a certain distribution of wealth that would have been different if the system were different. Discussions over how to construct the economy that ignore questions of distribution represent an implicit judgement that it does not matter, typically accompanied by a focus on growth or efficiency instead.

The topic of inequality illustrates perfectly why economics would benefit from being more grounded in institutional, social and political analysis. Inequality today has emerged as a result of specific historical circumstances and as such any study of it must be at least partly historical in nature. Inequality is also impacted by, and impacts, social and political forces and so cannot be studied only as a purely 'economic' phenomenon.

Thomas Piketty's best-selling *Capital in the Twenty-First Century*, a 600-page discussion of trends in income and wealth inequality in Western countries, is a good example of how historical understanding can shape economic understanding. Piketty is an economist whose analysis actually leans on neoclassical economics in places,[52] but his account is largely historical and emphasises how small changes can result in a great increase of inequality over time as the already-wealthy cement their position.[53] Piketty argues that 'the history of the distribution of wealth has always been deeply political, and it cannot be reduced to purely economic mechanisms'.[54] He uses the example of changes in corporate governance in the UK since the 1980s, which have seen boards legally obliged to maximise shareholder value. In Germany, in contrast, firms typically have worker representatives on their boards, who are naturally less enthusiastic about higher shareholder pay-outs and executive pay, and income inequality is lower than in the UK or US.[55] Another example is the expansion of patents, which has allowed ideas such as forms of computer software to become profitable due to legal protections from the government.[56]

These institutional arrangements are political choices rather than the outcome of fundamental economic forces, and the desirability of inequality itself may depend on the needs or wants of the institutions connected with it. Seeing the economy as a separate sphere disconnected from politics and society limits economists' ability to understand and potentially address inequality as an issue.

These three case studies illustrate that needlessly restricting our thinking about the economy to the neoclassical perspective leaves us with blind spots and shortcomings in our understanding of complex social reality, and means that we are less well equipped to build innovative, sustainable, fair and stable societies. We already face the task of making complex, challenging and urgent political decisions in all these areas, which will define the future course of our societies, and the broader knowledge and tools provided by a pluralist economics can only help us make better informed decisions. In the next section we show how pluralism in economics can help to improve the political process through which we will have to make these decisions.

The politics of neoclassical economics

The relationship between economics and politics is inescapable: as the economist Joan Robinson once pointed out, 'The answers to economic problems are only political questions.'[57] In this section we show how the dominance of the neoclassical way of thinking in economics shapes political thinking in subtle ways, undermining the quality of political debate. Pluralism is necessary because, by providing different ways of thinking about economics, it forces people to question how they think and brings issues that are often taken for granted back into the sphere of political discussion.

It is not uncommon to hear the claim that economics is inherently right wing. Much popular criticism of economics paints (neoclassical) economic theory as supporting the 'free market' or 'neoliberal' worldview that many believe has been dominant since the 1980s. Broadly speaking, this is the idea that a market economy will achieve the best possible outcome and that government intervention in the form of regulations, redistribution of wealth or public programmes will only make things worse. The rejoinder from economists is that they are not politically biased, and that those who criticise economics do so on their own, ideologically motivated grounds.

It is true that, particularly at undergraduate level, neoclassical economic theory contains a lot of models that depict markets and capitalism as producing the best possible outcome. For example, standard demand–supply analysis teaches students that policies in areas such as taxes, rent controls or the minimum wage will only serve to make things worse, so the market should be left to reach a 'socially optimal' equilibrium by itself.

Basic macroeconomic theory is similar: 'Real Business Cycle Theory' (RBCT) portrays periods of high unemployment as resulting from rational individual decisions and therefore as unproblematic; the idea is that workers are *choosing* to take time off work. This has been mocked for reducing recessions such as the Great Depression in the 1930s to the 'Great Vacation'. Similarly, financial economic theories such as the Efficient Markets Hypothesis (EMH) imply that financial markets adjust quickly to all available information and therefore need not (or cannot) be regulated. They are often associated with the drive to deregulate the financial sector before the financial crisis in 2008.

Economists will plead that these are only basic models which are developed in more advanced study, but many students may not go much further in studying economics, so these are the ideas that will shape how they think about the economy. The economist Adair Turner has warned that policymakers may be 'slaves to a simplified version of the conventional wisdom'.[58] There is evidence that those who have studied only undergraduate economics – and have therefore seen mostly only the core models – start to favour certain types of 'free market' policies as a result, despite the fact that most economists would agree that these beliefs are based on oversimplified versions of neoclassical economics.[59]

Even for those who learn about the various ways markets might fail, the debate is loaded towards a pro-market view. This is because, as we saw in the microeconomics section in Chapter 2, an 'ideal' model is used as the baseline and various 'frictions' are added to create the possibility of market failure. In other words, the 'underlying' tendency is for everything to work well, while for whatever reason – transaction costs, imperfect information – incidental problems may arise. This approach of setting up a perfect market as the baseline of analysis, and exploring the reasons why the real world does not conform to this baseline, means that even if students are taught about market failures, the 'perfect market' is still the focal point for their thoughts. When the perfect market is the norm and market failure is the exception, the exceptions can be dismissed.

Despite this, there is nothing in economics that says that someone who studies it has to have a particular political view. Neoclassical economics is a broad church that can be used to justify many political views. Surveys suggest that most academic economists support policies such as anti-discrimination laws and public healthcare and education, policies not typically associated with 'neoliberalism'.[60] Moreover, basic macroeconomic theory is firmly to the left of the political spectrum on one of the big political issues of our time, arguing against 'fiscal austerity' (cuts in government spending and tax rises) and for 'fiscal stimulus' (expansions of government spending and tax cuts). It is therefore untrue to characterise economists and economics as simply 'neoliberal' or as 'free market fundamentalists'.

In our opinion, one of the key problems with economics is not so much that it supports this or that view, but how it frames political debate. We often think of politics in terms of a series of dichotomies: free markets versus state intervention, individual freedom versus equality, private enterprise versus public ownership, individual responsibility versus social solidarity and left versus right. Neoclassical thinking has contributed to these dichotomies.

An example of this is the loaded idea of the government 'intervening' in the market discussed in the previous chapter. This idea paints markets as a naturally occurring, mechanical system and the government as an external engineer who may want to make some tweaks or corrections should this system fail to deliver. It polarises debate – with some on the side of 'markets' and others on the side of 'government'. Most crucially, it ignores the important role that governments have in creating markets in the first place. For trade to take place markets rely on systems of ownership: rules about who owns what and what that entails, rules that are written and enforced by the state. Most trade also entails state-enforced agreements such as employment contracts, promises to provide services, or other agreements such as wills. Many laws are so common that we don't even view them as restrictive: laws that make store owners give receipts and accept returns; laws against child and slave labour; and laws banning trade in things such as votes or identities.[61] Corporations themselves could not exist in the form we recognise without laws that protect shareholder's rights, grant the corporation limited liability for its debts should it go bankrupt, and define the structures of corporate governance. The free market versus state dichotomy is therefore a false one.

The result is that most economic debates aren't really about who favours 'governments' and who favours 'markets' but about the different ways people want markets and governments to be constructed. And perhaps the fact that economics places the existing market structure outside debate is one reason it attracts criticism from those who are unhappy with this system as it stands. More fundamental criticisms of the existing system are usually absent from economists' thinking. This narrows political debate by forcing it to fit into the neoclassical framework and pushes many topics off the table entirely.

At a fundamental level, each person's view of economic and political issues is shaped by the economic perspective that they subscribe to, and a lack of awareness of other perspectives results in a one-sided approach. Ha-Joon Chang has pointed out that your idea of whether a market is 'working' or not may depend on your school of thought:

> What you see as a market failure depends on your economic theory. So neoclassical economists when they see a monopoly will freak out and think that we have to regulate it. But for Hayek or especially Schumpeter a monopoly is a sign that the market is actually succeeding because for Schumpeter a monopoly actually comes into being because someone has innovated. For Schumpeterians a lack of monopoly is a sign of a stagnant economy because it means that no one has innovated.

Objections to the neoclassical framework therefore exist from all points on the political spectrum. Austrians like Hayek have also argued that many standard textbook examples of 'market failure' are not borne out in the real world, for reasons that are hard to understand using neoclassical economics.[62] On the other hand, it could be pointed out that Marxists view the social relations of markets as intolerable, regardless of their efficiency. Institutionalists may even object to the idea that 'markets' are the appropriate object of analysis, preferring to focus on the internal dynamics of firms.[63] The approach of viewing everything relative to a single, mechanical 'ideal' thwarts a full scrutiny of the benefits and drawbacks of markets from a variety of perspectives.

Pluralism in economics expands the scope of understanding, and it can also show that the current political dichotomies grossly over-simplify complex political questions and undermine the possibility for thoughtful political debate. If people are aware of different ways of thinking about the economy, they will be more aware of how they play a background role shaping political discussion. This can only be good for democracy.

Pluralism and econocracy

In this chapter we have made a number of separate but overlapping arguments for pluralism in economics. Pluralism is necessary to ensure that the next generation of economic experts are not indoctrinated into a single perspective. Pluralist economists have a broader, more accurate understanding of our complex and changing society and are more aware of the shortcomings of any particular way of thinking. As a discipline, pluralist economics is more open, diverse and reflective and, as a result, better equipped to help society understand and address the major challenges it faces. Finally, pluralism can make individuals more aware of how economics currently shapes political choices and frames debate.

Returning to our arguments in Chapter 1, it is important to ask what the consequences of pluralism in economics would be for a society that has become an econocracy. Our answer is that it would challenge some of the central foundations of econocracy and in doing so open the way to a revitalised democracy. By showing the contested nature of economics, pluralism highlights the fact that experts are unable to make neutral decisions and as a result it puts economic decision making firmly back into the realm of politics. Pluralism in economics lays the foundations for the reconnection of economics with politics and society after the dead end of the twentieth century when, as we have seen, the idea of the economy came to be seen as separate from the rest of society.

In a broader sense, ideas from different economic perspectives pose a deep challenge to the technocrat's ability to measure, forecast and fine-tune the economy. Evolutionary economics conceptualises the economy as a complex system with many interdependent parts whose behaviour is hard to predict.[64] Post-Keynesian economics stresses the 'radical uncertainty' of the future, with unknowns that cannot even be assigned a probability, such as the success of a new product or business.[65] Austrian economics emphasises the importance of the individual's local knowledge and preferences, which are inherently unknowable using the top-down, centralised decision making common in an econocracy.[66] Pluralist economic experts realise that they cannot pick out the 'optimal policy' and must instead give more humble advice to politicians and citizens.

Pluralist economics recognises that understanding the economy requires an understanding of its social foundations. The neoclassical way of thinking supports the belief that experts are able to isolate 'economic' forces that operate largely independently of political, institutional and cultural context and therefore avoid messy questions about history, ethics and practicality.

But there is no adequate definition of 'the economy' which is independent of these contexts. Even simple choices about measurement, such as whether or not to include house prices in inflation statistics, will feed into our understanding of the economy. House prices are not included in the measure of inflation used by most central banks, but if they had been prior to 2008 it would have been more obvious to policymakers and the public that a bubble was brewing. Policy may well have changed as a result of this. Political decisions determine both what the economy is and how it works, and should be brought out into the realm of public discussion rather than hidden in economic theory.

Pluralist economics, by highlighting different visions of the economy, illustrates that economics does not concretely exist outside of society. This is the crucial point. What we call the economy is often assumed to be universal but is in fact a description of a particular form of social organisation, and could always be something different. This means that defining the purpose of the economy, how to judge whether it is successful and how it is organised are once again political issues.

If any single way of thinking about the economy comes to dominate academic and political discourse in the way neoclassical economics has, it will end up restricting political choices to those that make sense from within that framework. Neoclassical economics has pigeonholed the kinds of economic debates we have, and means that the people who run our economy are unable to address some of the issues most important to our societies. It prevents us imagining alternatives and limits the tools we have to construct them. Pluralism in economics lays the foundations for a different kind of politics. We now turn to ask how the monopoly of neoclassical economics came about and how to challenge it, and in the final chapter we return to the question of reinvigorating democracy.

Notes

1 Oxford Dictionaries, published online. Available at: http://www.oxford dictionaries.com/definition/english/indoctrinate (accessed 22 April 2016).
2 This section draws heavily on the work of Alan Freeman and other long-standing advocates of pluralism. Sincere thanks go to all of them. See, for example, Alan Freeman, 'The economists of tomorrow: the case for a pluralist subject benchmark statement for economics', *International Review of Economics Education* 8(2) (2009): 23–40.
3 Quoted in Edward Fullbrook, 'To observe or not to observe: complementary pluralism in physics and economics', *Real-World Economics Review* 62(4) (2012): 20–8.
4 Any attempt to place economic perspectives into separate schools with such brevity inevitably makes some oversimplifications and misses out some perspectives. There is the behaviourist perspective typically associated with Herbert Simon, two varieties of institutional economics ('old' and 'new'), the German Historical School, and so forth. We chose these examples because we think they emphasise a broad array of different ways of looking at economics, which in many case overlap with the excluded schools. For example, the evolutionary idea that people 'act "sensibly" but not optimally' is quite similar to Simon's 'bounded rationality'. Herbert A. Simon, *Models of Bounded Rationality*, Cambridge, MA: MIT Press, 1997. It should also be noted that these perspectives are not competing or mutually exclusive. For example, while feminist economics may emphasise that the financial crisis was 'related to male domination in finance, and its impact was stratified by gender', that is perfectly compatible with the institutionalist view that it was 'a consequence of the concentration of firms and poor financial regulation'. The point of this table is that each perspective has particular focuses, tools and insights which can broaden our understanding of economics, rather than that one must choose between them.
5 This experience has been reported by students at multiple universities.
6 The Russell Group actually comprises 24 universities but Imperial does not offer straight economics degrees at undergraduate level.
7 John Kay, 'We can reform the economics curriculum without creating new disciplines', 15 April 2015. Available at: http://www.johnkay. com/2015/04/15/we-can-reform-the-economics-curriculum-without-creating-new-disciplines (accessed 21 April 2016).
8 That economists don't have answers to some of these questions is openly admitted by the prominent economist Raj Chetty. See Raj Chetty, 'Yes, economics is a science', *New York Times*, 20 October 2013. Available

at: http://www.nytimes.com/2013/10/21/opinion/yes-economics-is-a-science.html (accessed 21 April 2016).

9 Economist Gary Becker was the first and most prominent economist to attempt to apply neoclassical economics to the family, modelling it as a problem of optimal allocation. Here marriage takes place because the individuals involved can increase their consumption by getting married, and once married total resources are allocated by the household head. Apart from being rather Victorian in its outlook on the family, it is quite clear that this approach leaves out the fundamental role of household production emphasised by feminist economics, instead shoehorning the family into neoclassical analysis by explaining it in terms of individual consumption. See Gary S. Becker, *A Treatise on the Family*, Cambridge, MA: Harvard University Press, 1981.

10 Marilyn Waring, *If Women Counted: A New Feminist Economics*, San Francisco: Harper & Row, 1988.

11 This dates back at least to Nicholas Kaldor in *The Scourge of Monetarism*, Oxford: Oxford University Press, 1982. Modern exponents include Marc Lavoie, 'A primer on endogenous credit-money', in Louis-Philippe Rochon and Sergio Rossi, *Modern Theories of Money: The Nature and Role of Money in Capitalist Economies*, Cheltenham: Edward Elgar, 2003, 506–43.

12 The Bank of England released a quarterly bulletin in 2014 stating that money is created privately by banks: Michael McLeay, Amar Radia and Thomas Ryland, 'Money creation in the modern economy', *Bank of England Quarterly Bullet, Q1 2014*. Available at: http://www.bankofengland.co.uk/publications/documents/quarterlybulletin/2014/qb14q1prereleasemoneycreation.pdf (accessed 24 April 2016).

13 For an overview of the NAIRU, see Laurence Ball and Gregory N. Mankiw, 'The NAIRU in theory and practice', *Journal of Economic Perspectives* 16(4) (2002): 115–36.

14 See Karl Marx, *Capital Vol. I – Chapter Twenty-Five*, 1867 [online]. Available at: https://www.marxists.org/archive/marx/works/1867-c1/ch25.htm#S3. (accessed 24 April 2016).

15 The 2012 Nobel Prize in Economics was awarded to Al Roth and Lloyd Shapley for their work in matching theory.

16 This means that if interest rates go up, inflation goes down and vice versa.

17 Ben Bernanke, 'Deflation: making sure it doesn't happen again', speech, National Economists Club, Washington DC, 2002. Available at: http://www.federalreserve.gov/boarddocs/speeches/2002/20021121/default.htm (accessed 24 April 2016).

18 Robert E. Lucas, 'Macroeconomic priorities', *American Economic Review* 93(1) (2003): 1–14.

19 Olivier Blanchard, 'The state of macro', *NBER Working Paper* no. 14259, 2008.

20 Just a few examples are John Lanchester, *Whoops! Why Everyone Owes Everyone and No One Can Pay*, London: Allen Lane, 2010; Yves Smith, *ECONned: How Unenlightened Self Interest Damaged Democracy and Corrupted Capitalism*, New York: Palgrave Macmillan, 2010; Adair Turner, *Between Debt and the Devil*, Oxford: Princeton University Press, 2015.

21 In 2006 the deputy governor of the Bank of England reported that 'the largest contributions to OFC money growth have, in fact, come from … what the statisticians label "Other Financial Intermediaries"'. This is a clear example of how a simple (lack of) definition can completely change the way regulators view the economy. See Gillian Tett, 'Economists' tribal thinking', *The Atlantic*, 1 September 2015. Available at: http:// www.theatlantic.com/business/archive/2015/09/economists-tribal-thinking/403075/ (accessed 24 April 2016).

22 One such example was the Black–Scholes equation introduced in Chapter 1, which now has the impressive record of being associated with financial crises in 1987, 1999 and 2008. See also Tim Harford, 'Black-Scholes: the maths formula linked to the financial crash', BBC, 2012. Available at: http://www.bbc.co.uk/news/magazine-17866646 (accessed 24 April 2016).

23 Andrew Haldane, 'The revolution in economics', foreword to the Post-Crash Economics Society Report *Economics, Education and Unlearning: Economics Education at the University of Manchester*, April 2015, 3–6. Available at: http://www.post-crasheconomics.com/economics-education-and-unlearning/ (accessed 22 April 2016).

24 The letter from Besley and Hennessy is available at: http://www.feed-charity.org/user/image/besley-hennessy2009a.pdf (accessed 24 April 2016).

25 Robert Solow, 'Dumb and dumber in macroeconomics', address at Joe Stiglitz's 60th birthday conference, 25 October 2013. Available at: http://textlab.io/doc/927882/dumb-and-dumber-in-macroeconomics-robert-m.-solow-so (accessed 27 April 2016); Paul Krugman, 'How did economists get it so wrong?', *New York Times*, 2 September 2009. http://www.nytimes.com/2009/09/06/magazine/06Economic-t. html?pagewanted=print. (accessed 21 April 2016).

26 Hyman P. Minsky, 'The Financial Instability Hypothesis', *Levy Economics Institute Working Paper* No. 74, 1992.

27 Paul Krugman, 'Why weren't alarm bells ringing?', *The New York Review of Books*, 23 October 2014. Available at: http://www.nybooks.com/articles/2014/10/23/why-werent-alarm-bells-ringing/ (accessed 21 April 2016).

28 See Dirk Bezemer, *No One Saw This Coming. Understanding Financial Crisis through Accounting Models*, University of Groningen, Research Institute SOM (Systems, Organisations and Management), 2009; James K. Galbraith, 'Who are these economists, anyway?', *The NEA Higher Education Journal* (Fall 2009).

29 Art Rolnick, 'Interview with Thomas Sargent', Federal Reserve Bank of Minneapolis, 2010. Available at: https://minneapolisfed.org/publications/the-region/interview-with-thomas-sargent (accessed 21 April 2016).

30 Timothy Cogley and Thomas J. Sargent, 'The market price of risk and the equity premium: a legacy of the Great Depression?', *Journal of Monetary Economics* 55(3) (2008): 454–76. Credit is due to Jonathan Aldred for pointing this out, in his forthcoming paper 'Reforming economics education: assessing the mainstream response'.

31 Naomi Oreskes, 'Beyond the ivory tower: the scientific consensus on climate change', *Science* 306(5702) (2004): 1686.

32 See http://www.fund-model.org/

33 Environmental economics may work for some more specific environmental problems than climate change, such as creating a market for permits to emit sulphur dioxide in the US. See Roger Backhouse, *The Puzzle of Modern Economics: Science or Ideology*, New York: Cambridge University Press, 2010, 22–3.

34 Roger Perman, Yue Ma and James McGilvray, *Natural Resource and Environmental Economics*, London: Longman, 1996, 411–54.

35 Extrapolating these risks can easily be shown to be absurd. For example, if Ted values a 1-in-1,000 increased risk of death at £100, does this mean he values a 1-in-10 increased risk of death at £10,000? Certain death at £100,000? Climate change analysis frequently makes these kinds of leaps by transferring the estimated values to other contexts and scaling them up. This is a version of an argument made by Jonathan Aldred in a critique of Stern and CBA as applied to the environment. See Jonathan Aldred, 'Ethics and climate change cost–benefit analysis: Stern and after', *Environmental Economy and Policy Research Discussion Paper Series*, 2009.

36 Frank Ackerman and Elizabeth A. Stanton, *Climate Economics: The State of the Art*, report, Stockholm Environment Institute-US Center, 2011, 73–104.

37 Nicholas Stern, *Stern Review: Report on the Economics of Climate Change*, report, HM Treasury, 2006, vi.

38 Richard Tol, 'Bogus prophecies of doom will not fix the climate', *Financial Times*, 31 March 2014. Available at: https://next.ft.com/content/e8d011fa-b8b5-11e3-835e-00144feabdc0. (accessed 21 April 2016).

39 This was pointed out in a letter in response to Tol in the *Financial Times*: Cameron Hepburn, 'Incomplete climate models lead to complacency', *Financial Times*, 1 April 2014. Available at: https://next.ft.com/__anon-opt-in/cms/s/0/d54c0de6-b8e2-11e3-835e-00144feabdc0.html (accessed 27 April 2016).

40 Nicholas Stern, 'Economics: current climate models are grossly misleading', *Nature* 530(7591) (2016): 407–9.

41 See Mark Buchanan, 'Economists are blind to the limits of growth', *Bloomberg View*, 5 October 2014. Available at: http://www.bloom bergview.com/articles/2014-10-05/economists-are-blind-to-the-limits-of-growth (accessed 24 April 2016).

42 Herman E. Daly, *Ecological Economics and the Ecology of Economics: Essays in Criticism*, Northampton, MA: Edward Elgar, 1999.

43 The Equality Trust, 'How has inequality changed?', 2016. Available at: https://www.equalitytrust.org.uk/how-has-inequality-changed (accessed 24 April 2016).

44 John Gapper, 'Capitalism: in search of balance – FT.Com', *Financial Times*, 23 December 2013. Available at: http://www.ft.com/cms/s/0/4a0b8168-6bc0-11e3-a216-00144feabdc0.html#axzz46k4tODTg (accessed 24 April 2016).

45 Amartya Sen and James E. Foster, *On Economic Inequality*, Oxford: Clarendon Press, 1997, 16.

46 For a more comprehensive critique of SWFs, see Peter Self, *Econocrats and the Policy Process*, London: Macmillan, 1975, 14–25.

47 *Briefing 43: the poorest regions of the UK are the poorest in North-West Europe*, Inequality Briefing, 2016. Available at: http://inequality briefing.org/brief/briefing-43-the-poorest-regions-of-the-uk-are-the-poorest-in-northern- (accessed 24 April 2016).

48 'The thinking behind feminist economics', *The Economist*, 20 October 2015. Available at: http://www.economist.com/blogs/economist-explains/2015/10/economist-explains-17 (accessed 27 April 2016).

49 Robert E. Lucas, '2003 annual report essay – the Industrial Revolution: past and future', *Federal Reserve Bank of Minneapolis*, 2003.

50 Reported in Alexander Stille, 'Grounded by an income gap', *New York Times*, 15 December 2001. Available at: http://www.nytimes.com/2001/12/15/arts/15GAP.html?pagewanted=all (accessed 24 April 2016).

51 Paul Krugman, 'Economists and inequality', *New York Times*, 8 January 2016. Available at: http://krugman.blogs.nytimes.com/2016/01/08/economists-and-inequality/ (accessed 24 April 2016).

52 Piketty himself has criticised the discipline on similar grounds to us and has signed the state of the International Student Initiative for Pluralism In Economics (ISIPE) in support of economic pluralism. See http://www.isipe.net/supportus/

53 Similarly, the economist Tony Atkinson recently published an excellent book that in many ways takes neoclassical economics as its framework, but also uses a detailed, case-study approach to real-world policies that affect inequality. Moreover, Atkinson himself criticised the economics profession and its approach to inequality, saying it should be more central to the study of economics. See Tony Atkinson, *Inequality: What Can Be Done*, Cambridge, MA: Harvard University Press, 2015.

54 Thomas Piketty, *Capital in the Twenty-First Century*, Cambridge, MA: Harvard University Press, 2014, 35.

55 Data available at https://en.wikipedia.org/wiki/List_of_countries_by_income_equality.

56 John D. Wisman, 'What drives inequality?', Working Papers, American University, Department of Economics, 2015.

57 Joan Robinson, *Collected Economic Papers Volume II*, Oxford: B. Blackwell, 1951, iv.

58 This is a reworking of a quote from John Maynard Keynes: 'Practical men, who believe themselves to be quite exempt from any intellectual influence, are usually the slaves of some defunct economist.' See John M. Keynes, *The General Theory of Employment, Interest and Money*, New York: Harcourt, Brace & World, 1936, 383–4.

59 See Sam Allgood, William Bosshardt, Wilbert van der Klaauw and Michael Watts, 'Is economics coursework, or majoring in economics, associated with different civic behaviors?', *The Journal of Economics Education* 43(3) (2012): 248–68.

60 Daniel B. Klein and Charlotta Stern, 'Is there a free-market economist in the house? The policy views of American Economic Association members', *American Journal of Economics and Sociology* 66(2) (2007): 309–34.

61 Ha-Joon Chang, *23 Things They Don't Tell You About Capitalism*, New York: Bloomsbury, 2011, 8–10.

62 Daniel F. Spulber, *Famous Fables of Economics*, Malden, MA: Blackwell Publishers, 2002.

63 See William Lazonick, *Business Organization and the Myth of the Market Economy*, Cambridge: Cambridge University Press, 1991; John Kenneth Galbraith, *The New Industrial State*, Boston: Houghton Mifflin, 1967.

64 Jason Potts, *The New Evolutionary Microeconomics*, Cheltenham: Edward Elgar, 2000.

65 For an introduction to the post-Keynesian concept of uncertainty, see Fernando Ferrari-Filho and Octavio Conceicao, 'The concept of uncertainty in post-Keynesian theory and in Institutional Economics', *Journal of Economic Issues* 39(3) (2005): 579–94.

66 Friedrich A. Hayek, 'The use of knowledge in society', *American Economic Review* 35(4) (1945): 519–30.

Chapter 4

The struggle for the soul of economics

Economic thought is today dominated by a single perspective, which seriously limits the ability of economic experts to deal with many of the problems faced by society. The belief in this one perspective goes right to the heart of the profession. For example, the 2014 Nobel Laureate in Economics, Jean Tirole, stated that it is 'important for the community of academics ... and researchers to be endowed with a *single* scientific assessment standard'.[1] Thus, while economists often criticise the existence of monopolies – particularly Tirole, whose research is focused on this very topic[2] – they would argue that in this case it is the fit and proper situation. We therefore think it is important to present a narrative that challenges the idea that neoclassical economics has become dominant solely on grounds of quality. In fact, as we have shown in the preceding chapter, in many ways neoclassical economics is in crisis.

This chapter is dedicated to placing the dominance of neoclassical economics in context. We first trace the development of the discipline from its roots as a diverse moral science to the uniform, narrow theory that it is today, focusing on the specific type of mathematical modelling we have seen, which economists often term 'formal' modelling. We then show how it has entrenched its position by capitalising on certain institutional developments in order to exclude other opinions. Our work is focused on this process in the UK, but we believe this has happened in other countries, as it has been documented by numerous sources.[3]

The failure of economics as a discipline to predict or comprehend the financial crisis, as well as its limited relevance to some of society's most pressing problems, has not gone unnoticed. Consequently, the final section of this chapter documents how students are campaigning to persuade the discipline to renew itself. We recount the modern struggle for the soul of economics that is taking place in universities across the world.

The rise of econocracy and the narrowing of economics as a discipline are not historically coincidental. By presenting economics as a single, unified theoretical framework that can provide unique insights about the economy, economists have secured for themselves a position of great power. For politicians and policymakers, economics provides the allure of transforming complex, value-laden, ethically challenging and uncertain decisions into technical puzzles with clear right and wrong answers. To maintain this façade economics must exclude those with alternative perspectives who, by fundamentally challenging neoclassical economics, undermine the discipline's claims to scientific truth. In the long run this stifles the development of the discipline and prevents it from adapting to a changing world. The next section shows how economics came to this dead end.

Dreams of a unified science

> The master-economist must possess a rare combination of gifts ... He must be mathematician, historian, statesman, philosopher – in some degree. He must understand symbols and speak in words ... He must study the present in the light of the past for the purposes of the future. No part of man's nature or his institutions must be entirely outside his regard.
>
> John Maynard Keynes, 1924[4]

> The combined assumptions of maximizing behavior, stable preferences, and market equilibrium, used relentlessly and unflinchingly, form the heart of the economic approach as I see it.
>
> Gary Becker, 1976[5]

The above quotes represent two conflicting views of what is required to understand the economy. Over the past century or so, and especially over the past few decades, it is the latter definition that has come to dominate economics. Economics has exhibited dangerous trends towards homogenisation and the silencing of dissenting perspectives through exclusion, which has led to the single paradigm outlined in the previous two chapters.

The dominance of this form of economics is in many ways surprising, given the origins of economic thought. The birth of the discipline is usually seen as the publication of Adam Smith's *Wealth of Nations*, which coincided – not coincidentally – with the birth of the market economy. Smith was one of the first to argue that the mechanisms of price, supply and demand contained predictable laws that held society together. The insight for which Smith is best remembered is that even if everyone acts in their own self-interest, competition bids down price and leads to the most efficient and effective system for producing wealth, as if society is guided by an 'invisible hand'.[6]

Although Smith is commonly considered to have invented the idea of *homo economicus* – a long-running tendency within economics to model humans as rational and self-interested – *The Wealth of Nations* is not a book of abstract formalisms but a detailed, descriptive text. Moreover, in an earlier work, *A Theory of Moral Sentiments*, Smith argued for a much more complex understanding of human nature than simple self-interest.[7] Although he favoured a market economy, he was also prepared to confront its perceived shortcomings, criticising the degrading effects of repetitive labour[8] and arguing that meetings between industrialists often resulted in a 'conspiracy against the public'.[9]

During the nineteenth century, what is now economics was known as 'political economy'. Smith, Karl Marx and other great economists of the time, such as John Stuart Mill, considered economics a moral science that could not be separated from wider bodies of thought or reduced to simple abstraction. So while Mill's work focused on the 'laws' of the market, and Marx believed he had 'scientifically' shown why capitalism would produce volatility and misery, there were many other dimensions to their work. Marx's analysis centred on ideas of power, income distribution and instability. Mill always remained a philosopher and a social critic as well as an economist, and recognised that one could not separate the sphere of the economy from politics and society.[10]

This recognition of the fundamental openness and diversity of economics persisted even as the discipline became professionalised. In 1891 the British Economic Association's (now called the Royal Economic Society) first issue of the *Economic Journal* began by stating:

> The British Economic Association is open to all schools and parties; no person is excluded because of his opinions. The Economic Journal, issued under the authority of the Association, will be conducted in a similar spirit of toleration … the most opposite doctrine may meet here as on a fair field … nor will it be attempted to prescribe the method, any more than the result, of scientific investigation.[11]

Across the Atlantic, the American Economic Association's (AEA) Charter of Incorporation committed itself to 'the encouragement of economic research, especially the historical study of the actual conditions of economic life', as well as to 'the encouragement of perfect freedom of economic discussion'. 'The Association as such [took] no partisan attitude, nor commit[ted] its members to any position on practical economic questions.'[12] The Secretary of the AEA in 1909 described how in its earliest days the Association was split between two groups, one of which 'desired to make [it] a propagandist party leading a reaction against … laissez faire doctrines', and another of which 'opposed any form of propagandism'. He suggested that the latter group had won and that as a result the Association was to be kept a 'purely scientific body, with perfect freedom of discussion, and [with] room for every possible difference of individual opinion'.[13]

Yet this left economists with a problem. In its nascent, pluralist years, economics could not command the respect and power economists felt it deserved. This anxiety was expressed by the economist Irving Fisher in 1902, when he bemoaned that 'economists have altogether too little influence; they are too silent on public questions, and when they do speak their opinion commands less respect than it deserves'.[14] Fisher felt that economists needed to make the public and its politicians aware of the fundamental principles of economics to illustrate the scientific character of economic discourse and the rigorousness of its theory as a guide to policy.[15] Economists recognised that those in charge want clear, authoritative answers, not academic debate. Winston Churchill summed this up when he allegedly claimed that 'if you put two economists in a room, you get two opinions'.[16]

Economics was already developing in a way that would assuage Churchill's frustration. A key part of forming an authoritative intellectual community is to develop a distinct identity for the body of knowledge which can then be used to establish its boundaries, evaluate good and bad practice, define the terms of membership of the community and ensure its continued existence. This is done through setting up learned societies, journals, conferences, graduate training programmes, professorships and departmental rankings. In practice and over time the commitment to openness and diversity was subsumed by the perception that a single body of scientific economic knowledge was taking shape along with the greater confidence this gave to economists as a distinct intellectual community.

Economists who wanted the discipline to gain recognition and influence in the world felt that economics had to present itself as scientific, which meant agreeing on a shared approach for generating objective and rigorous knowledge. This resulted in a conscious attempt to manage and minimise disagreement within the discipline. In 1922, a decade after becoming editor of the AER, John Dewey declared that 'economics ha[d] abandoned the controversial stages and begun to work under the cooperati[on] of investigation and analysis'. While 'there [might] be, here and there, a cantankerous controversialist left who [would] insist upon defending his own point of view regardless of the facts', Dewey felt increasingly justified in 'leaving them by the wayside whenever [he] detect[ed] that quality' in submissions.[17] Dewey clearly saw himself as objective but his actions, along with an earlier commitment from the AER not to publish Marxist economics due to scares over communism, represented early attempts to police the borders of the discipline and enforce homogeneity.

From a theoretical perspective, the movement of economics away from its wider social, political and historical contexts and towards Becker's definition gained ground during the 'marginal revolution' of the late nineteenth century. Over this period, a number of prominent economists released similar books – sometimes independently of one another – detailing the kinds of formal models that would still be recognisable to an economics undergraduate today. One of these economists, Stanley Jevons, summed up his drive to create a mathematical approach: '[Economics] must be mathematical, simply because it deals with quantities.'[18]

Modern economic notions such as 'utility functions', 'supply and demand' and 'equilibrium' became prevalent as a result of these books. Jevons also introduced 'the single convenient term economics' in place of the previous label 'political economy', and this suggestion stuck, making it easier for the discipline to shed its political context.[19] In 1891 Alfred Marshall produced *Principles*, the discipline's first major textbook which would be used by students for generations.[20] *Principles* represented a milestone because it outlined a body of knowledge that one had to know to become an economist, standardising the shared understandings of future generations of economists and shaping the tools the discipline would use to understand the world.

In 1932 Lionel Robbins published a call for a new understanding of economics which was to change the direction of the discipline. He argued that defining economics in terms of material needs was too narrow. Instead he proposed the definition 'Economics is the science which studies human behavior as a relationship between ends and scarce means which have alternative uses.'[21] Previously economics had been particularly but not exclusively concerned with how to satisfy human needs. In contrast, Robbins's definition made economics the study of any goods that someone desired. This shifted the focus of economics from the production and distribution of goods to their exchange.[22] Curiously, this seemingly narrower definition would later allow economics to apply its methods beyond traditional spheres into vastly expanded areas of social policy such as crime, addiction and the family.[23]

John Maynard Keynes, who was quoted at the beginning of this section, was somebody whose views about the tools economists need were probably closer to our own. His book, *The General Theory of Employment, Interest and Money* – which intertwined economics with philosophy, ethics and history – seemed like it might disrupt the increasing technicalisation and abstraction of economics. However, following a script that would become familiar, neoclassical economics incorporated Keynes's ideas about recessions as a 'special case' and discarded his broader points about which skills and knowledge economists needed to have. Economists also had to reject Keynes's ideas about radical uncertainty, which did not fit easily into their models, in order to keep them mathematically tractable.[24]

Paul Samuelson's 'neo-Keynesian' *Foundations of Economic Analysis*, released after Keynes died shortly after the Second World War, crystallised and consolidated many of the key ideas in economics into a common mathematical framework. Soon after this Samuelson wrote a textbook called *Economics*, which set the stage for education in the discipline as it stands now. The London School of Economics still recommends an updated version of Samuelson's textbook, as well as the similar, 50-year-old *Positive Economics* by Richard Lipsey, as pre-requisites to their second year microeconomics course.[25] At around this time other crucial branches of economics were developed, such as econometrics and game theory.[26]

The drive towards formalism and a single paradigm partly reflected the USA's rise to political dominance, and historical circumstance. As we have seen, economics is closely tied up with politics and this means that economists' political and academic identities are often interwoven. The heightened tensions of the Cold War put pressure on the discipline to ensure political acceptability and this was done by redoubling the effort to make economics appear scientific and objective. According to the historian Michael Bernstein:

> The homogenization of opinion within the social sciences often took place along the dimension of academic peer review rather than overt political repression. With the exception of Paul Baran, a left-wing economist was rarely fired or harassed for 'political' reasons during the McCarthyite hysteria; unlike, say, a mathematician expelled from a faculty appointment and ultimately imprisoned for refusing to answer questions about his

political beliefs, an economist of radical loyalties could be denied promotion and advancement, left without research funding, and sequestered from journal editorial boards all on the basis of professional 'vetting' regarded as apolitical and rational.[27]

By controlling how economics is defined and subsequently what constitutes good and bad economics, influential organisations like the AEA can act as gatekeepers to the discipline and prevent those with alternative perspectives from attaining the necessary credentials to be appointed and promoted to academic posts. These processes are vital for the creation and maintenance of a single perspective within an academic discipline.

The growing consensus was briefly interrupted during the economic crisis of the 1970s. Samuelson's 'neo-Keynesian' economics had emphasised management of the macroeconomy based on observed statistical relationships: if inflation went up then unemployment would always go down. However, during the 1970s relationships like this broke down and the economy experienced 'stagflation', economists' imaginative term for a stagnant economy where inflation and unemployment are both going up at the same time. A young economist named Robert Lucas proposed that these models had failed because they were simply based on observed statistical relationships and not grounded in the decisions of economic agents.[28] According to Lucas, inflation is not a thing in itself but a result of the interaction of millions of different economic agents, and these agents are capable of learning about the system they are operating in. Therefore, if agents change their behaviour in response to a policy change, a previously observed relationship might break down. For example, if inflation was high, workers might demand higher wages to compensate, meaning that higher inflation would *not* result in lower labour costs, and therefore would not reduce unemployment as the older models had predicted.

Lucas's solution was to model the economy starting from the individual agent – taken from microeconomics – who had 'rational expectations', meaning that agents understood the economy as a whole and incorporated it into their decision making. The result was that the discipline became more technical, more mathematically complex and in many ways further detached from the real world. Economists model people as knowing exactly how the economy works, whereas we would argue that they themselves do not have the full picture.

As the neoclassical economist Paul Krugman has admitted, the homogeneity of the discipline and its crisis of hubris came from 'the desire for an all-encompassing, intellectually elegant approach that also gave economists a chance to show off their mathematical prowess'.[29] Economics lost a great deal on the way from its roots to the modern day – much of it we would argue for the worse. By shedding ethical, political and historical considerations, and adopting a particular, narrow style of modelling, economics became a consolidated formal framework. As the economist Mark Blaug has put it, economists developed an 'absolute preference for the form of an economic argument over its content'.[30] Most economists spoke a common language and used a common set of tools. Those who didn't were increasingly pushed to the fringes.

The cleansing of economics departments[31]

The development of economics in the early twentieth century led to a neoclassical 'mainstream' developing, but the situation that students of economics face now – where they are only exposed to one economic perspective – is relatively new. As Chris Giles, the Economics Editor of the *Financial Times*, has put it:

> There was a time when any self-respecting economics undergraduate could distinguish between neo-Keynesian, new-Keynesian and post-Keynesian thinking; they would write essays on the difference between Marxist and monetarist policies; and they would have to know how classical economists, such as Adam Smith, influenced the neoclassical school and how new classical economics developed subsequently in the 1970s. Economics teaching was about understanding the way the world worked; how the discipline had changed; and how to make the world a better place.[32]

This sentiment is echoed by many top economists we spoke to during research for this book. Martin Wolf, also of the *FT*, stressed how his degree was less technical and dogmatic, and that it allowed him to explore ideas. He said that if he were an undergraduate today, he would not pursue a degree in economics. Diane Coyle argued that, while it was perhaps not as different as Giles's quote suggests, it was certainly less restrictive. The economist Pat Devine perhaps best summarised the situation when he said that his education 'allowed one to be critical'. Neoclassical economics may have been dominant, but dissenting ideas still had their part to play.

In contrast, economics education today does not expose students to alternative perspectives and does not allow them to be critical.

The main reason for this shift is that non-neoclassical economists have been systematically excluded from economics departments across the UK. The result is that departments are neither willing nor able to teach alternative perspectives in environments that promote critical discussion.

This change can be seen clearly at the University of Manchester. The state of the department in the 1970s would seem alien to anyone familiar with a modern economics department. In departmental reports, the eminent post-Keynesian economist Joan Robinson was labelled as a 'distinguished visitor'. The department was filled with post-Keynesians, feminists and other economists with alternative perspectives, alongside the econometricians and neoclassical micro and macro professors who dominate the department today. It was in this environment that Diane Elson became an economist. She recollects that the atmosphere of pluralism and tolerance 'meant that you could look at institutions, not confined by neoclassical welfare economics'. Diane has played a significant role in the development of feminist economics as a distinct economic perspective, with its own research agenda and methodological framework, which now stands as a widely practised tradition.[33] She has been a member of the UN Committee for Development Policy, worked at some of the UK's most prestigious universities and now chairs the UK's Women's Budget Group, which analyses the gender implications of UK economic policy. She is by any measure a successful economist. And yet her contribution is not recognised by most economics departments in the UK. Like so many others who have diverged from neoclassical economics, she has been banished from economics departments across the UK.

In the UK the Research Assessment Exercise (RAE), first conducted in 1986, has created an institutional system that has gradually cleansed economics departments of academics who don't follow the neoclassical research agenda. The RAE – changed to the Research Excellence Framework (REF) in 2014 – is carried out about once every five years, and every university department submits two pieces of work from each of its academics to be given a score between one and four, where four represents internationally recognised, world-leading research. Each university department is then given an overall score for research quality and research 'power' (broadly, quality multiplied by size). This system provides a disincentive for departments to enter those academics it thinks will do badly.

The RAE left non-neoclassical economists in a vulnerable position. The power to define economics had always shaped the development of the discipline, but once state funding was attached to evaluations of quality this became doubly important. In the RAE/REF this ranking is done by a panel of leading academics from each discipline and external members from business and government. The system creates and reproduces 'monolithic notions of what constitutes quality'[34] because it allows a small group of academics to make fundamental decisions about how to define good and bad economics in private without any explanation of their criteria. Alternative or new approaches that don't use the dominant theoretical framework could be deemed to be bad economics and their author would in turn be seen as a bad economist.

The make-up of the panel would determine how open and diverse economics would be. The assessors for the 1989[35] assessment were selected by the Royal Economics Society,[36] which seemed to pay little attention to the promotion of intellectual diversity when it picked panel members. The result of this was that the early RAEs had panels overwhelmingly made up of established neoclassical economists who had little or no exposure to or knowledge of other forms of economics.[37] The trend has continued to this day and has arguably developed even further, with many assessors for the recent 2014 REF being editors of major neoclassical journals.[38]

This is in no way the result of a conspiracy. The cleansing of departments does not represent a conscious attempt to oust dissenting opinion; it is the result of a mindset in which dissenting opinion cannot even be considered because the discipline is defined by a particular framework. By rejecting this framework, non-neoclassical economists become outsiders. The distance between outsiders and insiders can be seen in surveys of citations from journals between 1986 and 1993, a period after the introduction of the RAE, during which mainstream neoclassical journals rarely cited the work of non-mainstream ones.[39] It is almost as if they were speaking different languages.

The belief that non-neoclassical economics does not have much to offer can be seen in the defence of the RAE process given by one former chair interviewed by us. On being asked whether he thought the process might be biased against those from outside the mainstream, his reply included the comment that 'if it had these criteria and it wasn't just Keynes said this, Keynes said that, which some of them unfortunately were, which we all know, we can read Keynes, thank you'. This illustrates a belief on the part of at least some panel members that non-mainstream work had nothing new to add and merely wanted to take economics back to an earlier period.

Moreover, it reflects a belief that we do not need to remember some of the old lessons of economics because its modern form has in some way progressed away from them. Influenced by the vision of economics as a single, unified science, panel members could now indirectly determine who was hired by university economics departments.

Prior to the RAE, universities and academics received funding that was related to the number of students that they were teaching. It was assumed that all academics were devoting part of their time to research, and questions of quality were resolved by peer-review but not directly linked to funding. In contrast, allocation of contemporary funding for research is largely based on REF scores. The first assessment exercise was not very significant in terms of funding, but over the course of the next few assessments the percentage of research funding allocated through these exercises increased: in the second exercise in 1989, it stood at 50 per cent; by 1992, it was over 90 per cent.[40] A brief glance at the University of Manchester archives shows how this changed the atmosphere in the department. Before the change, reports focused on the pressures of increasing student numbers and meeting savings targets; after the change one report reads '1996 was dominated by the RAE; the preparation, the waiting and the result, which was a 4 [out of a possible 5] ... sights have to be set higher for the next round'.[41]

Universities realised that to gain high research rankings in neoclassical economics they needed to hire and promote economists who either had published or would publish in the top-ranked, mostly American, neoclassical economics journals in order to bring in the most funding. Departments came under increasing pressure from senior management to secure funding and move up the league tables, and this led to the reconceptualisation of the academic as an economic agent or 'unit of resource', which was to be maximised to earn the university funding and prestige.[42] Through this lens it makes sense to hire only mainstream neoclassical economists. As early as 1994 the University of Manchester was advertising in the *Guardian* newspaper specifically for 'mainstream economists' who could help boost their research profile.[43]

As a result, a small number of the discipline's leading economists have been given the power to narrow the definition of what constitutes economics. University management, in order to maintain funding and prestige, then had to reshape their economics departments according to those criteria. The imposition of hiring and promotion strategies to achieve these goals in turn sent clear signals to young economists that to succeed they needed to produce a certain type of economic research. Researchers became more aware of the kinds of economics required to get published in a top mainstream neoclassical journal, knowing that such publications were the best pathway to career advancement.[44]

Academic freedom has been defined as being 'free to question and test received wisdom, and to put forward new ideas and controversial or unpopular opinions'.[45] Because the theoretical framework which academics must work within in order to be hired and promoted is so narrowly defined, would-be economists are effectively forced to follow a particular agenda if they are to be successful. Therefore the status quo does not allow this kind of academic freedom.

Pat Devine described the departure of non-neoclassical economists as a process of attrition. Many moved into business schools, others into other social science departments. Diane Elson described an 'implicit agreement' whereby her colleagues increasingly disrespected the work of non-neoclassical economists, or were too pressured by the RAE to be able to accept it, and so it was considered best for everyone if these economists moved on. Another colleague reported that he was told he would be left 'to wither on the vine' if he stayed in the department.

The introduction of the RAE has led to a cycle from which economics cannot escape. Economics tasks itself with understanding our world in all its complexities and propensities for sudden change, yet the discipline has allowed institutional inertia to set in. However, the narrowing of economics has not occurred without resistance from sources both inside and outside the discipline. We now turn to chronicling such dissent.

The struggle for the soul of economics

We the undersigned are concerned with the threat to economic science posed by intellectual monopoly. Economists today enforce a monopoly of method or core assumptions, often defended on no better ground than it constitutes the 'mainstream'. Economists will advocate free competition, but will not practice it in the marketplace of ideas.

The 1992 Plea for Pluralistic Economics[46]

The quote above comes from an open letter signed by 44 leading economists – including four Nobel Laureates – and published as an advertisement in the May 1992 edition of the *American Economic Review*. The letter goes on to call 'for a new spirit of pluralism in economics, involving critical conversation and tolerant communication between different approaches'. This letter illustrates that there have been fairly widespread concerns from many quarters about the state of economics for a long time.

It would take until the turn of the century for the battle for the soul of economics to be picked up, this time by economics students. In June 2000 students at the French University Ecole Normale Supérieure launched a petition calling for economic pluralism. While dissenting economists had tried in vain to interrupt the march of academic economics towards monopolisation and homogenisation, this petition represented the first organised attempt by students to articulate the flaws in their education. It also highlighted the gap between the expectations students had of studying economics and the reality they found, which was to be echoed time and time again:

> Most of us have chosen to study economics so as to acquire a deep under-standing of economic phenomena with which the citizens of today are confronted. But the teaching that is offered, that is to say for the most part neoclassical theory or approaches derived from it, does not gener-ally answer this expectation. Indeed, even when the theory legitimately detaches itself from contingencies in the first instance, it rarely carries out the necessary return to the facts. The empirical side (historical facts, functioning of institutions, study of the behaviours and strategies of agents...) is almost non-existent. Furthermore, this gap in the teaching, this disregard for concrete realities, poses an enormous problem for those who would like to render themselves useful economic and social actors.[47]

The petition led to a certain amount of disquiet within the profes-sion. Some of the students' teachers launched a petition in support of their protests, and similar grievances were later aired at Cambridge in a petition that was signed by 700 academics.[48] A network of dis-satisfied economists which is now called the Real World Economics Association was launched.[49] The student group in France consisted mostly of PhD students and when they moved on there was no one to continue their campaign, so it ground to a halt. This challenge of keeping momentum between generations of students is one that would also face student groups in the future, including our own.

When the Post-Crash Economics Society (PCES) first wrote an email to economics students at Manchester in October 2012 'calling all econosceptics' to an open meeting, we were motivated by frustra-tion and the vaguest idea that something was wrong. Five people turned up and we tried to explain, using a hastily prepared Power Point presentation, what was wrong with our education. It was all rather homemade but there was enough energy among the group to set up a society by the start of the second semester in January 2013.

Early on we made contact with students from a few different universities in the UK who were setting up a group called Rethinking Economics. This aimed to provide an international network to connect students and citizens who wanted to open up and reinvigorate economics. We used Facebook and Skype to communicate and while all of us dislike the crackle of a slow Skype connection, we recognise that the international student movement to reform economics could not exist without it. We are very much a movement of our time and could not have existed in the same way ten years ago.

Little did we know at the time but students in France had regrouped in 2011 and founded *PEPS-Economie* (*Pour un Enseignement Pluraliste dans le Supérieure en Economie*, or 'For a Pluralistic Teaching in Higher Education in Economics'). The French students carried out a survey of all the economics courses in France to analyse what was taught, leading to a French Government Commission into the teaching of economics.[50] Similarly, in Germany there was a thriving *Netzwerk Plurale Ökonomik*.

In Manchester we began to flesh out the aims of our society. Our search for a language and ideas to describe what was wrong with our economics education had led us to dusty books in the library outlining approaches to economics we had never heard of before. We stumbled across the feedback from the Association for Heterodox Economics to the 2008 'QAA economics subject benchmark consultation', which compared economics to other subjects and argued that it was 'less critical of its prescriptions than theology and … attaches less importance to diversity than accountancy'.[51] It then called for pluralism in economics, and although pluralism isn't the most glamorous of causes, it seemed to go a long way to addressing the intuitive criticisms we had of our economics education to date.

We started drafting a petition that would articulate our criticisms and which we could then use to communicate what was wrong to students. Getting students to sign would allow us to demonstrate to the economics department and university management that we had widespread support and were not just a bunch of renegades. Our four criticisms in the petition were of the lack of real-world application, the absence of alternative perspectives, the lack of history and the lack of critical thinking. Chapter 2 illustrates how our critique has developed since then but the petition was an important first step to articulate what had previously been unfocused frustration.

In March 2013 we held our launch event, 'Are Economics Graduates Fit for Purpose?', which was a panel discussion between economists of different stripes. We got the idea from a Bank of England conference of the same name which had been held in 2012. Seeing this was important validation for us because we felt that if powerful institutions were asking these questions there must be some substance to the criticisms we had of our education. At the event our then Head of Department compared alternative perspectives to the outdated use of tobacco-smoke enemas (the practice of blowing smoke up a patient's bottom) in medicine. Despite this, the event saw some good engagement between different types of economists and the positive feedback from the two hundred students who attended increased our confidence immeasurably.

Finding sources of confidence and validation for one's sanity in challenging an entire discipline has been a crucial part of the growth of the global student movement. One Danish student talked of reading an article about a student group in Copenhagen called *Kritiske Politter* (Critical Students of Economics) and a critical professor called Katarina Juselius, saying how 'for the first time [he] felt like [he] was not alone'. For another, the fact that so many student groups 'have all appeared independently but with almost the exact same idea and the same criticism … should perhaps be interpreted as a sign that there is something to the criticism'. As the student movement grew, we were able to challenge the internal doubt and the external criticism that we were isolated and ultimately misguided rebels without a cause.

We were clear now that the society would consist of events for students to illustrate the value and interest of what they were not currently being taught; self-education activities to fill the gaps; and an active campaign to increase student support for curriculum reform, communicating this to the department. We agreed that our campaign had to engage constructively with the department to be successful and we were aware that criticism from students could be threatening. Therefore, we always tried to stress that we weren't arguing that neoclassical economics was wrong; simply that it couldn't justify a monopoly in British economics departments.

This approach to campaigning was mirrored by student groups across the world. We were told time and again that local groups had 'good and constructive' relationships with their departments and had 'received support from a number of the academics in the Faculty of Economics, many of whom share at least some of the concerns put forward'. The image of students seeking to overthrow departments and obstinate economists blindly opposing reform is not an accurate one. In reality attitudes within departments are often varied, with a number of academics who are supportive of at least some of our aims, many with mixed feelings and a few who are hostile. We attribute our existence in Manchester to a few teaching assistants who went beyond their remit and asked us to think critically about what we were learning.

Our schedule for the 2013/14 academic year was ambitious and reflected our growing confidence, with new students joining the committee. We organised a monthly lecture series called 'What You Won't Learn in an Economics Degree', introducing students to alternative perspectives, as well as an evening not-for-credit course called 'Bubbles, Panics and Crashes', which covered the history of and policy responses to financial crises from multiple economic perspectives. The latter was run by one of our lecturers, Devrim Yilmaz, who was one of the few non-neoclassical economists in the department. He was unable to get the module accredited in time the previous year, so instead he ran it for us in his own time. We helped to organise and advertise it, hoping also that it would be put on as an official part of the course the following year.

Our campaign strategy for the year consisted of pushing our petition (which now had over 150 signatures), seeking media attention to raise awareness, and trying to arrange meetings with our department and senior management to make our case. We wrote a press pack explaining what was wrong with economics education and why it should matter to non-economists. On 24 October 2013 we appeared in the *Guardian* with an article that was eventually shared on Facebook 22,627 times. It received a lot of follow-up media coverage and suddenly we were receiving hundreds of messages of support from people all over the world as well as packages with books, and even plays, about economics. Most unexpectedly, the article provoked in the Houses of Parliament the Early Day Motion 641, which was a symbolic gesture of support from the 12 MPs who signed it.

The Early Day Motion and the media coverage highlighted a significant challenge for our society and the student movement more broadly. We were clear from the start that our society should not promote either left- or right-wing politics. We were calling for pluralism in our education, which included both Austrian economics – typically understood to be right-wing – and Marxism, which is of course left-wing. We also recognised that the political impact of neoclassical economics is itself complex, as we discussed in Chapter 3.

In our press pack we tried to avoid being pigeonholed as a rebellious left-wing student group by stating:

> Our society is not about left-wing or right-wing politics or economics; it is about the dire state of national economics education today ... We firmly believe that Hayek as well as Keynes would both be turning in their graves if they knew what an undergraduate economics education consisted of today. More importantly, we believe that our economics education system is not able to produce economists of the calibre of Keynes or Hayek anymore and it is society that will pay the price. Keynes and Hayek were both well versed in a broad range of economic thought and history, they both had vastly developed critical capabilities, they were great writers and communicators as well as economists and, most importantly, they were both free thinkers who overturned existing ideas and norms to build their respective theories. All that is now lost...

However, we weren't able to escape the established 'left vs right' narrative in some of our media coverage, and the Early Day Motion supported us in our supposed aim of combating 'orthodox neoliberal globalised free market teaching'.[52] This framing oversimplifies a more complex political issue and undermines the possibility of constructive dialogue. For us it illustrated how entrenched this left versus right understanding of the world is and the scale of the challenge we face in catalysing public debate about economics education without simply falling back into these tired and outdated stereotypes.

In the autumn of 2013 we had separate meetings with the Head of Social Sciences and Head of Humanities. These were exciting events for us because we felt that we were finally making an impact, and we prepared our arguments carefully. We had spent the past few months researching and writing a report that analysed all the economics modules at Manchester and was a precursor to the curriculum review described in Chapter 2. We took the empirical evidence gained from this report to our meetings with the firm hope that, combined with the press coverage, it would have a real impact. It turned out to be difficult to pin down who was responsible for what and we became frustrated as we felt we were being passed around different people – from the head of Humanities to macroeconomic lecturers – without making any substantive progress. This experience inspired us to research in more depth who had responsibility for what within the university, and who had the power to set in motion some of the reforms we desired.

In May 2014 we published our report 'Economics, Education and Unlearning'.[53] Unbelievably, we had managed to get Andrew Haldane, who was at the time Director for Financial Stability at the Bank of England, to write the foreword. The report was covered in the media around the world and was downloaded over 16,000 times in six months. We could not believe that this many people wanted to read about economics education! The report also provoked critical responses on the blogosphere from some of the world's leading economists, including Simon Wren-Lewis, Roger Farmer and Paul Krugman, and rebuttals supportive of PCES from other economists.[54]

In the end, the University of Manchester decided not to renew Devrim's (temporary) contract and rejected running 'Bubbles, Panics and Crashes' as a for-credit module, citing budgetary constraints as the reason. In that same year it hired at least five new academic staff in the economics department. This illustrates that research considerations drive recruitment strategy and create conditions in which departments do not feel they can justify allocating resources to academics like Devrim, even if they are consistently recognised by students to be great teachers who can bring diversity to the department.[55]

While we had been plugging away in Manchester there had been big changes on the international scene. Rethinking Economics was growing as a network as new groups from the UK and around the world joined it, giving students a chance to meet (virtually), share experiences, plan joint projects and – most importantly – take confidence and inspiration from each other. One of the founders of RE, Yuan Yang, spoke of the excitement of being on a Skype call with students who between them could speak over ten languages, all brought together by this common cause.

In April 2014 students from PEPs, Rethinking Economics, the Netzwerk and others decided to get together and draft a global open letter calling for pluralism in economics. A drafting group wrote the letter using Google docs (another piece of technology the student movement would not exist without). The final Skype meeting has entered the pluralist campaigning folklore as it was twelve hours long and involved students from eight different countries. The open letter was published on 5 May under the banner of a new global umbrella group, the International Student Initiative for Pluralism in Economics.[56] It was covered in media outlets across the world and has now been signed by 65 student groups in 30 countries and by over 3,000 individuals. In our interviews for this book, students told us of the importance of these networks in supporting and inspiring local groups. On finding and joining the international student movement, one said:

> Suddenly our horizon expanded, and I was incredibly excited about that. It was like getting to know that you have family that you have never met. Because we are all fighting a cause, moving against the current. Sometimes it is very difficult to keep faith, when no one else seems to care too much about your struggle. Being part of a larger community is very encouraging and crucial for us to ever receive attention and be taken seriously by our fellow students, professors, the media etc.

At the end of the 2013/14 academic year the first generation of Post-Crash students finished university and moved on. We had been preparing for this and had recruited returning students for all the different committee roles so that there would be a six-month crossover period, enabling them to carry on the campaign. In comparison to the longevity of an academic career, student life is fleeting, and maintaining momentum across different generations of students is one of the biggest challenges the pluralist movement faces. We realised that the national and international networks were vital because they act as hubs that can store and pass on experience and learning. Because of this, in the summer of 2014, the UK national movement launched funding bids to set up a charity that would support student local group campaigns. Thankfully, they were accepted.

Before the student movement, curriculum reform wasn't being discussed. Now, there is widespread agreement that things need to change. The debate has become about how far this change should go.

To stay the same we must change

When people demand a revolution and those in power regard the demand to be a serious threat, the outcome is often incremental reform. The origins of modern welfare states can be traced back to attempts by Germany's first chancellor, Otto Von Bismarck, to diminish the allure of socialist parties and radical thinking. The key for those in power in such a situation is to find a set of reforms that can extend the lifespan of the status quo by making it more palatable, while still maintaining the central elements that they favour.

In the face of student demands for change in economics a reform proposal called CORE has gained prominence. CORE's advocates seem genuinely committed to improving economics education, but to us this appears to be the kind of reform that ends up preserving much of the status quo and undermining more fundamental calls for change. Economists who would usually oppose any change to curricula might, in the face of rising student discontent, accept the reforms CORE offers in the belief that 'to stay the same we must change'.

CORE is an online open-access textbook designed to be used as part of a revised economics curriculum that aims to ground economics education in real-world, historical and interdisciplinary knowledge.[57] Currently it consists of an introductory first-year module that covers both microeconomics and macroeconomics and is designed to replace the existing classes, which the advocates of CORE argue are too focused on abstract theory and regurgitation. CORE has been trialled at several universities including University College London, Bristol, the University of Sydney, Sciences Po (Paris), the University of Chile, UMASS Boston and Columbia University. It seems likely that further universities will adopt it as time goes on.

In many ways it is a positive thing to see a push for change coming from within the discipline. It is even more positive that some of CORE's aims – to relate economics to reality and to present it within historical, political and social contexts – chime with those of the student movement. The CORE online textbook is a big improvement on many of the established textbooks and it is particularly impressive that its authors are translating and adding local examples so that it is more relevant to the real world. However, the architects of CORE have reached a diagnosis of the problems with economics education that is very different from the one we set out in this book. As a result they prescribe an alternative that in our view will not meaningfully improve the situation.

CORE appears to rest on the assumption that the cause of the problem is to be found in economics education rather than economics itself. CORE's chief designer, Wendy Carlin, encapsulated such a view when she said that 'economics explains our world, economics degrees don't'.[58] CORE is marketed as 'teaching economics as if the last three decades had happened', implying that the answer to the problem is just to teach neoclassical theory in a more engaged and up-to-date manner. In this sense, CORE has striking similarities with previous reform efforts that occurred in economics during the 1980s in the USA. After surveys revealed that students on economics PhD programmes were disenchanted with the subject and that they lacked the broad knowledge needed to teach in Liberal Arts colleges, a Commission on Graduate Education in Economics was set up by the American Economics Association. While flaws in the curriculum were recognised, the solution was seen as 'providing students with applications of the tools to economic problems'.[59] There was no reason to challenge the 'core [which] should be regarded as the basic unit in which those things common to all economists should be taught'.[60]

In a similar way, economists Simon Wren-Lewis and Diane Coyle have argued in defence of CORE on the grounds that 'we need reform in the way economics is taught, but not a revolution'.[61] These reformers from within the discipline appear to share the view that the neoclassical framework provides the scientific way to do economics, and the feeling that the only problem is that it is not taught well enough.

In contrast, this book has argued that the shortcomings of economics education are the result of deeper problems in the discipline. We feel that CORE's approach is treating a symptom rather than the cause of the problem. To echo Lord Robert Skidelsky, who has criticised CORE and proposed developing an alternative syllabus more in line with the student movement's vision, 'the heart of the problem [with CORE] lies in the claim of mainstream economics to an authority which is intellectually illegitimate'.[62] CORE continues in the tradition of believing that only one perspective is valid in economics.

We applied the methodology from our curriculum review in Chapter 2 to the CORE curriculum at University College London to make an honest comparison.[63] The course guide suggests some interesting innovations, including formative assessment (assessment that doesn't count towards your final grade) such as a group video assignment and an individual writing project. CORE promisingly claims that students will use 'historically and methodologically informed narrative' as well as graphical and mathematical models. It also claims that it will show the 'contested nature of the subject' through its 'Past Economists' section. However, like the History of Economic Thought modules discussed in Chapter 2, this suggests that the big debates within economics are confined to antiquity.

The assessment for CORE relies heavily on multiple choice, with 60 per cent of the final grade given for multiple-choice questions, highlighting a similarity with standard macro and micro modules. The final 40 per cent is given for more comprehensive questions, but these do not entail much, if any, critical evaluation of economic theory. Using our methodology, we found that over half of these questions were still 'operate a model' (and only 6 per cent of those questions made any reference to the real world), 16 per cent were descriptive and 30 per cent were evaluative. On this basis CORE does require more independent judgement than the standard core modules we analysed in Chapter 2, but the scope of this judgement is limited.

In our view, the nature of the evaluation questions remains unnecessarily limited. In more than one instance the student is asked to give their judgement on a particular real-world phenomenon, but is then pushed towards a certain answer by explicit guidelines in the question, such as 'define and use the following terms in your answer' or 'to answer this, you may find it useful to refer to [a given section of the textbook]'. The exam does not use the words 'evaluate', 'discuss', 'debate' or 'critique' at all. Therefore, while CORE may represent an attempt to teach students to apply economic theory to the real world, it does not encourage critical evaluation of these theories.

Importantly, students are not encouraged to question neoclassical economics anywhere in the CORE syllabus. The three prongs of neoclassical economics outlined in Chapter 2 – individualism, optimisation and equilibrium – are simply accepted as true throughout. An example used by Lord Skidelsky is the discussion in Unit 3 of the CORE curriculum about why societies have taken so much of their increased real earnings in consumption rather than free time. While this is an interesting question, the discussion is almost entirely in terms of individual consumer choice. 'The way advertising, labour market structure, and distribution of income enter into these "individual" choices, while briefly mentioned in the conclusion, is not part of the analysis.'[64] Because the textbook fails to introduce other perspectives that would approach the question differently, the first prong of neoclassical economics– individualism – is accepted as a given.

Those sections of the online textbook that attempt to place economic theory in a historical context are similarly one-sided and often feel like an afterthought to the economic models. As it does with economic theory, CORE interprets historical events from only one, contested perspective without acknowledging that it is doing so. Chapter 1 opens by discussing the Industrial Revolution, arguing that technological progress and capitalism caused a 'hockey stick'-shaped take-off in economic growth. The focus is on 'the economy' as a separate, self-sustaining process, with an implied inevitability of growth and technical change. This narrative leaves the student believing that at one time 'the economy' took off and there has been no going back since.

According to the historian Aashish Velkar, the CORE textbook paints a false picture of the Industrial Revolution as the sudden displacement of the 'old' by the 'new'. This ignores the fact that technological progress was piecemeal and that 'old and new methods co-existed well into the nineteenth-century'. A short section introduces elements of the broader political and social context of the Industrial Revolution, such as the establishment of property rights, but the focus quickly shifts to familiar-looking neoclassical economic models. One such model claims to predict the 'timing and location of the industrial revolution' through the 'optimal' decisions of firms to introduce new technologies – the second prong of neoclassical economics – which Velkar states 'leaves out a whole set of sociological and historical conditions'. The non-economic may be present, but it is not incorporated rigorously into the analysis and the focus remains firmly on neoclassical economics.[65]

George Cooper, an ex-financier and writer, highlights a particular line from the textbook that is symbolic of CORE's approach: 'We explain how policymakers can improve well-being by stabilising shocks using fiscal and monetary policy.'[66] He points out that this sentence rests on 'the assumption that any instability in the economy comes from an exogenous shock which of course is necessary if you've got an equilibrium-based theory'.[67] In contrast, Cooper argues that disequilibrium-based theories are much more realistic because in these the destabilising shocks come from inside the economy. This quote illustrates how CORE takes the third prong of neoclassical economics – equilibrium – as a given, ignoring perspectives that disagree, and as a consequence leads the student to believe that there is only one right way to study the economy.

We believe that disagreement is a healthy and vital part of any academic discipline and something economics sorely needs. CORE, in failing to introduce students in any substantive way to alternative perspectives, fails to deliver this. We are grateful to Wendy Carlin and her collaborators because they have been proactive and willing to attend student-organised debates about the future of economics education. However, less positively we feel that CORE is positioning itself publicly (at the moment quite successfully) as the answer to our calls for reform, despite the fact that its authors know very well how much our visions differ. Following a BBC radio programme in March 2016 on the student movement, Wendy Carlin responded to the presenter in a letter, subsequently published on the BBC's website, strongly implying that CORE answers our demands:

> Students looking for economics teaching that deals with financial crises, the contributions of thinkers from Hayek to Marx, and issues like inequality, the environment and innovation, will find these subjects are already on our courses ... our work has already created a plural, practical, global economics course that produces better economists.[68]

Despite the positioning of CORE, we have demonstrated in this chapter that there are real and fundamental differences between our proposals for reform, and it is important that students, universities, policymakers and the public are aware of this. With CORE it remains the case that a narrow, fixed body of knowledge is handed down from one generation to the next, leaving little room for debate. This pedagogy is flawed because it fails to prepare students for living and working in a complex, diverse world in which knowledge is fluid, uncertain and contested.

A challenge to economists

The CORE curriculum shows that the rejection of other approaches is deeply embedded in the discipline. Even at a time when many neoclassical economists are introspectively assessing the state of economics education, they are unwilling to learn from outsiders. This is emblematic of a problem within economics that acts as a barrier to calls for pluralism. Currently, most economics departments could not transition to a pluralist ethos due to the fixed mind-set of both neoclassical economists towards alternative work, and of alternative economists towards neoclassical work. Disputes between economists of different stripes are about professional identities and people's careers and so the stakes are high. However, there is a reluctance on both sides to acknowledge the benefits of each other's work. This can result in unsavoury working environments. For example, an economics department in Canada had to be temporarily chaired by a political scientist when non-neoclassical members of the department claimed that they were being systematically ostracised, while the neoclassical members denied the charge.[69]

Therefore, one of the obstacles that may ultimately have to be overcome if economics is to change is the attitude of economists. Neoclassical economists are extremely proud of their discipline. In 2015 a paper found that 57.3 per cent of economists disagreed with the statement 'In general, interdisciplinary knowledge is better than knowledge obtained by a single discipline.' In contrast, a considerable majority from all other social sciences, from history to psychology, agreed with the statement, illustrating that economists are unique in their belief that their discipline has all the answers.[70] Economists are often ever more dismissive of alternative economic theories and the response that most economists give to their discipline being challenged is to accuse the dissident of not fully understanding what they are criticising. On the other hand, economists

from alternative perspectives often claim that neoclassical economics is entirely useless and should be completely abandoned.[71] We
feel that neither of these positions is particularly becoming of the
academics who espouse them. Unless such attitudes change, it is
hard to see a way forward.

Economic pluralism *does* complicate matters and there is no way of
getting around this fact. The whole idea of pluralism is that it opens
up a debate about economics, and debates require more energy from
their participants than perpetual consensus does. Yet we hope we
have demonstrated that pluralism and debate are crucial. The dominance of neoclassical economics comes to the detriment of society.
Economists therefore need to overcome their tribal differences.

However, it must also be admitted that there are barriers to providing a pluralist education in the modern university department
that go beyond economics departments. Pluralist economics requires
a pedagogy that is less about transferring knowledge into passive
students, as modern economics curricula and the CORE syllabus
are. In the next chapter, we argue that the answer to the problems
of economics lies in the idea of a liberal education and outline the
challenges of achieving meaningful reform.

Notes

1   This quote comes from a letter that Tirole wrote in response to inter-
    esting developments in France that are similar to ones in the UK that
    we discuss in this chapter. In France there are a very different set of
    institutional pressures on universities but there has been a similar
    homogenisation of economics education. In reaction to this, and to halt
    the otherwise inevitable narrowing of economics, it was proposed that
    a new academic programme called 'Economics and Society', encourag-
    ing a liberal education as opposed to a technical training, would be
    established across the country. Around a sixth of academic economists
    working in France signed a petition calling for it and the Ministry of
    Education appeared to be in favour. Tirole wrote the letter asking for
    these plans to be halted. They were eventually scrapped, but whether
    this was due to Tirole's intervention is difficult to ascertain. An English
    translation of the letter can be found at http://assoeconomiepolitique.
    org/wp-content/uploads/TIROLE_Letter.pdf.
2   See Jean Tirole, 'Market power and regulation', *Economic Sciences Prize
    Committee of the Royal Swedish Academy of Sciences* (2014): 1–54.
3   For example, see Marion Fourcade, *Economists and Societies: Discipline
    and Profession in the United States, Britain, and France, 1890s to 1990s*,
    Oxford: Princeton University Press, 2009.

4 John M. Keynes, 'Alfred Marshall, 1842–1924', *The Economic Journal* 34(135) (1924): 322.
5 Gary S. Becker, *The Economic Approach to Human Behavior*, Chicago: University of Chicago Press, 1976, 5.
6 Although Smith, famously, only used the term once in *The Wealth of Nations*.
7 Adam Smith, *The Theory of Moral Sentiments*, Cambridge: Cambridge University Press, 1790, 4.
8 Smith said 'The man whose whole life is spent in performing a few simple operations, of which the effects are perhaps always the same, or very nearly the same, has no occasion to exert his understanding or to exercise his invention in finding out expedients for removing difficulties which never occur. He naturally loses, therefore, the habit of such exertion, and generally becomes as stupid and ignorant as it is possible for a human creature to become'; Adam Smith, *An Inquiry into the Nature and Causes of the Wealth of Nations*, London: Methuen, 1904, Book 5, Chapter 1.
9 Ibid., Book 1, Chapter 10.
10 Roger E. Backhouse, *The Penguin History of Economics*, London: Penguin, 2002.
11 British Economic Association, 'The British Economic Association', *The Economic Journal* 1(1) (1891): 1.
12 Michael A. Bernstein, *A Perilous Progress: Economists and Public Purpose in Twentieth Century America*, Woodstock: Princeton University Press, 2001, 16.
13 Ibid., 17.
14 Ibid., 15.
15 Ibid., 20–1.
16 This quote may be apocryphal as it is difficult to source. However, contemporary economists often report encountering a similar attitude from politicians. See Michael Reay, 'The flexible unity of economics', *American Journal of Sociology* 118(1) (2012): 65–7.
17 Bernstein, *A Perilous Progress*, 2.
18 William S. Jevons, *The Theory of Political Economy*, London: Macmillan, 2nd edn, 1879, Introduction.
19 Ibid.
20 Writers such as Marshall and Jevons also understood the limitations of the neoclassical framework, seeing their toolkit as only one way of exploring the social world; Ben Fine and Dimitris Milonakis, *From Economics Imperialism to Freakonomics: The Shifting Boundaries between Economics and Other Social Sciences*, London: Routledge, 2009, 32.
21 Lionel Robbins, *An Essay on the Nature and Significance of Economic Science*, London: Macmillan, 2nd edn, 1935: 15.
22 Robert Cooter and Peter Rappoport, 'Were the Ordinalists wrong about

welfare economics?', *Journal of Economic Literature* 22(2) (1984): 507–30.

23 Fine and Milonakis, *Economics Imperialism*, 32.

24 Particular examples were John Hicks, who originated the modern IS/LM model in John R. Hicks, 'Mr. Keynes and the "Classics": a suggested interpretation', *Econometrica* 5(2) (1937): 147–59, but later admitted his mistake in Hicks, '"IS-LM": an explanation', *Journal of Post Keynesian Economics* 3(2) (1980–81): 139–54.

25 London School of Economics, 'EC201 Microeconomic Principles 1'. Available at: http://www.lse.ac.uk/resources/calendar/courseGuides/EC/2015_EC201.htm (accessed 20 April 2016).

26 Commonly believed to be founded by John von Neumann and Oskar Morgenstern in *The Theory of Games and Economic Behaviour*, Princeton, NJ: Princeton University Press, 1944.

27 Bernstein, *A Perilous Progress*, 122.

28 Robert Lucas, 'Econometric policy evaluation: a critique', in Karl Brunner and Allan Meltzer (eds), *The Phillips Curve and Labor Markets*, New York: North Holland, 1976, 19–46.

29 Paul Krugman, 'How did economists get it so wrong?', *New York Times*, 2 September, 2009. Available at: http://www.nytimes.com/2009/09/06/magazine/06Economic-t.html?pagewanted=print&_r=0 (accessed 27 April 2016).

30 Mark Blaug, 'The formalist revolution of the 1950s', *Journal of History of Economic Thought* 25(2) (2003): 145.

31 Special thanks go to Frederic Lee for much of the research that supports this section; Frederic sadly passed away in October 2014 before we could thank him personally.

32 Chris Giles, 'A formula for teaching economics', *Financial Times*, 11 November 2013. Available at: http://www.ft.com/cms/s/0/12e558da-4adc-11e3-8c4c-00144feabdc0.html#axzz46qDSIEtb (accessed 27 April 2016).

33 The fact that feminist economics is a widely practised tradition might at first glance seem to contradict our argument about the dominance of neoclassical economics. The point is that feminist economists generally have institutional affiliations outside economics departments, in geography and politics departments or research institutes, which explains the fact that there were no feminist economics modules at all the universities we studied in our curriculum review.

34 Louise Morley, *Theorising Quality in Higher Education*, London: Institute of Education, 2014, 2.

35 The aforementioned 1986 RAE was described by one of the panellists, in an interview for this book, as a 'training exercise' and so is not deemed significant.

36 Which was commissioned by the University Grants Committee.

37 The only two panel members who could be considered as at least

partially non-neoclassical economists were Philip Aristis and Meghnad Desai.

38 For example, the deputy chair of the 2014 REF was Rachel Griffith, who is also editor of the *Economic Journal*, a journal published on behalf of the Royal Economics Society.

39 Frederic S. Lee and Sandra Harley, 'Peer review, the Research Assessment Exercise and the demise of non-mainstream economics', *Capital and Class* 66 (1998): 23–51.

40 Frederic S. Lee, Xuan Pham and Gyun Gu, 'The UK Research Assessment Exercise and the narrowing of UK economics', *Cambridge Journal of Economics* 37(4) (2013): 693–717.

41 University of Manchester Archives, 'Faculty of Economic and Social Studies – School of Economic Studies – Report of Council to the University Court 1996 Volume IA', 1996, 189.

42 Morley, *Theorising Quality*.

43 Lee and Harley, 'Peer review', 25.

44 The classic example of this came from this article, now known as the Diamond list: Arthur Diamond, 'The core journals of economics', *Current Contents* 21 (January 1989): 4–11.

45 Education Reform Act, United Kingdom Parliament, 1988: Part IV, Section 202.

46 Foundation for European Economic Development, 'Plea for a pluralistic and rigorous economics', *American Economic Review* 82(2) (1992): xxv.

47 Post-Autistic Economics Network, 'Open letter from economics students to professors and others responsible for the teaching of this discipline', 2000. Available at: http://www.paecon.net/PAEtexts/a-e-petition.htm (accessed 27 April 2016).

48 Post-Autistic Economics Network, 'Opening up economics: a proposal by Cambridge students', 14 June 2001. Available at: http://www.paecon.net/petitions/Camproposal.htm. (accessed 27 April 2016).

49 It was originally distastefully named the Post-Autistic Economics Network.

50 *L'avenir des sciences économiques à l'Université en France*, report, Government of France, 5 June 2014. Available at: http://cache.media.enseignementsup-recherche.gouv.fr/file/Formations_et_diplomes/05/1/Rapport_Hautcoeur2014_328051.pdf (accessed 25 May 2016).

51 Association of Heterodox Economists, 'Submission from the Association of Heterodox Economics to the consultation on the QAA Benchmark Statement on Economics', 2016: 7. Available at: https://www.business.unsw.edu.au/research-site/societyofheterodoxeconomists-site/Documents/QAA Benchmark.pdf (accessed 27 April 2016).

52 Early Day Motion 641: Formation of the Post-Crash Economics Society at Manchester University, UK Parliament, 2013.

53 *Economics, Education and Unlearning: Economics Education at the University of Manchester*, report, the Post-Crash Economics Society,

2014, 17. Available at: http://www.post-crasheconomics.com/econom
ics-education-and-unlearning/ (accessed 27 April 2016).

54 For responses to the report by neoclassical economists, see Roger
Farmer, 'Teaching economics', 23 April 2014. Available at: http://roger
farmerblog.blogspot.co.uk/2014/04/teaching-economics.html (accessed
25 April 2016); Paul Krugman, 'Frustrations of the heterodox', *New
York Times*, 25 April 2014. Available at: http://krugman.blogs.nytimes.
com/2014/04/25/frustrations-of-the-heterodox (accessed 25 April
2016); Simon Wren-Lewis, 'When economics students rebel', 24 April
2014. Available at: http://mainlymacro.blogspot.co.uk/2014/04/when-
economics-students-rebel.html (accessed 25 April 2016). For rebuttals
see Alex Marsh, 'Economics budo', 26 April 2014. Available at: http://
www.alexsarchives.org/2014/04/economics-budo/ (accessed 25 April
2016); Steve Keen, 'Why Krugman needs a new school of thought', *The
Australian*, 28 April 2014. Available at: http://www.theaustralian.com.
au/business/business-spectator/why-krugman-needs-a-new-school-of-
thought/news-story/7e36b530ca7bb990a1258596e49a8214 (accessed
25 April 2016).

55 A petition to put the module on was signed by over 240 economics
students.

56 *An International Student Call for Pluralism in Economics*, International
Student Initiative for Pluralism in Economics, 5 May 2014. Available at:
http://www.isipe.net/open-letter/ (accessed 27 April 2016).

57 CORE is available as a free open resource at: http://www.core-econ.org/

58 Wendy Carlin, 'Economics explains our world – but economics degrees
don't', *Financial Times*, 17 November 2013. Available at: http://www.
ft.com/cms/s/0/74cd0b94-4de6-11e3-8fa5-00144feabdc0.html#axzz46
qYfHtC0 (accessed 18 July 2016).

59 Anne Krueger, 'Report of the Commission on Graduate Education in
Economics', *Journal of Economic Literature* 29(3) (1991): 1052.

60 Ibid.

61 Diane Coyle and Simon Wren-Lewis, 'A note from Diane Coyle and
Simon Wren-Lewis', *Royal Economic Society Newsletter* 169 (April
2015): 15.

62 Robert Skidelsky, 'Reforming economics', 19 December 2014. Available
at: http://www.skidelskyr.com/site/article/reforming-economics/ (accessed 18 July 2016).

63 We thank UCL for agreeing to provide us with the materials.

64 Skidelsky, 'Reforming economics'.

65 Velkar Aashish, 'Review of CORE eBook', 2016. Available at: http://
www.post-crasheconomics.com/review-of-core-ebook/ (accessed 18 July
2016).

66 'How should economics change? With Steve Keen, Diane Coyle and
George Cooper', Post-Crash Economics Society. Available at: https://
www.youtube.com/watch?v=shZJNG1F6MM (accessed 18 July 2016).

67 Ibid.
68 Peter Day, 'Changing how economics is taught', BBC, 3 March 2016. Available at: http://www.bbc.co.uk/news/business-35686623 (accessed 18 July 2016).
69 The Canadian Association of University Teachers wrote a report criticising the neoclassical economists and senior management at the university. See Allan Manson, Pamela McCallum and Larry Halven, *Report of the Ad Hoc Investigatory Committee into the Department of Economics at the University of Manitoba*, report, Canadian Association of University Teachers, 2015.
70 Marion Fourcade, Etienne Ollion and Yann Algan, 'The superiority of economists', *Journal of Economic Perspectives* 21(1) (2015): 95.
71 We have no intention of naming these people. However, we expect those familiar with the debates in economics will recognise this picture.

Chapter 5

Rediscovering liberal education

Economics as a pluralist, liberal education

[The purpose of universities] is not to make skilful lawyers, or physicians, or engineers, but capable and cultivated human beings.

John Stuart Mill, 1867[1]

The School again is not a place of technical education fitting you for one and only one profession. It makes you better for every occupation, it does help you get on in life ... But you will lose most of the value of the School if you regard it solely as a means of getting on in life. Regard it as a means of learning, to advance science and civilization.

William Beveridge, 1924[2]

These quotes from two of Britain's most famous economists set out an approach to education that contrasts radically with economics education today. It is an approach called 'liberal education' and in this chapter we argue that it provides a set of principles that can be used to reform economics degrees. In this section we introduce the idea of liberal education and in the next we explore the history and state of the English higher education (HE) system since 1945 and show how far liberal principles have been neglected. Finally, we set out some ways in which these principles can be used to reform economics within our current system.

The roots of liberal education are as old as Western civilisation itself. In Ancient Greece the philosopher Socrates developed a method of teaching now called the 'Socratic dialogue' in which he challenged his opponents to develop and defend their opinions and beliefs using reason and logic. Socratic pedagogy emphasised the role of reason in education, the importance of challenging authority and accepted thought, and the importance of self-criticism. This approach has important implications for education today. It tells us that the ability to develop independent, reasoned judgements while being critical of one's own traditions and beliefs is a prerequisite of thinking for oneself and ultimately being a free individual.

Socrates' approach was radical because it implied that social norms were changeable, not fixed – and that ultimately it is our collective responsibility to examine, question and challenge these norms if necessary.[3] The next generation of economic experts must be made aware that there are different ways of thinking about the economy so that they can engage critically with theories that are currently handed down to them unquestioningly.

What a liberal education has meant in practice in British universities has varied greatly over time and, as a consequence, the concept has many different and even contradictory meanings.[4] Liberal educational principles are shaped by their wider social and political contexts. They can be used to both defend the social status quo by giving elites a shared sense of identity as in eighteenth-century Britain, or to challenge and question accepted norms as Socrates did in Greece.[5] In our view, both the transmission of civilisation, culture and common standards of citizenship as well as the encouragement of original, critical thinking are important parts of any educational philosophy. Finding ways to do both is one of the great challenges of any form of education.

So what are the core principles of a liberal education? All versions of liberal education reject instrumental approaches, narrowly defined as training for work. Whereas in training success has been achieved when the student has mastered what the teacher has taught, in liberal education success has been achieved when the student has subjected that teacher to severe questioning. The distinction between education and training here is crucial because undergraduate economics currently provides only training in neoclassical economics. Toby Young captures the sentiment when he argues that 'independence of mind, not compliance with socio-economic expectations, is the goal of a good education'.[6] This is a principle which, as we shall see, has been lost in HE today.

A modern formulation of the purpose of a liberal education is given by the Association of American Colleges and Universities (AACU):

An approach to college learning that empowers individuals and prepares them to deal with complexity, diversity, and change. This approach emphasizes broad knowledge of the wider world (e.g., science, culture, and society) as well as in-depth achievement in a specific field of interest. It helps students develop a sense of social responsibility; strong intellectual and practical skills that span all major fields of study, such as communication, analytical, and problem-solving skills; and the demonstrated ability to apply knowledge and skills in real-world settings.[7]

We use this definition as a basic guide to what we mean when we call for a liberal education in economics. We take liberal education to be an ideal, which is to be valued and sought after, but recognise that it is difficult for individuals and institutions to achieve this, as we explore in the next section. However, the degree to which they do is, in our view, a mark of their quality.[8]

The AACU argues that liberal education is a way of teaching (pedagogy) as much as any particular content (syllabus), although choices about one clearly affect the other. Our analysis of economics education at Cambridge University illustrates the centrality of pluralism to any meaningful liberal education. We introduced the concept of pluralism in Chapter 3, and Exhibit 3.1 illustrated a number of different important economic perspectives of which all economics students should have at least a basic knowledge. The historical wealth of Cambridge and Oxford means that now, of all the universities in Britain, they are best placed to provide students with a liberal education. This is apparent in our curriculum review. At Cambridge there is less of a reliance on textbooks and more engagement with economic literature; multiple-choice tests are not used; and they provide small-group supervision with academics instead of large tutorials with graduate students.[9] Other universities cannot provide the same resources per student and so struggle to develop the personalised relationship between student and academic that is such an important part of liberal education.

However, our curriculum review showed that the actual content of Cambridge modules was very similar to content at other universities, and there were very few references to non-neoclassical perspectives. Exposure to diverse ways of thinking about the world distinguishes education from narrow technical training and prepares students to deal with the complexity, diversity and change that they will encounter in their lives. When you are taught that there is only one way to do economics you are only taught one way to think, and if you are not given the tools to critically engage with your learning, it is difficult to develop these deeper skills. Pluralism is for these reasons a necessary condition for a liberal education.

This is illustrated by the Cambridge Society for Economic Pluralism, which did a survey of 250 economics students and alumni. The survey found that over the course of their studies 60 per cent of respondents reported zero or negative improvement in verbal communication skills, 47 per cent reported the same effect for written communication, and 35 per cent reported it for critical and independent thinking skills.[10] Despite its resource advantages, economics education at Cambridge fails to develop some of the core values of liberal education including independent thinking, social responsibility and critical intellect.

Undergraduate economics today undermines liberal education with its narrow focus on employability. The response we get from academic economists when we argue that pluralist economics is better for students illustrates this point. The first thing they tell us is that economics graduates have one of the highest average starting salaries of any discipline and therefore economics education must be getting something right. This reply illustrates the instrumental approach economists take to education and, in our view, mistakes correlation for causation (assuming that because people with an economics education often have high salaries that the former causes the latter). Recent research (by economists) shows that ten years after leaving university, economics graduates have on average the second highest average starting salary of graduates from any course in the UK (only behind medicine).[11] So yes, economics graduates are highly employable and do receive a high starting salary, but that is not a direct result of the quality of the education graduates receive. Instead, it is a result of the prestige and influence economists have managed to gain and which we outlined in Chapter 1.

Economics plays a vital role in modern government and business, so those graduates who have better qualifications in the subject have a set of credentials that gives their holder a relatively high chance of employment and a high starting salary. Economics graduates are in demand because they are clever people who can speak a specialist vocabulary and are familiar with a narrow set of analytical tools. It is not because their education has helped them understand the economy or its history, nor because it has developed in them many of the skills necessary to thrive in life and work.

There is discontent among employers about the lack of skills many economics graduates display. One survey carried out by the Economics Network showed that a considerable number of employers believe that the economics graduates they employ have 'not very high' critical self-awareness (28 per cent), general creative and imaginative powers (23 per cent), ability to communicate clearly in writing (22 per cent) or ability to apply what has been learned in a wider context (25 per cent).[12] In a letter to applicants, the deputy director of the Government Economic Service stated that

'government economics is about dilemmas not lemmas' (technical
results that help prove a theory), advised against a 'dogged adherence
to ... a set of axiomatic rules for theoretic consistency' and looked
for candidates who were 'intellectually pluralistic'.[13] Andy Haldane,
Chief Economist at the Bank of England, has stated that:

> Answering effectively public policy questions of the future requires an
> understanding of the past. It also requires eclecticism in the choice of
> methodology, a knowledge of political economy, an appreciation of
> institutions, an understanding of money and banking. A revamped eco-
> nomics curriculum could serve these needs, and hence those of public
> policy, well.[14]

This endorsement of critical, pluralist economics from some of the
largest employers of economics graduates highlights the disconnect
between what they are are looking for and the knowledge and skills
economics graduates are currently being provided with. The somewhat
counter-intuitive argument is that while liberal education doesn't
focus directly on employability, it actually better prepares graduates
to thrive in work than narrower, supposedly vocational training.

We argued in Chapter 2 that undergraduate economics education
amounts to indoctrination and demonstrated the consequences of
the monopoly of a particular way of thinking about the economy
for the discipline and for society. In contrast, a liberal, pluralist economics education would be designed to develop individuals who are
independent, creative and critical in both their professional practice
and as citizens.

Educationalists have for a long time studied the links between
education and democracy. Writing in 1915, John Dewey argued that
education should actively seek to develop the skills necessary for individuals to participate in democratic life. For Dewey democracy was a
culture and a set of practices, not merely a formal system. This meant
schools could develop these skills by involving students in establishing the rules by which the classroom is governed, debating ideas
for the improvement of classroom life, and participating in setting
the objectives of their own learning in order to instil the culture of
democracy and teach the necessary skills for it to work effectively.
On this view dissent and disagreement are valued as central to both
academia and democracy. The starting point is that societies and
academic disciplines are home to individuals and communities with
diverse perspectives, backgrounds and interests. The same human
skills of listening, independence of mind, ethical judgement, respect,

openness to diversity, reflectiveness and inquisitiveness allow individuals to engage constructively with each other, whether that be at the level of academic economic debate or democracy.[15]

A further stage is for students to be able to reflect on why they think what they think and to be critical of their own beliefs and values as well as those of others. By reintegrating ethics and politics into the study of economics, a pluralist, liberal education takes steps towards this. By making clear the values and assumptions in economic theory and exploring how they fit with their own views, economists become aware of possible influences on their professional judgements, including their own world view and, moral, cultural, historical, religious, spiritual, societal and professional values and biases.[16]

Importantly, a growing number of important economists do recognise the need for a more pluralist, liberal education.[17] There has been a wave of significant curriculum reform in the UK at Greenwich, Kingston and Goldsmith universities, which has seen both fundamental curriculum redesign and completely new courses set up.[18] This isn't incremental change, it is bold and it embraces the principles of pluralism and liberal education. When we met Sara Gorgoni, the academic responsible for coordinating Greenwich's curriculum reform, what was most striking was her open, broad-minded demeanour as she argued that 'the ultimate purpose [of economics] is to understand the complexity of reality'.[19] Here what defines economics is the object of study – the economy – not a particular way of thinking about it. Redefining economics in this way is a bold and important step towards a liberal, pluralist and critical economics education.

Undoubtedly there is still work to be done. At another economics department that claims to be pluralist, a student candidly told us: 'At most universities they say, "Here's the mainstream, it's all correct so learn it." Here they say, "Here's the mainstream, it's all wrong but learn it anyway."'[20] Integrating pluralism into syllabuses is difficult; the discipline is defined as neoclassical economics, and so universities feel that they must focus on this to allow their students to go on to postgraduate study at prestigious institutions. However, universities like Greenwich are pathfinders in hiring new staff, redesigning courses and changing assessment procedures. Changes like these will in time, we hope, change the direction of economics.

It is, however, important to recognise that the future of economics education will not be determined solely by academic debate between economists and students. Attempts to reform economics face many institutional constraints. By hiring economists from outside the mainstream of neoclassical economics, departments might perform worse in future Research Excellence Frameworks. This translates into lower rankings in league tables and as a result potential students go elsewhere. The straitjacket of neoclassical economics can be hard to escape because its dominance has become institutionalised in the system. This situation is a result of wider changes to HE in the UK that make it increasingly difficult to provide the resources per student necessary for a good quality liberal education.

Higher education as a sausage factory

Part 1: Taking meat out of the sausage

A pack of value sausages from a supermarket often contains less than 30 per cent meat. More than two-thirds of the contents of these sausages consists of water mixed with rusk, fat, starches, additives and various other ingredients, including a red colouring to give the sausage a 'meaty' look. Taking meat out of the sausage reduces costs and allows more to be made with the same inputs. In the seventy years since 1945, English HE has followed a similar logic. Over that period it has seen a massive expansion in student numbers from 3 per cent to 47 per cent of 18+ school leavers.[21] In isolation, this development is hugely positive, as we strongly believe that university is an opportunity that should be open to all. However, more students are now processed through the system with greatly diminished funding per student. Changes have been made to management, funding, research and teaching to try to increase efficiency and maintain standards of education but, like the red colouring in sausages, they have so far only served to conceal deficiencies. It is in this context that we must reform economics education and the challenges are great.

This story is also closely bound up with the rise of econocracy. The dominant view of education in an econocracy is symbolised by the former leader of the Labour Party Ed Miliband's argument that 'education today [is] for the economy of tomorrow'.[22] Neoclassical economic logic has, through 'human capital' theory and endogenous growth models, provided an influential rationale for increasing student numbers and powerful levers that successive governments have used to try to reform the sector. An implication of both of these theories is that investment in education will increase the future productivity of individuals and of the economy as a whole, which increases earnings and potential growth. The purpose of HE has become narrower over time at least partly as a result of this approach, and has turned away from the development of the skills necessary for active citizenship.

Our story starts in 1946 when the UK education system was made up of a group of 16 elite universities that were largely self-governing.[23] The University Grants Committee (UGC) acted as a 'buffer' between the universities and government, allowing universities a large degree of autonomy around funding and university policy. University education at this time was only for a small elite but it did provide the necessary resources for liberal education.

Expansion began in earnest in the 1950s when the UGC started building eight new universities. The importance of personalised teaching was recognised and a commitment was made to maintain staff–student ratios of 1:8.[24] Expansion then continued in a slightly different guise: in 1966 the government set out plans to open 28 polytechnics. However, the polytechnics remained under local authority control, creating a two-tier system.[25] The case for mass HE had now been made but, for a time, expansion was still possible while maintaining the resources needed for a liberal education.

Government spending on universities as a proportion of university income rose from 34.3 per cent in 1935–36 to 63.9 per cent in 1949–50.[26] This influenced a shift in how they were viewed from being seen as independent institutions with public funding to a public service with considerable independence. In the 1950s and 1960s the Treasury changed how departmental budgets were set by restricting overall spending and forcing departments to negotiate with it to get their budget agreed.[27] This made the Treasury more powerful because it gained a greater ability to control the HE budget. These two changes would become important later because, first, they justified increased government intervention and, secondly, they gave government an effective lever by which to do this.

After nearly a decade of economic crisis the incoming government in 1979 set about trying to reduce public expenditure. Budget cuts in 1980/81 led to the UGC reducing overall student numbers by 5 per cent in order to maintain resources per student. The decision was justified on the basis that this was the minimum needed to provide a good-quality education and it highlights a continued commitment to providing the necessary resources for liberal education.[28] At the start of the 1970s, the participation rate of 18+ school leavers in HE was 15 per cent, and it stayed there for nearly two decades. However, during this time the purpose of HE was changing, and the influence of econocracy can be seen in this shift. In its 1985 Green

Paper the government of the day argued that 'it is vital for our higher education to contribute more effectively to the improvement of the performance of the economy'.[29] As we saw in Chapter 2, neoclassical economics implies that education plays a major role in economic growth, either in terms of developing human capital or technological development.[30] The growing influence of these models in the Treasury and in politics more broadly provided a strong intellectual rationale pushing for further growth in student numbers.

As compelling as arguments for the expansion of student numbers were, the government still had to find a way to fund this growth within broader fiscal limits. Here economic ideas also played a crucial role. After being stung by the decision of the UGC to cut student numbers in 1980/81 to preserve resources, the government abolished the UGC in 1988 and replaced it with the University Finance Council (UFC), which would have a greatly restricted remit. The abolition of the UGC signified a loss of autonomy for HE that was symptomatic of the wider decline of informal government and the rise of the more technocratic approaches that symbolise an econocracy.[31] Kenneth Baker, Education Secretary from 1986–89, rejected the UGC's arguments that there should be a fixed amount of resources per student and promoted growth in student numbers at 'marginal cost', an idea with its roots in neoclassical economics.[32] In 1989 the UFC developed a new market-based funding system through which HE institutions were expected to bid for student numbers. The idea was that new student funding should be worked out by estimating the cost of adding one more student to the existing numbers (marginal cost), rather than adding a fixed amount of funding for each new student (unit of resource). On this view, if a class had twenty students, adding one more would not increase teaching costs by much, if at all, which made expansion seem like a more attractive prospect.

Under this new system all universities could bid for students at a fixed guide price, but they were also encouraged to enter bids at a second lower price for additional student numbers. If the market worked, competition between universities for extra students would drive down prices to the point at which, for each university, adding one more student would equal the costs of accepting one more student, or in other words equilibrium. Detaching student numbers from resources per student provided a technical fix that avoided difficult political conversations about whether there was enough funding to provide a quality education. This is a common feature of economic decision making in an econocracy. However, in practice the universities colluded to bid for a 19 per cent increase in student numbers but only at the higher price, thus effectively resisting the attempt to allocate funding for students at marginal cost.[33]

In 1992 the Further and Higher Education Act abolished the two-tier system of polytechnics and universities, thus increasing the number of universities in the UK from 47 to 88. In the newly unified system there were over a million students, up from 85,000 in 1949, and this caused severe financial pressures. To give an indication of the scale of the growth in HE, staff numbers in 1990 were the same as student numbers in 1950.[34] Between 1976 and 1995 funding per student fell by 40 per cent and this was a major contributing factor to the average staff–student ratio more than doubling from 1:8 in 1950 to 1:18 by 2000.[35]

It was in response to this erosion of the resources per student that university leaders threatened to impose tuition fees independently in the mid-1990s. The incoming Labour government's answer was to introduce the first means-tested up-front tuition fee of £1,000. Then in 2004 it passed legislation introducing variable 'top-up' fees of up to £3,000. The idea was to allow universities to charge fees that reflected their quality in order to give the country's leading universities the extra funding needed to compete internationally and allow them to expand.[36] However, almost all universities resisted attempts to create a differentiated market by setting their fees at £3,000.

The 'top-up' fees were to be funded through income contingent repayment (ICR) loans. ICR loans – another idea developed by economists – came to be seen as the silver bullet that would allow both expansion and proper resourcing of HE.[37] The basic idea is that instead of students paying up-front, the government provides loans to students to pay their tuition fees, and the students then pay the loans back after they have graduated and are earning more than a certain threshold. The loans are income contingent because repayments are determined by the income of the graduate, not by how much they have borrowed. The ICR loans are premised on the idea of 'human capital': students invest in themselves by taking out loans and the productivity gains are evidenced in the labour market by the reward of higher graduate earnings, which means that they can then pay the loans back.[38]

In 2010 there were large-scale reforms to the HE sector based on ICR loans. The wider context of these reforms was a comprehensive spending review that sought to reduce public expenditure by 25 per cent after the financial crisis in 2008. The HE teaching budget received enormous cuts of around 80 per cent, going from about £5 billion in 2009/10 to about £1 billion in 2015/16.[39] The funding gap was filled by raising the tuition fee cap to £9,000. The terms of these ICR loans are complicated but broadly involve graduates paying back a percentage of any income they earn over £21,000 until the loan is repaid.[40] The government now puts much more cash into HE than before but the expansion of ICR loans means that it expects to get that money back at some point in the future. Before September 2015 universities had specific recruitment caps that they were not able to breach without financial penalties, but now there are no limits to undergraduate recruitment. In this system universities compete to recruit undergraduates, and the 2010 reforms included other attempts to make the HE sector more like a competitive market. There was a concerted effort to remove so-called 'barriers to entry' – which prevented new providers from entering the sector – in order to increase competition and choice. This process is ongoing but has included cutting the block grants to universities that allow them to subsidise tuition fees; allowing certain private providers to give student loans (up to £6,000); and loosening up regulations around who can use the title 'university'.[41]

Over the period we have examined, the purpose of HE shifted from focusing on the broad educational and holistic development of individuals to becoming, in large part, a means for improving human capital and contributing to economic growth. This shift is reflected in its journey through Whitehall. In 1945 universities were independent institutions with public funding negotiated directly with the Treasury. Then were then moved to the Department of Education, and now they fall under the Department for Business, Innovation and Skills (BIS). A recent BIS select report on teaching quality, in a section entitled 'The quality of UK higher education', states that 'in 2011 higher education made up 2.8 per cent of UK GDP and the sector generated £10.7 billion of export earnings'.[42] Good quality in HE is increasingly framed in terms of its contribution to the economy.

The story we have told here is a prime example of economic ideas that have been used at a macro level to reshape a whole sector in certain ways so that individuals and institutions are incentivised to act according to the logic of neoclassical economics.

Part 2: The modern university

HE funding after the 2010 reforms is supposed to be on a sounder footing. Higher up-front tuition fees provide an important additional revenue stream for universities while full ICR loans available to all students mean that HE is free at the point of consumption and graduates only have to pay loans back if they secure relatively higher earnings in the labour market. This allows the government to claim that it is providing universities with the resources necessary to provide a liberal education. However, in this section we show how this claim ignores the reality of university business models and the competing resource claims of teaching and research.

The decisions modern universities make about fee levels, student numbers, marketing and recruitment and research strategies mean that educational quality is neglected. As a result, many universities would find it difficult to improve the quality of economics education even if they tried. Successful university business models don't aim to provide good-quality education; they aim to maximise student satisfaction, the institution's place in the research rankings and applications from international students. A combination of good levels of student satisfaction and research rankings secures a decent place in the league tables, which – combined with effective marketing and historically accumulated prestige – secures undergraduate applicants who bring in revenue.

The 2010 reform raised the tuition fee cap to £9,000, leaving universities with important decisions to make. When introducing this reform the government stated that the cap of £9,000 'should apply only in exceptional circumstances', and that the average tuition fee would be set at £7,500.[43] In practice the average tuition fee was £8,100, and many institutions set their fees at the full £9,000.[44] This average was brought down by some universities such as Coventry, which set up 'no frills', Ryanair-style undergraduate courses that cost £4,800 per year, but on these courses students were not even able to borrow books from the library.

Why did the market not behave as the government hoped? An Econ 101 course would suggest that price is inversely related to demand and so the higher the price of a degree the lower the demand for it. However, university education isn't a standard consumer good, but a 'positional' good: institutions and subjects are ranked in a hierarchy with entry restricted by A-level results, and the qualification received significantly determines the consumer's future opportunities relative to those who have gained qualifications from other universities. As a consequence, setting low prices may send the wrong signal to potential applicants by implying that a university is sub-par. Many universities also concluded that since students were already seeing fees more than doubling, it would be wise to set fees as high as possible to generate additional resources to make improvements, including upgrading facilities and raising contact hours.[45]

David Willetts, the Universities Minister in 2010, believed the sector had too little incentive to focus on teaching and argued that giving students more power as consumers would force universities to improve teaching quality. The idea was that in competing for students, universities would be forced to focus on improving student experience and standards across the board would be driven up. The Browne Review suggested that 'students are best placed to make the judgment about what they want to get from participating in higher education'.[46] But knowing what you want is not the same as being able to evaluate the quality of the course on offer before you sign up.[47] Unless one has a relative or friend within the institution, it is difficult to get a real idea of what the education will be like before one starts. Applicants' lack of knowledge of the subject area before they begin studying makes it virtually impossible to assess in advance the quality of different approaches to content and teaching style. In the absence of information about course quality, applicants are forced to fall back on symbolic proxies such as prestige and the stylised indicators in the league tables.

Successive governments have realised that for such a system to work, consumers must be able to make informed choices, and so they have promoted the importance of widely available information to facilitate these choices. However, as Andrew McGettigan has argued, 'it is not clear that information about courses can rectify the fundamental difference between education and other consumer goods, no matter how reliable and accessible such information is made'.[48] One example of this is that university league tables – which are a key source of information for prospective students – base their rankings on 'inputs' such as the selectivity of the institution, the students who attend, and the research ranking of the institution or spend per student – rather than pedagogical experience. Many of the economics courses we analysed in Chapter 2 score highly in league tables despite their clear shortcomings precisely because the tables fail to accurately measure educational quality.

It is not clear that students are gaining greater power from being treated as consumers once they have started their course, or that this is forcing universities to improve teaching quality. The single most important annual student feedback mechanism is the National Student Survey (NSS) carried out with students in their final year at the end of each academic year. The importance of this feedback process to universities is not because of the urgency of directly responding to the consumer feedback, but because NSS results are fed into the league tables and influence overall and subject area rankings for the next year. The commotion on university campuses across the UK at the NSS time of year is truly astounding with a frenzy of activity to persuade students to respond positively: free chocolate and pizza; prize draws for iPads or cash; and banners everywhere to remind students of all that the university and their academic department have done for them.

The consequence of feeding NSS results into league tables is that there is a direct disincentive for students to give negative feedback because it potentially lowers the ranking of their university and subsequently devalues their degree. Also, this feedback mechanism is only open to students who will have left the university by the time the results are processed. This engenders a 'What's the point? None of this will change anything for me' attitude; as one academic put it, in the end many students fill it in 'just so we'll stop bothering them'.[49]

Most universities also run module feedback surveys at the end of each semester. These surveys are also completed once the module is finished and so lose any chance of collaborative engagement. Their individualised, anonymous nature lends itself to either unconstructive criticism of the lecturer, or fairly narrow requests such as that lectures be podcast. These forms of student engagement undermine any idea that through open dialogue student power is to be used to positively shape courses and universities in partnership with other stakeholders, and they reproduce a culture of passivity and disengagement.

The growing view of education among students as a financial investment encourages the minimum effort and engagement necessary to get a satisfactory grade and undermines many of the core principles of a liberal education.[50] Once this is the case, students begin to expect not to be failed and there can be significant pressures from both students and managers on academics to make exams easier and apply mark schemes generously.[51] The inadequacy of both top-down performance management and bottom-up consumer pressure means that universities are failing to improve educational standards; instead, they are encouraged to improve the packaging of what they offer, in the same way a sweet company might redesign the wrapper of a chocolate bar to give the perception of change when the wrapper ultimately contains the same product.

Measures such as student satisfaction are also an inaccurate proxy for educational quality because they do not offer any genuine measure of what students have learned. Universities may even dumb down the education if students – who understandably want to do well in their courses – complain that modules or exams are too hard, giving the university higher student satisfaction scores if their modules are made easier.[52] As a result of all this, potential students cannot have enough information to interrogate the relationship between price and quality for different courses at different institutions and so the link between the two is broken. Setting high fees is a simple way to project an image of quality and prestige, which gives an incentive for universities to set fees at the maximum level, knowing that students cannot truly evaluate their education until they get there.

Economics has become an increasingly popular subject at university level: between 2003/04 and 2011/12 the number of students studying economics rose even more than the sector as a whole, rising from about 26,000 to 39,000 (an increase of 49 per cent).[53] From a business perspective, economics is a desirable subject because of this popularity and because in comparison to laboratory and medical subjects it is cheap to teach. Exhibit 5.1 shows tuition fees and government grants for different bands of subjects before and after the 2010 reforms. Economics is a 'Band D' subject and so universities receive £2,916 more in funding per student after the 2010 reforms.

Exhibit 5.1 Comparative funding for full-time undergraduate study per student before and after 2010 reforms

Indicative subjects	Band	Typical Grant in 2011/12	Grant plus £3,375 tuition fee	Typical Grant in 2012/13	Grant plus maximum £9,000 tuition fee
Clinical medicine & clinical dentistry, veterinary science	A	£14,601	£17,976	£10,000	£19,000
Laboratory-based subjects (science, pre-clinical medicine), engineering & technology	B	£5,484	£8,859	£1,500	£10,500
Intensive teaching, studio or fieldwork, inc. art, design & mathematics	C	£3,898	£7,273	None	£9,000
Arts & humanities Law & economics	D	£2,709	£6,084	None	£9,000

Source: redrawn from Andrew McGettigan, The Great University Gamble: Money, Markets and the Future of Higher Education, London: Pluto Press, 2013, 27

All universities charging £9,000 per student for economics should be able to generate a considerable surplus that can be used to subsidise other parts of the university. This, combined with the demand for economics education, gives university management a strong incentive to seek to increase student numbers in economics.

This pressure to increase student numbers on economics courses has been present since at least the early 1990s. The University of Manchester economics department's annual report in 1992 highlighted a 'big expansion in student numbers' which was stimulated by the 'Vice-Chancellor's incentive scheme (50 per cent bonus on the resulting fee income)'.[54] As a consequence, the economics department admitted 522 new undergraduates in 1992, compared to 375 in 1991.[55] A similar story is true at universities with strong economics departments across the UK, and the continued upward pressure on staff–student ratios is a major barrier that prevents any shift to a more personalised, critical liberal education.

In this context the technicalisation of economics education and the corresponding move towards multiple-choice exams and copying set answers off the board in tutorials can also be seen as a way of coping with volume. This isn't to say that internal developments within the discipline of economics haven't been influential too; just that this trend conveniently allowed universities to teach more students with fewer resources. There is widespread support among a number of leading academic economists for the reintroduction of essays and discussion in tutorials but the wider university context makes this difficult to achieve in practice.[56] Twenty-five years ago it was common to have tutorials with three students where it would have been viable to discuss critically a range of economic theories in relation to a current economic issue, but this seems near impossible now. Despite the staff–student ratio rising from 1:8 to 1:18, labour costs were 55 per cent of total expenditure in HE in 2014/15 and are deemed a barrier to increasing efficiency further.[57] Many universities have attempted to cut labour costs by reducing pay and changing the terms and conditions of employment, a process critics call 'casualisation'. Casual contracts are often short term, do not support staff development or training and don't account for preparation time for classes. By 2014 at least 15.5 per cent of all teaching staff working in HE were employed on this type of contract.[58]

The status quo in many institutions now involves tutorials of twenty students with under-trained graduate teachers; it is this context in which the economics education we described in Chapter 2 takes place. At our lectures in Manchester there were 500 students in the core first and second year economics modules. In this context multiple-choice exams are less costly to mark than essays because the whole process can be automated. Seven or eight graduate students are needed to take tutorials, each with groups of 20–30 students. Graduate students are chosen for their research skills, not for their teaching ability, and they often receive little training or support with teaching. When this is combined with large class sizes it is little wonder that copying problem sets from the board becomes the most attractive option. Mathematical problems and multiple-choice questions have fixed 'right' and 'wrong' answers which can be provided to teaching assistants on a crib sheet, avoiding the need for the costly training and support that would facilitate critical group discussion.

This trend underpins the rise of a global multimillion-pound market in economics textbooks, lecture slides and stock exam questions which save staff preparation time and mean that less experienced teachers can take lectures and tutorials. As we discussed in Chapter 2, these textbooks are largely abstracted from any real-world context, at least partly because they are designed to be generic so as to be sold to students across the world. Because economics textbooks have a global market, whereas politics and sociology textbooks need to be much more country specific, successful authors are offered huge fees. It has been estimated that Gregory Mankiw has earned royalties of $42 million from his *Principles of Economics* textbook, which is in its seventh edition and has sold over a million copies, and it is rumoured that Richard Lipsey earned so much from his textbook he didn't know what to do with it and ended up buying a chicken farm.[59] It is considered to be too expensive for academics to spend time preparing case studies on current affairs or working out real-world examples against which students can evaluate theory.

There is a vital 'if' here: economics courses are a money-earner for universities *if* they are viable at all. While there has been a 49 per cent increase in students studying economics, there has been a corresponding reduction in the number of universities that offer economics. Between 2003/04 and 2011/12, 16 universities – 14 of which were post-1992 universities – withdrew economics programmes from their prospectuses.[60] This has led to a stratification of economics provision across the HE sector:

> old universities [are] much more likely to offer undergraduate economics degrees than new universities. Indeed whether a university is categorised as old or new is probably the best predictor of whether it offers an

economics degree. In 2011/12, three quarters of new universities did not offer an economics title. Of the 66 universities offering single degrees in at least one of the three most common titles 48 were old and just 18 new. North of a line between Preston and Sheffield there are no single economics degrees on offer in the new university sector.[61]

A system that only gives access to the study of higher-level economics to those who are willing and able to meet the financial and academic demands of the UK's older universities is one that risks further restricting access to places of influence in an econocracy. Skewing access to the study of economics in this way has the potential not only to harm the career prospects of the socially disadvantaged, but also to impoverish wider social and political debate on economic issues.

Once more, a major factor in this stratification is the research selectivity exercises started in the mid-1980s. The number of universities submitting to the economics Research Assessment Exercise fell steadily from 60 in 1992 to 35 in 2008, with submissions from the new universities falling from twelve to three.[62] Having a strong research base may be a good reason to retain economics programmes and, conversely, having little or no research base is a good reason to withdraw them. New universities have performed poorly in successive research exercises, prompting withdrawal of their economics submissions, so that the three that entered in 2008 all performed much worse than the 32 older universities.[63] Research ranking is not only important because of the cash it brings in but also because of the prestige it grants. Research ranking is a major determinant of league tables, which students are encouraged to use to decide where to study, and as a consequence it has significant value for recruiting students.

Despite the purpose of HE becoming narrower over time, university documents that set out the desired outcomes of an education at that institution still affirm a commitment to the principles of a liberal education. At Manchester an undergraduate education will 'promote mastery of a discipline' and 'prepare graduates for citizenship and leadership in diverse, global environments',[64] while graduates from Glasgow will be able to 'defend their ideas in dialogue with peers and challenge disciplinary assumptions'.[65] These claims are mirrored across all the universities we studied, which illustrates that the *rhetoric* of liberal education at least is alive and well.

As we have shown, in the case of economics the rhetoric is far from the reality. HE provision has increasingly been shaped into a good for private consumption and the funding and business models of universities now reflect this. Other public purposes of universities such as promoting democracy, transmitting culture, shaping active citizens and holding authority accountable are given lip service but have no place in current university business models or in government funding structures. While universities have not always in practice fulfilled these roles very well, they are a core part of the liberal educational ideal and have potential to add great value to the health and wealth of the nation – potential that is lost in the current system.

What is to be done?

Liberal education in the UK has only ever been tried in an elite HE system in which less than 3 per cent of 18+ school leavers attended university. Now that around 45 per cent of this cohort enrol in HE the resource pressures are far greater. We cannot simply transplant pre-Second World War liberal education models into our universities today because they were premised on a completely different society. We must instead use the principles of liberal education to develop new models of teaching and learning.

The purpose of this chapter's focus on the wider history and context of HE is to show that reforming economics education to better serve its students, the discipline and society will be extremely difficult without a change of direction in university and government policy. It is clearly necessary to look in depth at HE funding and business models and to have a serious political conversation about whether funding needs to be increased or redirected to increase the resources per student and lower staff–student ratios. However, there are ways in which pluralist, critical, liberal education can be practised in universities today which would improve the quality of education and be popular with students. Here we outline a set of constructive ideas for how reform in economics education could be approached in practice. Our vision is not fixed or final – it is the start of a conversation, not the end – but we hope that it illustrates that there are credible alternatives.

Many of the changes we have described in this chapter have been attempts to deliver a mass education while reducing the resources per student. The basic formula has been to 'pack 'em in and stack 'em up' while improving productivity through virtual learning, modular degrees, bigger lecture theatres and less contact time. Any reform to economics education must also depart from established methods of teaching which might have worked in 1945 for a small elite but do not work now.

A key underlying aim of reform should be to move from the idea of a passive student body – whose only input into their education is a tick-box feedback form – to active student co-production of education. The status quo is dependent on the tacit understanding that education is a kind of 'knowledge transfer' from teacher to student. With the 'transfer' metaphor for education, the teacher instructs and directs the students, who are empty receptacles waiting for knowledge to be poured into them. The metaphor of education as a journey is, though slightly cheesy, in our view a much better way to describe a good-quality education. On this view education is a joint exploration between the students and the teacher, where the outcome is unclear at the outset and depends on the contributions of all participants.[66] According to this view, students should play a part in setting learning aims in dialogue with their lecturers, and should bring their own experience into the classroom.[67] Facilitating learning and understanding is not simply a matter of transference, but rather of creating the conditions that enable learners to construct and apprehend meaning through individual and group activities and processes.[68]

An important extension of the above aim would be the reconfiguration of the relationship between different generations of economists. This is essential for the renewal and advancement of the discipline of economics because it means less is taken for granted. Also, wider critical debate increases the likelihood of 'disruptive innovation' in methods and theory. As for giving economics students an active role in co-producing their education, this can be achieved quite easily at undergraduate level; however, to achieve it throughout the discipline requires the reform of graduate training as well as the institutional landscape for early career economists, which currently forces adherence to the core neoclassical way of thinking if graduates want to be successful.

Now we will briefly outline some of the key features of a pluralist, liberal economics curriculum and pedagogy. As we have seen, currently almost all economics modules introduce economic theory in the abstract and then evaluate how well it fits the data (although most never get on to the evaluation stage). We believe that modules should instead take an inductive approach, meaning that they would start with empirical evidence and real-world issues and then introduce theory afterwards. Modules that utilise an inductive, problem-first approach to economics would almost by definition require engagement with other disciplines such as politics, history and philosophy. Core modules could be used to introduce the complex, major issues in economics (such as development, business cycles and financial markets) and then go on to show how different approaches can be used to understand these issues and how policies can (or cannot) influence them.

Greater use of peer-to-peer learning is one important way of making students co-producers of their education. England has fewer teaching and study hours attached to courses than other countries. About one-third of students study for twenty hours a week or less, meaning that they are paying to be full-time but actually technically only doing a part-time course.[69] Students from the same class could organise peer-led discussions or manage a course blog open for everyone to contribute to. More advanced students could facilitate classes for newer students, and because teaching is also a great way to learn, this could be a required part of the course for the more senior students too. It has been argued that there has already been a 'significant change in the nature of relations between learners and teachers, as the former draw increasingly on their peers to explore and consolidate their own learning',[70] and this should be actively developed in positive ways. Peer-to-peer learning, if done well, has additional non-academic benefits such as improving organisational and communication skills and increasing students' sensitivity to power and privilege in group discussions.

We need bold, imaginative experiments to address the shortcomings of the lecture/tutorial format of economics education as we are not yet in the position of being able to significantly increase staff–student ratios. Student assignments and assessments in economics could be much more varied and could include reflection journals which students fill out every week, policy briefings put together in small groups, mock strategic plans for governments and businesses outlining different economic strategies, comment pieces for the student newspaper, podcasts in which students have to find local participants to interview, and presentations of all of the above.

A little creativity would go a long way, and while we recognise that the pressures on academics are great and that some academics do try these kinds of experiments, they are far too rare and need much greater institutional support and encouragement. Longer-term tasks could require each student to follow the economic news of a particular country over a year or a term, keep a dossier of key developments and analysis, and feed this back to the class periodically. This kind of work is intrinsically connected to and embedded in the real world, and would give students the opportunity to understand how economies work (or don't) in practice.

Problem-based learning (PBL), which is widely used in medicine, could be used more widely in economics education.[71] PBL is centred on students being given an economics-related problem, such as 'How should, if at all, the UK government respond to falling oil prices?' or 'Examine three historical economic events and analyse a) how agents made decisions, b) how decisions were influenced by market structures, and c) what, if anything, this illustrates about incentives, behaviour and preferences', along with a number of readings and some structured questions. A problem could be completed over different timescales depending on its complexity and could include both group work as well as independent research. Exercises could be assessed by a portfolio detailing research carried out, answers to the questions and reflections on the process, for example methodology and limitations. Working effectively in a team and having to deal with the complexity and messiness of difficult economic problems is excellent training for professional work and life.

Economics education can and should relate to students' lives and to civic society. Students could do presentations on the local economy in their home area and use reflection journals to think about when and how their lives have been shaped by the wider economy. Communicating economic ideas to lay audiences is one of the skills employers find lacking in graduates today, so groups could be responsible for organising and running accessible workshops for schools and the wider public. Connecting economics education with civic society in ways like this would help students understand how important their knowledge is to their wider community.

Last but definitely not least, critical thinking and reflection must be at the heart of any reformed economics education. The principal intentions of a university are that it should promote the ability to think critically, and consider evidence while being discriminating in its selection and use – it is a travesty that this purpose is so absent from economics courses.[72] As we argued in section 1 of this chapter, pluralism is an essential part of developing the ability to think critically about economic theory. Critical reflection also requires an understanding of the reasons why you and others think as you do, and this involves being conscious of one's values, assumptions and intellectual framework and vigorously criticising them.[73] This could be done through assessed debates in class, but also through reverse debates, where the objective is to understand *exactly what* the other person is arguing (which is harder than it sounds) and *why*.

Taken together, these proposals represent a radical departure from the lecture/tutorial format of much university education today.

They place much more emphasis on the student as an active learner engaging their peers and the world around them to gain mastery of an academic discipline. Here the academic is a facilitator and a guide, not an imparter of mass-produced lectures, and the discipline is not an esoteric set of theories to be memorised in the abstract but a living body of knowledge embedded in wider society. The role of universities is to inspire students to want to learn, not provide a mechanical pathway of lectures and exams.

That being said, in the short term we recognise that many students will be unwilling to do the work unless it is clearly signposted that it is going to be assessed. This is not an excuse for avoiding reform or an argument against it, and it is the teacher's and the institution's responsibility to challenge the ethos in which the qualification is all that matters and create a more holistic educational culture. However, the assessment in economics education described in Chapter 2 must clearly be reformed root and branch, and this reform can be used to change the culture immediately. Modules should, where possible, run for a whole year to encourage deep learning and, however long they are, they should have continuous small-percentage assessment. For example, a module could have five assignments that each constituted 10 per cent of the total grade, one essay that was 20 per cent and one exam that was 30 per cent. The barrier to this is the cost of marking all these assessments; one way to address this is to say that only two of the five assignments will be marked, but they will be chosen at random.

These are only brief sketches of the urgent reform that must be experimented with and implemented in economics courses across the country. We hope we have demonstrated that pluralism and debate are crucial to the discipline. While better education will produce better experts, this alone isn't enough. We therefore turn to the final chapter of this book, in which we set out our vision of how econocracies must change to become more democratic.

Notes

1 John S. Mill, *Inaugural Address Delivered to the University of St Andrews*, London: Longmans, Green, Reader, and Dyer, 1867, 5. Available at: https://archive.org/details/inauguraladdres00millgoog (accessed 22 April 2016).
2 Sue Donelly, 'William Beveridge's advice for new students', London School of Economics History, 7 October 2014. Available at: http://blogs.lse.ac.uk/lsehistory/2014/10/07/william-beveridges-advice-for-new-students/ (accessed 22 April 2016).

3 Carl Gombrich, 'Liberal education for a complex world: the challenge of remaining open'. Available at: http://www.carlgombrich.org/liberal-education-for-a-complex-world/ (accessed 22 April 2016).
4 In eighteenth-century England one of the key functions of education was to form a close-knit ruling class and, as a result, liberal education stressed the concepts of politeness and sociability. Just across the border, different political and social circumstances meant that the Scottish tradition of liberal education emphasised much more the value of exposing the student to a wide range of literary, philosophical and scientific modes of thinking. See Robert Anderson, *British Universities Past and Present*, London: Hambledon Continuum, 2006, 41.
5 In eighteenth-century England academics weren't expected to do original research and their sole role was as a teacher and mentor of students. In contrast, the German universities were developing the idea that academics should be active researchers making original contributions to their discipline. Reformers in the UK wanted British universities to emulate their German counterparts and there was a tension between those who felt that education should promote tradition and continuity and those who felt that it should encourage critical questioning and be pushing the frontiers of knowledge. In this debate liberal educational principles were used to defend the status quo and it was argued that 'the problem and special work of the university, is not how to advance science, nor how to make discoveries ... but to form minds religiously, morally, intellectually' and to 'transmit the civilization of past generations to future ones'. See Anderson, *British Universities*, 42.
6 Toby Young, 'A classical liberal education', *The Telegraph*, 19 April 2013. Available at: http://blogs.telegraph.co.uk/news/tobyyoung/100213007/a-classical-liberal-education/ (accessed 8 June 2015).
7 Association of American Schools and Colleges, 'What Is a 21st century liberal education?' Available at: https://www.aacu.org/leap/what-is-a-liberal-education (accessed 22 April 16).
8 Trevor Hussey and Patrick Smith, *The Trouble with Higher Education: A Critical Examination of our Universities*, Abingdon: Routledge, 2010, ix.
9 Actual levels of supervision appear to vary significantly between colleges. See Phelim Brady, 'Mind the supervision gap', *Varsity*, 10 March 2013. Available at: http://www.varsity.co.uk/news/5787 (accessed 22 April 2016).
10 *CSEP Survey of Economics Students: Is it Time for Change at Cambridge?*, report, Cambridge Society of Economic Pluralism, June 2014, 6–10.
11 Jack Britton, Lorraine Dearden, Neil Shephard and Anna Vignoles, *How English Domiciled Graduate Earnings Vary with Gender, Institution Attended, Subject and Socioeconomic Background*, report, Institute for Fiscal Studies, 2016.

12 The Economics Network, 'Economics Employers' Survey 2014–15'. Available at: https://www.economicsnetwork.ac.uk/projects/surveys/employers14–15 (accessed 22 April 2016).
13 Andrew Ross, 'Message to applicants from Deputy Director GES', The Government Economic Service, undated. Available at: https://www.jiscmail.ac.uk/cgi-bin/webadmin?A3=ind1209&L=CHUDE&E=base64&P=4477856&B=--_003_799B56EC23F30340810F2D7B762611FD10F92CMBXP09dsmanacuk_&T=application%2Fmsword;%20name=%22Message%20to%20Applicants%20from%20Deputy%20Director%20GES.doc%22&N=Message%20to%20Applicants%20from%20Deputy%20Director%20GES.doc&attachment=q. (accessed 25 April 2016).
14 Andrew Haldane, 'The revolution in economics', foreword to the Post-Crash Economics Society Report *Economics, Education and Unlearning*, April 2015, 3–6. Available at: http://www.post-crasheconomics.com/economics-education-and-unlearning/ (accessed 22 April 2016).
15 Modern advocates of liberal education are similarly explicit about the value of skills learned in the classroom to diverse and healthy societies. See for example Martha Nussbaum, *Not for Profit: Why Democracy Needs the Humanities*, Princeton, NJ: Princeton University Press, 2012.
16 Other professions such as social work have formalised the importance of this kind of ethical awareness in their professional code of conduct. See British Association of Social Workers, 'The Code of Ethics for Social Work Statement of Principles', 2012. Available at: https://www.basw.co.uk/codeofethics/ (accessed 22 April 2016).
17 Martin Wolf, Adair Turner and Andy Haldane are just a few of the major public figures who have argued for reform in economics education in the last few years. Haldane, 'The revolution in economics', 3–6; Martin Wolf, *The Shifts and the Shocks: What We've Learned—and Have Still to Learn—from the Financial Crisis*, London: Penguin, 2014; Adair Turner, 'Preface', in Cambridge Society for Economic Pluralism, *CSEP Survey of Economics Students*, 2.
18 For more details see Sara Gorgoni, 'University of Greenwich revises its economics programmes to enhance pluralism and real world economics', Rethinking Economics blog, 14 December 2014. Available at: http://rethinkingeconomics.blogspot.co.uk/2014/12/university-of-greenwich-revises-its.html (accessed 22 April 2016); Yuan Yang and Costas Repapis, 'Pluralism & real-world economics: a new curriculum at Goldsmiths', Rethinking Economics blog, 16 October 2016. Available at: http://www.rethinkeconomics.org/news/2015/10/pluralism-real-world-economics-a-new-curriculum-at-goldsmiths/ (accessed 22 April 2016); Steve Keen, 'For a pluralist education, come to Kingston', *Steve Keen's Debtwatch*, 8 May 2014. Available at: http://www.debtdeflation.com/blogs/2014/05/08/for-a-pluralist-education-come-to-kingston/ (accessed 22 April 2016).

19 In an interview we conducted with Sara Gorgoni for this book.

20 In an interview with a student conducted for this book.

21 Michael Shattock, *Making Policy in British Higher Education 1945–2011*, Maidenhead: Open University Press, 2012, 6; Department for Business, Innovation & Skills, *Participation Rates in Higher Education: Academic Years 2006/2007–2013/2014 (Provisional)*, report September 2015.

22 Holly Watt and Peter Dominiczak, 'Ed Miliband: school funding to rise under Labour', *The Telegraph*, 12 February 2015. Available at: http://www.telegraph.co.uk/news/politics/ed-miliband/11408627/Ed-Miliband-School-funding-to-rise-under-Labour.html (accessed 25 April 2016).

23 Shattock, *Making Policy*, 6.

24 Anderson, *British Universities*, 133–8.

25 Ibid., 152.

26 Shattock, *Making Policy*, 12.

27 Ibid., 5.

28 Ibid., 125

29 Ibid., 105.

30 For a more detailed but still fairly accessible explanation of endogenous growth models in the context of education, see Geraint Johnes, 'Education and economic growth', *Lancaster University Management School Working Paper 19*, 2006. Available at: http://www.lancaster.ac.uk/media/lancaster-university/content-assets/documents/lums/economics/working-papers/EducationEconomicGrowth.pdf (accessed 22 April 2016).

31 Mick, Moran, *The Regulatory State: High Modernism and Hyper-Innovation*, Oxford: Oxford University Press, 2003.

32 Shattock, *Making Policy*, 152.

33 Ibid., 152–4.

34 Ibid., 5.

35 The decline in funding per student is illustrated in a graph in Ronald Dearing, *The Dearing Report: Higher Education in the Learning Society*, London: Her Majesty's Stationery Office, 1997, 45. Available at: http://www.educationengland.org.uk/documents/dearing1997/dearing1997.html (accessed 24 April 2016). Polytechnics had on average considerably higher staff–student ratios and so the unification of the university system also contributed to this increase. See Anderson, *British Universities*, 169.

36 Shattock, *Making Policy*, 163–4.

37 See, for example, Nicholas Barr, 'Income-contingent student loans: an idea whose time has come', in G. K. Shaw (ed.), *Economics, Culture and Education – Essays in Honour of Mark Blaug*, Aldershot: Edward Elgar, 1991, 155–70.

38 For a more detailed discussion of human capital and education, see Milton Friedman, 'The role of government in education', in Robert A. Solow

(ed.), *Economics and the Public Interest*, New Brunswick, NJ: Rutgers University Press, 1955, 123–44.

39 See Figure 2 in *Guide to Funding 2015–16: How HEFCE Allocates its Funds*, report, Higher Education Funding Council England, March 2015, 16.

40 For what is in our view the most accessible explanation of these complex reforms, see Andrew McGettigan, *The Great University Gamble: Money, Markets and the Future of Higher Education*, London: Pluto Press, 2013.

41 Ibid., 4.

42 *The Teaching Excellence Framework: Assessing Quality in Higher Education*, Business Innovation and Skills Committee, Third Report of Session 2015–16, London: The Stationery Office, February 2016, 3.

43 McGettigan, *The Great University Gamble*, 27.

44 Ibid., 25.

45 Ibid., 34.

46 *Securing a Sustainable Future for Higher Education*, report, Independent Review of Higher Education Funding & Student Finance, October 2010, 25.

47 McGettigan, *The Great University Gamble*, 60.

48 Ibid., 59.

49 Frank Furedi, 'Satisfaction and its discontents', *Times Higher Education*, 8 March 2012. Available at: https://www.timeshighereducation.com/features/satisfaction-and-its-discontents/419238.article (accessed 22 April 2016).

50 McGettigan, *The Great University Gamble*, 64.

51 Furedi, 'Satisfaction and its discontents'.

52 For a critical perspective on this process, see Universities and College Union, 'The impact of student satisfaction surveys on staff in HE and FE institutions', October 2010. Available at: https://www.ucu.org.uk/brief_satissurveys (accessed 25 April 2016).

53 James Johnston, Alan Reeves and Steven Talbot, 'Has economics become an elite subject for elite UK universities?', *Oxford Review of Education*, 40(5) (2014): 591–2.

54 University of Manchester Archives, 'Faculty of Economic and Social Studies – Whole Faculty Overview – Report of Council to the University Court 1992', 1992, 166.

55 Ibid., 166.

56 This is a view that was widely expressed by attendees at a conference called 'Revisiting the State of Economics Education' held at the Bank of England on 17 March 2015.

57 Higher Education Statistics Authority, 'Income and expenditure of UK Higher Education providers 2014/15'. Available at: https://www.hesa.ac.uk/stats-finance (accessed 25 April 2016).

58 Will Pickering, 'Zero-hours contracts: a UCU briefing', University and College Union, March 2014, 4.

59 Richard Read, 'A $280 college textbook busts budgets, but Harvard author Gregory Mankiw defends royalties', *The Oregonian*, 12 February 2015. Available at: http://www.oregonlive.com/education/index.ssf/2015/02/a_280_college_textbook_busts_b.html (accessed 22 April 2016).

60 Johnston, Reeves and Talbot, 'Has economics become an elite subject', 597.

61 James Johnston and Alan Reeves, 'Economics is becoming an elite subject for elite UK universities', Politics and Policy blog, London School of Economics, 11 November 2014. Available at: http://blogs.lse.ac.uk/politicsandpolicy/the-growth-of-elitism-in-the-uks-higher-education-system-the-case-of-economics/ (accessed 22 April 2016).

62 Ibid.

63 Ibid.

64 University of Manchester, 'The purposes of a Manchester undergraduate education'. Available at: http://documents.manchester.ac.uk/display.aspx?DocID=9804 (accessed 22 April 2016).

65 University of Glasgow, 'University of Glasgow graduate attributes'. Available at: http://www.gla.ac.uk/media/media_183776_en.pdf (accessed 22 April 2016).

66 Hussey and Smith, *The Trouble with Higher Education*, 63.

67 Nussbaum, *Not for Profit*, 55.

68 Hussey and Smith, *The Trouble with Higher Education*, 68.

69 Ibid., 115.

70 Ibid., 107.

71 Diana Wood, 'Problem based learning', *British Medical Journal*, 8 February 2003. Available at: http://www.bmj.com/content/326/7384/328 (accessed 22 April 2016).

72 Hussey and Smith, *The Trouble with Higher Education*, 104.

73 Ibid., 103.

Chapter 6

Economics is for everyone

Renewing democracy

In the last chapter we set out our vision for how the education of economic experts could be improved, and the temptation might be to end there. However, this would at best be addressing only half of the problem. While we have been following one path to an important set of conclusions, there has been another path running alongside, just out of sight but interwoven with our story; neglecting its ultimate conclusions will only leave us at a dead end.

Throughout this book we have shown how economics underpins a technocratic system that marginalises citizens and restricts their ability to engage with economic issues. Econocracy is a system where some have access to economic knowledge and authority and others do not. While improving the quality of experts would undoubtedly be good for society, the wider system will still be incompatible with democracy and with some of our most deeply cherished political beliefs. Therefore, to finish we must return to the wider question of society and politics in order to show how we need more than just better experts; we need a new relationship between experts and society. This entails a new culture of open and inclusive economic dialogue that all citizens can take part in.

Our criticisms of econocracy should not be read as scepticism towards all forms of expertise. However, we have tried to show in this book that trust in economic experts should not be blind. Economics is inherently bundled up with politics and ethics. Moreover, as we have demonstrated, economists have frequently failed to live up to society's expectations and requirements.

The problem is that, as the sociologist Michel Callon has pointed out, 'when a citizen wishes to resolve the problems that the specialists were unable to foresee or to avoid, he finds himself back in their hands'.[1] Society cannot do without economic experts, and yet citizens have every reason to be sceptical of them. So where do we go from here? We believe that economics must be brought back into the spotlight of democratic scrutiny. Economic decisions must be taken as part of a public discussion. People should have an equal stake in deciding what kind of economy they want to live in, and citizens must claim this stake if, in Ha-Joon Chang's words, 'we are not to become passive victims of someone else's decisions'.[2]

Democracy can be conceptualised as the rule of the majority, but it can also be conceived in terms of certain institutions, as well as a form of public culture. A distinction can be drawn between ideas of 'thin' and 'broad' democracy, which can help us assess what kind of democracy is best able to address the problems presented by econocracy. Thin democracy envisages democracy as a formal set of institutions in which the general public vote for political parties that then represent their interests in Parliament. At the extremes of thin democracy are theories such as that of Joseph Schumpeter, who claims that democracy is merely a battle by political elites for the votes of passive citizens.[3] The act of people voting merely provides an incentive for elites to serve voters well.

In a broad democracy citizens take a more active part in the institutions and decision-making processes, and there is a strong public culture of democratic debate. Less power is delegated to representatives and more is exercised directly by individuals and communities through participatory and inclusive democratic institutions. Politics is seen less as something that is done to one and more as something that one takes part in. The ideas of thin and broad democracy are at either end of a spectrum that can be used to evaluate how democratic a society's institutions, processes and public culture are.

The status quo represents a danger, even for thin democracy. That economics has become so detached and obscure means that citizens often cannot even assess whether or not elites are serving them well. Recall that the public has never been consulted about GDP and many people are unsure what it means, yet its increase is almost universally represented as economic success. Economic ideas and statistics can be used to mask contentious political decisions and create confusion rather than clarity.

A functioning thin democracy would be preferable to the status quo but it is far from perfect. Therefore, over the course of this chapter we will make the case for moving towards making economic decisions in a way that is compatible with the idea of broad democracy.

In this book we hope that we have convincingly argued that economics should be a discipline that is open to public scrutiny and engages the public in a substantive, two-way dialogue. Questions about the economy go right to the heart of how we organise society, as well as our individual and collective values, and as a consequence we all have a right to shape it. Thin democracy does not offer this possibility as it delegates this responsibility to political parties and experts.

We believe that there is real potential for a public culture of economics, supported by a renewed and thriving discipline of economics. This culture can provide the foundations on which a set of participatory, democratic institutions can be built which facilitate the involvement of far greater numbers of people in economic discussion and decision making. It may be hard to imagine such a shift now when so many economic decisions are made behind closed doors and it would undoubtedly involve significant changes to daily life and the state, which the cynic could condemn as utopian. However, as we will demonstrate in this chapter, we are already working as a student movement to achieve some of these aspirations.

There is something intrinsically valuable about making decisions for ourselves and having autonomy over our lives. This is at the heart of our idea of freedom. Our modern word 'idiot' derives from the Ancient Greek *idiotes*, meaning a private individual, or someone not involved with public decision making. We all have a deeply ingrained sense of what is moral or just, which leads to a desire to take part in social and political life. Aristotle perhaps best captured this urge when he called humans 'political animals'.[4]

This need is strong and provides the raw material from which to build a set of participatory democratic institutions – even if that world is hard to imagine now. The kinds of skills and qualities needed by citizens for a broad democracy to function effectively are learned, not innate, and must be practised to be mastered. They include listening, compromise, the ability to critically evaluate verbal and numerical argument, and developing independent judgement. They can only come through practical experience of being involved in participatory democratic institutions. In this sense, moving towards a system of broad democracy is a process of learning by doing.

There is also a powerful economic argument for broad democracy. Friedrich Hayek argued that there was a 'fatal conceit' in socialist planning, which was the assumption that it was possible for planners to gain such comprehensive knowledge of the present and future that they could rationally plan the whole economy. For Hayek, effective economic organisation and progress is dependent on the use of knowledge 'which is not given to anyone in its totality' and is inherently imperfect.[5] He argued that markets, by facilitating the diffusion of knowledge dispersed among different actors through prices, were the best solution to this problem.

The assumptions about the economy that underpin an econocracy are very similar to those Hayek criticised, as economic experts presume that they have the necessary knowledge and expertise to successfully interpret, predict and shape the economy. Today's economic experts, like yesterday's socialist planners, govern a system that is unable to take into account the diverse preferences that make up society or incorporate relevant locally situated knowledge and expertise. As a result the decisions made are both undemocratic and, to use neoclassical language, socially suboptimal.[6]

A broad democracy must develop democratic processes through which collective agreement is reached, first locally and then nationally, on the way society and the economy should be organised. The resulting system would be one in which individuals and communities have real 'ownership' of local and central government. In a broad democracy the line between the state and the public is blurred and fluid because individuals are much more engaged in different parts of government. This means that policy problems are not only the domain of an elite, but of much wider parts of the population. Systems, making use of advances in technology, could be set up to collate knowledge and experience which could inform the development of policy. This kind of state is smarter, more efficient and a better problem solver.

A turn towards broad democracy is a turn away from the technocratic consensus that has dominated both the left and right of politics in the twentieth century. This view held that society could be designed and shaped according to rational, scientific criteria by experts and elites, usually with the backing of the state.[7] It is the ideology that underpins an econocracy.

Instead, authority and power must start with the broader citizenry and be delegated to particular experts on the basis of an explicit agreement. The public retain oversight and control through a parliament or some other method, have an ongoing critical relationship with those with delegated authority, and have the real option to recall that authority if they so choose. Experts must fulfil certain obligations to society in return for the power that they are given.

Too often books set out grand ideas and fail to address the specifics of their proposals, leaving the reader struggling to see how they would work in practice. We have therefore developed two concepts: 'Citizen Economics' and 'Public Interest Economics'. Such terms may seem grandiose but we feel they offer a real vision of how to reshape the role of economic experts in society so that they can better support citizens and encourage them to be involved in the economic decisions that are an increasing part of everyday life.

A new generation of citizen economists

We have tried to show how this thing we call 'the economy', which often seems to play such a central role in our individual and collective lives, is actually a fairly recent invention. What we call the economy, often assuming it to be universal and natural, is in fact a description of a particular form of social organisation. It is in this way that economics is the continuation of politics by other means. The crucial point is that the economy always could have been and always can be something different. We need to decide what we want it to be through public discussion, but in order to have that discussion everyone must first understand the language of the debate.

We therefore propose the idea of the 'Citizen Economist', an individual who has the basic knowledge, confidence and interest to engage critically with economic discourse in politics, the news and their local communities. Citizen Economists are able to see the links between their individual circumstances and the operation of the economy on a systemic level. They are able to engage with economic statements and narratives made by politicians, economists and media commentators about the performance of the economy and evaluate the values and assumptions behind their arguments. A society of Citizen Economists is one in which individuals have more understanding and thus control over their circumstances. It is a society where there are always alternatives and all of society plays an active role in proposing, debating and scrutinising them, ultimately deciding collectively and individually which paths to take.

Supporting the creation of a new generation of Citizen Economists is now a key aim of Rethinking Economics and we are developing a range of practical projects to democratise economics. We have developed schools workshops for 11–18 year olds, which introduce students to critical, pluralist economics in a fun and accessible manner. In the workshops we ask students to draw an economist: they invariably draw white men, some wearing top hats, others reading the *Financial Times*. One had a monocle and another was even standing on top of the world. These stereotypes about what kind of person an economist is must be challenged in order to create space for Citizen Economists and to make future generations of economic experts more diverse. We have a mirror that we bring to our workshops with 'This is what an economist looks like' written on it to illustrate our message.

In September 2015 we launched a pilot 'Community Crash-Course in Citizen Economics' in Manchester, a six-week evening class for adults providing a critical introduction to everyday economics. As students we feel that we are halfway between experts and citizens and that having a foot in both camps allows us to facilitate spaces where a new kind of Citizen Economics can be created. The topics of the first crash-course included 'What is economics?', poverty and inequality, work and tax, booms, busts and banking, and debt.

High demand for the crash-course has highlighted the appetite many people have to understand more about the economy. One participant said their reason for attending was that 'I feel that economics is so important currently, and people like myself are so powerless. This course is an opportunity for me to understand some basic economic ideas, to support or maybe even challenge some of the preconceptions I already have about the world.' This appetite is reflected in our YouGov survey. When asked whether people would like to know more about economics, only 13 per cent of respondents said no; the rest said yes (14 per cent), or yes but that either time (34 per cent) or resources (21 per cent) were a barrier. We are now working on developing a model in which student groups run crash-courses in their area with the support of academics from their universities and guest facilitators, while Rethinking Economics provides students with training and resources and also runs its own courses.

An important part of creating a generation of Citizen Economists is creating a public culture and a community. One crash-course participant reflected that 'everyone is so friendly and engaged. It's refreshing to come to a class with people from all walks of life, all wanting to contribute and chat about economics. I think the fact it was an evening class, and the affordability, made this possible.' We also hold conferences and encourage local groups to make all their speaker events open to the public to create spaces where people can engage with economic ideas, discuss and debate them, and build the relationships that are at the heart of our growing community of Citizen Economists. Every year we hold the Rethinking Weekender in London, a public conference aimed at bringing students, academics and the public together to discuss and rethink economics.

In March 2015 and April 2016 we held conferences in Manchester called 'Why Economics is for Everyone', each attended by hundreds of members of the public. We tried, as far as possible, to scrap the lecture format and instead ran discussions and workshops in which the distinction between audience and speaker was blurred. We gave speakers specific instructions to tailor their contributions to a lay audience and asked them to make their events as interactive as possible. We tried to create an environment in which people felt comfortable asking any question they had, no matter how simple it seemed, and expressing their views no matter how little they knew about economics.

Rethinking Economics also launched a current affairs website called 'Economy' (www.ecnmy.org) in March 2016. Its vision is to create a world in which every citizen is able to discuss economics with confidence and understanding, and critically engage with the economic and political narratives around them. The website has a 'Learn' section which includes videos and animations introducing users to a wider range of economic ideas. The centrepiece of the website is the 'Engage' section, which provides a forum for Citizen Economists from all over the world to contribute their own views, share stories and ask questions. Finally, the 'Act' section links to wider democratising economics projects and provides resources for people to set up their own discussion groups and events.

We've called the website 'Economy' – with the mantra 'It's Everyone's!' – because we want to reinvent what the word means to people.[8] Whereas currently the economy is an intimidating, complex and abstract idea, we want people to feel able to engage with it, to get beyond the jargon and to feel that they can shape it too, even if only in small ways. The message of Economy is that economics is really just seven billion people's stories, experiences and choices. It's about what we do, what we make and what we need. We hope that the website will help to catalyse a global community of Citizen Economists and spark vibrant conversations about economic issues which have seemed irrelevant and off-putting to most people for too long.

We have spent considerable time and energy thinking about the pedagogy we use for our public education activities because we are aware that embedding critical reflection and pluralism at their core is not easy. It would be easy to fall into teaching economics the way we have been taught, and it's easy to get carried away by the authority given to economic experts, even those who are still students. As a result, we are especially keen to reshape the relationships between teachers and students and recognise the value of the experience and contributions of all participants.

We make a crucial distinction between *formal literacy*, where the subject matter is a fixed body of knowledge which participants are encouraged to learn unquestioningly, and *substantive literacy*, where participants are encouraged to interrogate and critique the subject matter and develop their own independent judgements.[9] University economics education gives graduates a formal literacy in neoclassical economics. We hope to imbue Citizen Economists with a substantive economic literacy that will enable them to critically engage with economic narratives and arguments and rebalance their relationship with economists, politicians and media experts.

There are important questions about how much people can be expected to know about economics. The economy is enormously complex and we are asking people to develop an awareness and understanding of not just one economic perspective, but many. We recognise that most Citizen Economists won't have the time or resources to engage with different economic perspectives at an advanced theoretical level. This is why Citizen Economics isn't about gaining an elaborate knowledge of abstract theory (neoclassical or otherwise); it is about trying to make connections between peoples' lived experience and economic circumstances on the one hand, and the economy on a systemic level on the other. Understanding how changes in the economy influence people's personal cost of living, the education their children receive, and how much they and the people who live in their area are paid is also, in our view, a far more accessible way into economics than learning about abstract and arcane IS-LM models and utility functions.

In the spirit of this book, we have tried to emphasise to Citizen Economists that economists, politicians and media commentators generally know less about the functioning of the economy, and know it with less certainty, than it may seem and so the public should feel confident in engaging with them. The knowledge we are trying to provide Citizen Economists is not that of certain rules and laws about how the economy works, which in our view are unknowable even for experts. Instead, it is about different ways of understanding and engaging with narratives, theories and statistics that purport to describe the economy, and formulating arguments about what we can do to make it function better. Joan Robinson put it perfectly – if cynically – when she said, 'The purpose of studying economics is not to acquire a set of ready-made answers to economic questions, but to learn how to avoid being deceived by economists.'[10]

When this is achieved, then individuals and groups will have greater agency to shape the economy through political action on different scales. By committing to building a society of Citizen Economists we put in place one of the preconditions for a functioning and effective democracy.

The need for a new kind of expert

It is clear to us that we cannot have a society of Citizen Economists without radically reconfiguring the discipline of economics. Economic experts need to play a key role in providing economics education for citizens and creating more open and inclusive economic dialogue across society. However, there are currently four main features of the discipline that are fundamentally incompatible with developing a thriving society of Citizen Economists. Economic experts have not done enough to earn the trust of citizens; they tend to inform citizens of their economic analysis rather than engage them as equals; they too rarely acknowledge the limits of their expertise; and the discipline as a whole is highly unrepresentative of wider society.

In our YouGov survey we asked respondents how much they trust economists to take decisions in their interest: 2 per cent answered 'a great deal', 33 per cent 'a fair amount', 40 per cent 'not very much', and 11 per cent 'not at all' (the rest didn't know or didn't answer). This overall lack of trust does not create a healthy basis for economic experts to play a central role in educating a generation of Citizen Economists. There are many highly publicised examples of economic experts acting in unethical and unscrupulous ways, which must be openly addressed in order to rebuild trust.

Economic experts in the US have most obviously undermined public trust, and this has been popularised through films like *Inside Job*, which have in turn brought the whole profession into disrepute. For example, the Dodd–Frank Wall Street Reform and Consumer Act passed in 2010 regulates financial markets and institutions and was lobbied against vigorously by the financial sector. During 96 testimonies to Congress by 82 academic economists – under oath – *one third* failed to disclose that they were being paid for consulting by companies that would be regulated under Dodd–Frank.[11]

A more in-depth academic study analysed the 15 academics who co-authored the influential Squam Lake report on financial reform in the US, and found that economists fully reported their affiliations in their academic work only 2.3 per cent of the time, and gave the full extent of their affiliations in media appearances just 28 per cent of the time.[12] Charles Ferguson adapts the revolving-door metaphor for the US to argue it is now a 'three-way intersection' represented by 'the convergence of academic economics, Wall Street, and political power'.[13] While there is no similar record of bad behaviour in the UK, economic experts everywhere have been tarnished by scandals like these. Economics needs much stronger codes of professional ethics, and applied ethics must become a central part of undergraduate economics education.[14]

The second major barrier to a popular culture of Citizen Economics is the unequal intellectual relationship between economists and citizens. Popular economics books like *Freakonomics: A Rogue Economist Explores the Hidden Side of Everything*, *The Economic Naturalist: Why Economics Explains Almost Everything* and *The Logic of Life: Uncovering the New Economics of Everything* clearly show an effort to engage with the public. While we applaud the efforts of the authors of these books, as well as their readability, they are *informing* people about economics rather than *engaging* with them. The former takes the shape of an expert simply telling the public 'how it is'; the latter involves a dialogue between the public and the expert in which the participation of both is equally important.

Consider the widely read *Freakonomics*, starting with its subtitle, *A Rogue Economist Explores the Hidden Side of Everything*. This paints an image of the economist as someone who has a special set of tools with which they can reveal the 'hidden side of everything' to the public. The economist of the authorial duo, Steven Levitt, thinks 'economics is a science with excellent tools for gaining answers but a serious shortage of interesting questions' (clearly he doesn't pay much attention to current affairs).[15] One of these tools is the idea that 'people respond to incentives', and the authors state that 'the typical economist believes the world has not yet invented a problem that he cannot fix if given a free hand to design the proper incentive scheme'.[16] Such an approach is intrinsically paternalistic and gives economists free rein to decide both what constitutes a 'problem' and how they must try to influence citizens' behaviour to fix it. Here the citizen is passive; they are told what the economic experts know, which is presented as scientific, and there is no mention that the analysis rests on a set of methodological and ethical assumptions that the reader might dispute, if only they were given the chance.[17]

Thirdly, economic experts must do more to challenge the illusion, which they often actively advance, that they are the only people qualified to have a legitimate opinion on economic issues. A recent talk in New York with three of the most famous economists in the world – Paul Krugman, Joseph Stiglitz and Thomas Piketty – provides a demonstrative example. It illustrates the difference between modesty in economics and the current belief in technocratic expertise that we have argued is so dangerous. Krugman and Stiglitz to a large extent accepted the presenter's claim that they were 'considered geniuses in the field of economics' as she made references to their Nobel prizes. Krugman then excused his own and the profession's general failure to foresee the 2008 financial crisis, arguing that 'there's always going to be something that you miss'.

In startling contrast, Piketty admitted that the discipline 'spends a lot of time doing complicated mathematical models ... to impress others', chastised it for trying 'to pretend that they [as economists] have developed a science that is so sophisticated the rest of the world cannot understand it', claiming that 'this is a joke', and finally argued 'that we have to be modest ... if we want to be useful and it's not always clear that economists are so useful'. To underline the contrast, Stiglitz then declared that 'if we were running Europe, we would know how to get it out of its troubles', followed by Krugman jokingly adding that 'we're not geniuses; we're philosopher kings'.[18]

Some economists are trying, to some extent, to escape from this kind of thinking, but their progress is necessarily limited as long as they accept the current structure of the discipline. Probably one of the most highly regarded responses of the discipline to its recent crisis is *Economics Rules: The Rights and Wrongs of the Dismal Science* by Dani Rodrik. Rodrik chastises his fellow economists for being overconfident in their models and their political proclamations, but also defends economics against its critics, arguing that it remains a useful, semi-scientific tool for analysing the world. Rodrik's argument is reasonable in some places, but it remains firmly within the paradigm of the single approach to economics discussed in this book. Although Rodrik embraces a wide range of modelling techniques within neoclassical economics – acknowledging that these models are context-specific – he rejects pluralism without explicitly discussing any non-neoclassical theories.[19] Although he sees that economic as a discipline is elitist, at no point does he seriously consider the possibility that it has become too powerful and unaccountable, or that it should be more open to democratic scrutiny.

Rodrik acknowledges that economics rests on ethical assumptions that can be challenged, but he quickly slips back into reasserting the authority of the discipline without questioning his own values and assumptions. His 'Ten Commandments for Noneconomists' include informing readers that '*economics is a collection of models with no predetermined conclusions; reject any arguments otherwise*'; telling them to '*not criticize an economist's model because of its assumptions*; ask how the results would change if certain problematic assumptions were more realistic'; and assuring them that 'economists don't (all) worship markets, *but they know better how they work than you do*' (our emphasis).[20] At the core Rodrik retains the same confidence in his economic expertise and dismissive attitude towards the public that is characteristic of economics in an econocracy.

Finally, the academic discipline of economics is so unrepresentative of wider society that it cannot hope to understand or engage with many parts of the population. In Britain only one in four academic economists are women and the ratio is similar for students.[21] In contrast 56 per cent of undergraduates in the UK were women in 2013.[22] Meanwhile, in a 2010 survey of academic economists the Royal Economic Society found that 82 per cent of respondents were white, going up to 88 per cent for professors.[23] The 2010 survey appears to be the last of its kind, with the 2012 and 2014 surveys only focusing on gender balance.[24] Strikingly, of the 75 Economics Nobel Prize winners, only one is a woman and two are not white. This lack of diversity must be addressed urgently if we are to hope for a new, better kind of economic expert.

Economics is currently failing to take seriously every citizen's right to engage with economic discussion and decision making. Economic experts often present economic theory as identifying scientific truths while failing to admit the values and assumptions that the theories rest upon, and this cements unequal power relations between experts and citizens. Economics has never engaged in a political discussion about what kind of economy to build and fails to incorporate the public interest as an explicit criterion in many of its key decision-making mechanisms. Economics can either be a barrier or a bridge to a wider renewal of democratic society; currently it is a barrier. In the next section we set out how it can change to become a bridge.

Public interest economics

There are connections between neoclassical economics, how economists are taught and the rise of econocracy. We have argued that neoclassical economic theory provides important intellectual foundations for econocracy, justifying a particular understanding of the economy and a technical approach to economic decision making.

Economics education frames economic issues in terms of clearly defined problems and answers, depoliticises economics, devalues non-economic forms of knowledge and does not highlight the limits of what we currently know and what it is fundamentally possible to know. Taken together, these features underpin the view that the economy is something that can be detached from politics and society, and mapped, measured and shaped in an objective manner by a small number of experts. Wider changes to higher education have also contributed to the fundamental shortcomings of economics education in the UK today and, by making it difficult to reinstate pluralism and critical skills to the curriculum, have locked in the status quo.

A new generation of critical, socially engaged economic experts would form the heart of the system we envision. Therefore, we propose a new rationale for economics, one that changes what it means to be an economist and designates explicit social obligations in return for the authority economists are given. We call this 'Public Interest Economics'.

Public Interest Economists would try to hold the powerful to account. In doing this, they could draw on legal practice and theory. The British state can be thought of as three branches: the Cabinet which proposes laws, Parliament which votes on whether to accept them and the British legal system which interprets and applies them. A significant part of the role of the legal system is to hold the other branches of the government to account, either through representing individuals in the courts or through publishing legal opinions on the basis for and consequences of policy. Judges interpret the laws Parliament makes and often consider the public interest in coming to judgements. This system is based on the idea of checks and balances on power to ensure that those with power are held to account for their decisions.

Media organisations like the Bureau of Investigative Journalism (TBIJ) also have a clear public interest mission. The TBIJ conducts 'research, investigations, reporting and analysis which is of public benefit by undertaking in-depth research into the governance of public, private and third sector organisations and their influence' in order to 'help educate the public about the realities of power in today's world'.[25] This understanding of the public interest chimes closely with Edward Said's vision of the public intellectual, whose role is

> publicly to raise embarrassing questions, to confront orthodoxy and dogma (rather than to produce them), to be someone who cannot easily be co-opted by governments or corporations, and whose raison d'être is to represent all those people and issues that are routinely forgotten or swept under the rug.[26]

A central aim of Public Interest Economics would be to develop similar systems of checks and balances for the economy that scrutinised the decisions and actions of powerful public and private economic institutions and held them to account.

Public Interest Economists would also take seriously the challenges of creating democratic economic institutions. For example, while in the UK Parliament has the formal authority to repeal central bank independence, its ability to do this in practice is questionable. This is because there is now a widespread view, influenced by neoclassical economics, that political interference with independent central banks undermines their independence. This view then becomes a self-fulfilling prophecy as democratic attempts to scrutinise and direct central banks would lead to a loss of credibility in important financial markets.[27] So while Parliament has formal powers to revoke central bank independence, in practice the principle of independence requires central bank decision making to be taken outside of the political sphere. Public Interest Economists would challenge this status quo and find creative ways to make central banks more accountable, open and accessible to the wider public.

Public Interest Economists must not be technocrats operating behind closed doors but experts who help citizens understand the discipline and who facilitate public discussion. To achieve this, they could learn from the Science Communication movement and establish 'Economics Communication' as a discipline in itself. Science Communication has grown up in the past few decades and attempts to educate the public about key areas of science, with the multiple aims of improving society by educating its citizens, sharing knowledge and making science itself more democratic. This has resulted in a large movement, with qualifications such as Master's degrees now available in 'Science Communication' as a separate subject from science.

The Science Communication movement has long recognised that educating the public does not only flow in one direction from expert to public, but benefits both parties more if there is a two-way interaction. This is not only because people are more likely to learn when they feel engaged, but because scientists themselves can benefit from listening to the public about the issues they deem important, gleaning research ideas and new insights, and even getting direct help with gathering and interpreting data. Science Communication has come up with many innovative ideas for engaging with the public, and scientists who take part often report that they benefited from the experience immensely.[28]

Similarly, a key role for Public Interest Economists is to support the development of a culture of Citizen Economics by actively educating, engaging with and listening to the public. This might entail universities running evening courses, and broadcasters producing more educational economics programming and more accessible analysis of economic news. If universities ran crash-course style workshops nationally, they could quite quickly develop large numbers of Citizen Economists and possibly recruit some of them into academia, policy-making and economic journalism to widen the diversity and perspectives of economic experts. In a challenge to those who believe that this is idealistic, there is the story of Alan Kirman, a highly respected economist who has published in top-ranked economic journals; he was originally a geography teacher and only entered the profession after first taking courses at his local Workers Education Association.

Public Interest Economics could also be a core part of the economics syllabus, with students actively engaging with non-economists as part of their course, perhaps working with local community groups or participating in local economic debates. It is entirely feasible that universities could have modules entirely devoted to Public Interest Economics and Economics Communication, and posts for Public Interest Economists. Economists could sign up to become Public Interest Economists, and take part in the various initiatives that are in development to help engage the public. Of course, such a possibility would have to be allowed for by institutional change to combat the pressures of the 'publish or perish' culture dominant in universities today.

The key to Public Interest Economics is that the economist is always explicit about the theory behind their argument, when others disagree with their position, the limits and uncertainty of their empirical knowledge and their values and assumptions. By doing this, they fundamentally transform the relationship between citizen and expert. Instead of saying 'this is how the economy works', they are saying 'this is how I believe the economy works, others disagree with this for reason X, it's difficult to prove empirically and my argument rests on the belief that humans behave in this way'.

Public Interest Economics is already practised by some journalists and academics who communicate economics in an accessible, jargon-free manner and are transparent about their own opinions and perspectives.[29] However, in order to embed Public Interest Economics as a thriving culture within the discipline it is necessary to develop institutions that support academic economists in engaging with the public and ensuring that undergraduate courses provide a pluralist, liberal education. In the UK, about £4 billion of public money is spent on higher education every year, and tuition fees, which are publicly backed by the student loan system, are also a significant part of university income.[30] As UK taxpayers, we fund academic economics and have the right as a society to demand something in return. We should demand Public Interest Economics.

It is important to remember that Public Interest Economics is not a panacea. The 'public interest' is an ideal that is often neglected and sometimes used as justification for great injustices. The quest for a single, united 'public interest' is illusory as there are in fact many public interests which must be made explicit and discussed openly – the public interest is about a transparent process and being clear about conflicting interests rather than the pursuit of any particular goals. We would not want to set public economists up as bastions of truth; only as competent economists with explicit social obligations, an explicit ethical framework, transparent and democratic working interests and socially aware research topics. Public Interest Economists must be aware of their own biases and the limitations of economics itself.

Unlearning economics and relearning democracy

In this book we have highlighted the perils of leaving economics to the experts. In econocracies economics has become so important that citizens must be able to engage with it critically in order to scrutinise the actions of decision makers and articulate their own political views. However, there is a risk that in the process of arguing this we fetishize the economy even further and entrench econocracy. We have tried to challenge the idea that 'the economy' is a separate sphere from politics and society, and that there is only one way of approaching economic problems. However, escaping the ways of thinking that result from the intensive societal focus on the economy – as well as the further limitations that are imposed by an economics education – are difficult tasks.

Counterintuitively, the point of citizens learning economics might be so that they can articulate clearly in which decisions and spheres of life economic values and ways of thinking aren't appropriate. It is important that citizens are able to participate in economic debate because it is natural that experts are trained to see every issue as an economic one. Here we use two contemporary examples to highlight the importance of unlearning the economic ways of thinking that now dominate our political decisions.

The 2014 Scottish independence referendum debate centred on economic issues, with the 'No' campaign especially making an economic case against independence. It claimed that an independent Scotland would lose the pound and EU membership, that key businesses would move to England and that it would be unable to fund public expenditure without raising taxes significantly. A post-referendum poll asked respondents to name two or three of the most important issues in the referendum and among those who voted 'No' economic issues were all important: 57 per cent listed the pound, the highest of any of the categories, 21 per cent jobs and 32 per cent tax and public spending.[31]

As we saw in Chapter 1, political debate in the run up to the June 2016 EU referendum was also monopolised by economic issues. A focus on economic issues in these debates is clearly important and in many ways our main aim in this book has been to point out that these debates should be more inclusive and accessible.

That being said, the focus on economics has drowned out many non-economic arguments that are also important. As a member of Rethinking Economics has recently argued:

> the founding treaties of the EU declare its intention to create 'a society in which pluralism, non-discrimination, tolerance, justice, solidarity and equality between women and men prevail'. These words are not empty, as the EU has definitive mechanisms for bringing such a society about. For a country to become a member, it must have a stable democracy (including media freedom and an independent judiciary), the rule of law, respect for human rights and the abolition of the death penalty.[32]

Turning away from econocracy and relearning democracy requires rediscovering the importance of a wide range of non-economic values and ways of thinking.

The way forward

As we demonstrated in Chapter 1, politics is increasingly framed in terms of economics in a way that excludes the public and damages democratic culture and process. Trying to make democracy more meaningful, in either the thin or broad senses outlined earlier, will clearly necessitate democratising economics.

The first response by many to our calls for a Citizen Economics will be that most people are not interested in understanding economics, as if this state of affairs justifies the delegation of decision-making authority to economic experts. When economics is conducted in technical language and marketed as 'the dismal science', it is unsurprising that people are put off and intimidated by it. Despite this, our YouGov poll and public education activities show that people realise how important economics is to them and want to understand it better, and just need the time and support to do so.

The most obvious way to start breaking down the trepidation that many feel when talking about economics would be to start teaching economics in schools. Currently, our society marginalises attempts to promote the formation of active citizenship from a young age; subjects such as citizenship are often not taught or when they are, they are often not viewed as adequate qualifications for gaining entry to university. Workshops and courses could also be run for adults in community centres and universities, and through civil society and religious groups, addressing economic issues that are relevant locally and giving people the substantive economic literacy necessary to engage with economic discourse.

The second key shift needed for thin democracy to function is the regular provision of accessible and jargon-free analysis of economic arguments and narratives. This is a public good that must be accessible to every citizen and provided in newspapers and on the internet, television and radio. It should follow public interest principles by being explicit about the values and assumptions of viewpoints and the limits of what is currently known. It should also highlight where arguments are contested and where there are alternatives to particular decisions and policies in order to prevent situations in which there only appears to be one option on the table. The core of thin democracy is the ability to make informed choices and for this to be possible citizens must have substantive economic literacy.

As part of a move towards broad democracy we also need to discuss what we consider economic success to look like and how to measure it. Our YouGov poll suggests that when presented with alternative ways of measuring economic success, GDP, even with its almost complete dominance in politics and the media, is not considered the most desirable gauge by the general public. We asked respondents what two measures should be used to assess the effectiveness of government economic policies: 36 per cent favoured measures that tried to capture quality of life, 26 per cent favoured GDP and 25 per cent favoured measures of income distribution and inequality. We do not claim that our evidence is overwhelming, but it does show that we might collectively choose to base our economic policy on something else if only we could have a public discussion about it.

We have developed two ideas for institutions that could catalyse preliminary steps towards broader democracy, although we wish to stress that they are simply sketches, not fully developed plans. More importantly, we believe that any transition to broad democracy will not be the result of a blueprint set out on paper, but of a broad alliance of individuals, communities, experts and the state developing practical experiments and learning through experience the skills and values of broad democracy.

First, lay councils could be set up in both the Treasury and the Bank of England to scrutinise their decisions and policies. Like jury service, people would be paid to be on the lay council for a certain period of time. Policymakers would then have to explain and justify key decisions, such as whether or not the Monetary Policy Committee should raise interest rates, to these councils. The councils would not have the power of veto but would scrutinise and give feedback on policy proposals. Policymakers could be given a statutory duty to take feedback into account.

The need to explain such decisions would ensure that they are put forward in a language that ordinary people can understand, and this would mean that the lay council would then be able to give critical feedback and would be tasked with communicating the process to the general public. The benefits of the scheme would be to open up decision-making processes previously hidden behind closed doors and the promotion of a culture of public engagement with economic policymaking. If a policy were explained to the lay council and severely criticised by all involved, but then implemented anyway, it would directly suggest that public opinion was being overlooked.

Secondly, a national network of Citizens' Policy Groups at universities across the UK could be set up. Organising these groups could be part of the public mission of universities. Each group would consist of a representative cross-section of the local community, and groups would last for a year, with members being reimbursed expenses for their time. While not compulsory the scheme would need to be 'opt-out' to prevent it being dominated solely by those who have a pre-existing interest in politics and economics. The groups could be held regularly, reviewing policy areas identified as particularly important, challenging or controversial. Education would need to be provided on these topics before the group went out to gather information and develop their own ideas, before finally reporting back to the relevant parts of local and central government and publishing their reports on a website. Policy areas could range from issues such as health and education to competition and monetary policy or how to measure economic success.

Citizens' Policy Groups could provide a mechanism for people from all walks of life to have a much more active role in economic and political discussion, with substantial input into the development of government policy.[33] These groups would probably be more effective if they focused on broader principles and innovative ideas rather than highly technical policy areas – though it is essential they are not dumbed down. The key test would be whether these reports were actually fed into decision making in a meaningful way or whether they ended up gathering dust on some shelf in Whitehall.

These are just two ideas. They are a challenge to everyone to think creatively about how we could create a set of participatory democratic institutions that would enable much wider sectors of the population to be involved in political and economic discussion and debate. Ultimately, the authors of this book could sit in a room and come up with ideas all day long, but we need people with energy, determination and intelligence to take ideas like these and run with them. It is social innovation of the most urgent kind.

Economics is for everyone

The writing of this book has its origins in a campaign to reform the economics syllabus at the University of Manchester. Its finale has included suggestions for reconstructing some of our society's most powerful institutions. We understand that we may seem to have overstepped our brief. However, we hope that in this book we have demonstrated that how economic experts are trained should be the concern of everyone in society.

We know it is tempting to leave economics to the experts, particularly as this is part of the dominant political culture of the twentieth century, but in this case we cannot afford to. We are being sold short because the very knowledge and skills we need to address the great challenges humanity faces in the twenty-first century have been systematically left out of the education of those who go on to run our economy. We have shown that as a society this binds us in a mental straitjacket that prevents us imagining the economy in any other way. This in turn precludes any real discussions about what our collective values are, how we wish to organise the economy and how we should address the challenges we face. We must reform economics so that the next generation of economic experts have the skills needed to reinvigorate economics and to build a society in which economics is a dialogue people actively take part in.

The aim of the student movement, which this book has summarised, is to create spaces in which we can individually and collectively begin to rethink economics. In time we hope these spaces will become concrete institutions which enable mass participation in economic discussion and decision making. Ultimately we believe that economics must become a public dialogue and never again be left only to the experts.

Notes

1 Michel Callon, 'The democratization of democracy', in Michel Callon, Pierre Lascoumbes and Yannick Barthe, *Acting in an Uncertain World: An Essay on Technical Democracy*, Cambridge, MA: MIT Press, 2009, 227.

2 Ha-Joon Chang, *Economics: A Users Guide*, London: Penguin, 2014, 163.

3 See Joseph Schumpeter, *Capitalism, Socialism and Democracy*, New York: Harper & Brothers, 1942.

4 Aristotle, *The Politics*, London: Penguin, 1992, 1253a1–18.

5 Friedrich A. Hayek, 'The use of knowledge in society', *American Economic Review* 35(4) (1945): 519–30.

6 Adair Turner has made a similar argument, though we each arrived at it independently. Adair Turner, *Between Debt and the Devil*, Oxford: Princeton University Press, 2015.

7 James C. Scott, *Seeing Like a State: How Certain Schemes to Improve the Human Condition Have Failed*, New Haven, CT: Yale University Press, 1999.

8 See http://www.ecnmy.org/

9 In this distinction we draw on the educational theory and practice of Paulo Freire. See, for example, Paulo Freire, *Education: The Practice of Freedom*, London: Writers and Readers Publishing Cooperative, 1976.

10 Joan Robinson, *Marx, Marshall and Keynes*, Delhi: University of Delhi, 1955, 75.

11 Emily Flitter, Christina Cook and Pedro Da Costa, 'Special report: for some professors, disclosure is academic', *Reuters,* 20 December 2010. Available at: http://www.reuters.com/article/2010/12/20/us-academics-conflicts-idUSTRE6BJ3LF20101220 (accessed 21 April 2016).

12 Jessica Carrick-Hagenbath and Gerald Epstein, 'Dangerous interconnectedness: economists' conflicts of interest, ideology and financial crisis', *Cambridge Journal of Economics* 36 (January 2012): 43–63.

13 Charles Ferguson, 'Heist of the century: university corruption and the financial crisis', *The Guardian*, 21 May 2012. Available at: http://

www.theguardian.com/education/2012/may/21/heist-century-university-corruption (accessed 21 April 2016).

14 The American Economic Association released a code of ethics in 2009 (https://www.aeaweb.org/PDF_files/PR/AEA_Adopts_Extensions_ to_Principles_for_Author_Disclosure_01-05-12.pdf) which focuses on economists disclosing information about their sources of funding. It stops short of an explicit code of conduct in research practice, and does not include any call for economists to be explicit about their approach, values and the limits of their knowledge. For an attempt to develop a more comprehensive code of ethics for economists, see Sheila Dow, 'Codes of ethics for economists: a pluralist view', *Economic Thought* 2(1) (2013): 20–9.

15 Steven D. Levitt and Stephen J. Dubner, *Freakonomics: A Rogue Economist Explores the Hidden Side of Everything*, London: Penguin, 2007, ix.

16 Ibid., 20.

17 For a critique of this approach to human behaviour, see Jonathan Aldred, *The Skeptical Economist: Revealing the Ethics Inside Economics*, London: Earthscan, 2009; and Ben Fine and Dimitris Milonakis, *From Economics Imperialism to Freakonomics: The Shifting Boundaries between Economics and Other Social Sciences*, London: Routledge, 2009.

18 MSNBC, 'Thomas Piketty, Paul Krugman and Joseph Stiglitz: the genius of economics', YouTube, March 2015. Available at: https://www.youtube.com/watch?v=Si4iyyJDa7c (accessed 21 April 2016). It might be argued that given the faith placed in economic expertise, if these economists suddenly expressed doubts about their position it would be seen to undermine their credibility. Although unfortunate, this is a symptom of the problems we have outlined and must be overcome if economists are going to engage in open democratic debate.

19 Dani Rodrik, *Economics Rules: The Rights and Wrongs of the Dismal Science*, New York: W. W. Norton, 2015, 196–207.

20 Ibid., 214–15.

21 Victoria Bateman, 'Is economics a sexist science?', *Times Higher Education*, 15 September 2015. Available at: https://www.timeshighereducation.com/blog/is-economics-a-sexist-science (accessed 25 April 2016).

22 *Equality in Higher Education: Statistical Report 2013 Part 2: Students*, Equality Challenge Unit, November 2013, 31.

23 Laura Blanco and Karen Mumford, *Royal Economic Society Women's Committee Survey on the Gender and Ethnic Balance of Academic Economics 2010*, report, Royal Economics Society, October 2010, 20. Available at: http://www.res.org.uk/SpringboardWebApp/userfiles/res/file /Womens%20Committee/Biennial%20Report/Womens%20Committee %202010%20survey%20report%202010.pdf (accessed 25 April 2016).

24 See www.res.org.uk/view/publicationsWomensComm.html

25 The Bureau of Investigative Journalism, 'About the Bureau'. Available at: https://www.thebureauinvestigates.com/who/ (accessed 21 April 2016).
26 Edward Said, *Representations of the Intellectual: The 1993 Reith Lectures*, London: Vintage, 1994, 11.
27 It should be noted that if this were not the case and Parliament were free to revoke independence, then making central banks independent would have no effect at all as people would just expect Parliament to revoke this at any time.
28 See Robert A. Logan, 'Science mass communication: its conceptual history', *Science Communication* 23(2) (2001): 135–63; and Michael F. Weigold, 'Communicating science: a review of the literature', *Science Communication* 23(2) (2001): 164–93.
29 Examples include Simon Wren-Lewis, Ha-Joon Chang and Andy Haldane, all of whom we applaud for trying to engage with a wider audience
30 Higher Education Funding Council England, *Guide to Funding 2015–16: How HEFCE Allocates its Funds*, report, March 2015, 4–16.
31 'Scottish independence: poll reveals who voted, how and why', *The Guardian*, 20 September 2014. Available at: http://www.theguardian.com/politics/2014/sep/20/scottish-independence-lord-ashcroft-poll (accessed 25 April 2016).
32 Rafe Martyn, 'Beyond the economic: the true value of Europe', The Disraeli Room, Respublica, 23 March 2016. Available at: http://www.respublica.org.uk/disraeli-room-post/2016/03/23/beyond-economic-true-value-europe/ (accessed 25 April 2016).
33 Excitingly the RSA (The Royal Society for the Encouragement of Arts, Manufactures and Commerce) has come to a similar conclusion and is launching the Citizens' Economic Council Project. Matthew Taylor, 'The human welfare economy', Chief Executive's Lecture, RSA, July 2015. Available at: https://www.thersa.org/action-and-research/arc-news/chief-executives-lecture-2015-news/ (accessed 25 April 2016).

Appendix I
Technical appendix to curriculum review

This appendix is intended to set out a further critique of economics education for those who either remain to be convinced or who are simply interested in the field. It discusses our view of maths in economics, new developments in economics (in particular, behavioural economics) and econometrics. It is labelled as a 'technical' appendix because it zooms in more on the details, though we feel we have conveyed the most crucial ones in the main text. However, it is not especially mathematical or jargon filled and is still written with the lay reader in mind.

Economics doesn't add up

One of the first responses we hear to our criticisms is that we are anti-maths and anti-modelling. On the contrary, we are not against maths itself, but against the uncritical and unquestioning use of a particular type of maths and the relative denigration of qualitative argument and evidence. We believe that multiple types of maths – including those not currently taught in economics – as well as non-mathematical tools are vital to the study of economics.

In contrast, economists often seem to view their approach to modelling as the inevitable starting point of economic inquiry. When the economist Diane Coyle was presented with our figures for operating a model, she responded:

> I passionately defend modelling because I think that is just intellectual enquiry; historians model, they just don't call it that. If they're trying to think about the causes of the First World War they'll have a limited number of variables and they'll try to collect evidence about which ones are more important and which ones are less important. So we all do modelling and that's just a way of talking about how do you make sense of a very complicated and dynamic world.

There may be some truth in this statement but it conflates mathematical modelling with the more general idea of building arguments and theories. There is no reason to believe that the social world conforms to the kind of regularities necessitated by mathematical modelling. To say that the First World War was caused by Franz Ferdinand's assassination plus Britain's need for economic power times Russia's rivalry with Austria is virtually meaningless, since these things do not have quantifiable units and do not have a simple mechanical relationship with one another. Another example might be the focus within labour economics on wages and productivity, rather than aspects of work that are harder to quantify such as job satisfaction. To satisfy the fixation on maths and equations, economic models may have to leave important details behind, sometimes oversimplifying to the point of uselessness compared to the complexities that can be detailed by written argument.

Despite this, the subject nature of economics can clearly benefit from quantitative analysis and mathematical modelling, and the question is to which kinds of mathematics students should be introduced. We believe that the current focus on constrained maximisation – a mathematical technique that is used to represent the optimising individuals discussed in Chapter 2 – is necessarily limited and can be improved upon. A particular problem is that it is often static, dealing with either equilibrium points or a series of equilibrium points, when real economic issues are often dynamic, i.e. there are changes over time. We would therefore encourage economics departments to collaborate with mathematics departments to teach ordinary differential equations so that students can gain a better understanding of dynamic systems.[1]

Some economics students get a glimpse of this type of mathematics, but it is typically focused on the equilibrium the economy will (supposedly) eventually settle at over analysing immediate dynamics, and remains far more basic than the kind of mathematics taught in other complex sciences such as meteorology or chaos theory.[2] Economics students could also be taught basic programming packages such as MATLAB – as mathematics and engineering students currently are – or the programming techniques used in Agent-Based Computational Economics (ABM).[3] The result of all this would be that students would be able to work with, or at least prepare for, various comprehensive dynamic models that currently lie outside neoclassical economics.[4]

New vogues, same problems

A common rebuttal to criticisms such as ours is that the discipline is already in the process of changing, and that integrating these changes into the curriculum will be enough to answer our concerns. Some currently 'in-vogue' areas of economics include new institutional economics, the modern empirical 'credibility revolution' of Joshua Angrist and Stephen Pischke,[5] and behavioural economics. We do not have the space to comment on every one of these here, but we would like to illustrate that there is no reason to believe they will serve as a panacea for the discipline. To demonstrate this we will use the example of behavioural economics.

Behavioural economics investigates the biases ingrained into human reasoning which may contradict the behaviour of the super-rational *homo economicus*. The field is increasingly popular and, as we saw in Chapter 1 with the 'Nudge Unit', has made its way into politics. However, behavioural economics cannot solve the problems we outlined in Chapter 2 as it teaches students to approach economic problems from a particular, incomplete perspective. One policy-related idea from behavioural economics is that by studying individual behaviour 'as it is', we can recognise the biases people have in decision making and governments can then design policy to correct for these biases. Yet as economists George Loewenstein and Peter Ubel have argued, this can lead to a focus on the consumer as the solution to problems such as excessive energy usage or obesity, problems that have systemic origins (e.g. unhealthy food being cheaper) that are bigger than consumer biases.[6] Furthermore, it completely excludes the biases of other decision makers: firms, governments and even economists themselves are surely just as likely to suffer from these 'irrational' biases.

Our curriculum review supports the hypothesis that students are encouraged to think through problems almost exclusively from the perspective of the consumer's biases. Two of the behavioural economics exams we had available (from LSE and Glasgow) were both close to completely model based (95 per cent of marks were for operating a model, on average). Questions typically ask students to solve 'toy' examples where some bias is present and the standard utility-maximising framework must be adjusted to account for this. As Exhibit A illustrates, the focus is on solving yet another mathematical problem over the critical evaluation and application of key ideas, something the reader may recognise as remarkably similar to the macro and micro examples in Chapter 2. This particular example

Exhibit A Example of an 'operate a model' question from a behavioural economics exam

---

5. Consider an agent who may pre-order snacks online for delivery the following day. Snacks spoil and may therefore not be saved. Denote the agent's current hunger state by $h_t \in \{0,1\}$. Denote the quality of the snacks by b_t. If the agent consumes snacks in period t, he derives utility $b_t(1 + h_t)$ in period t, but bears a cost of d utils in the subsequent period. Not consuming snacks yields zero utility.

(a) [21 marks] Assume in this part that the agent does not discount the future, but exhibits simple projection bias of degree $\propto$ over his hunger state. Assume that hunger is drawn from an i.i.d. Bernoulli distribution, with $\Pr(h_t = 10 = \theta)$ for all t. The quality of snacks is unknown at the time of ordering, but is drawn from an i.i.d uniform distribution over the interval [0,8]. The future cost of consumption is always $d = 4$.

   (i) What is the expected utility in period 1 if the agent has already ordered a snack, and is hungry ($h_1 = 1$)? Note that the agent may choose not to consume the snack.

   (ii) What does a (partially) projection-biased agent predict is the expected utility of ordering a snack if he is hungry ($h_1 = 1$), as a function of his current state h_0?

   (iii) What is the maximum price that a (partially) projection-biased agent would pay to pre-order snacks for period 1, as a function of his current state h_0? Interpret the sign of the derivative of this WTP with respect to h_0?

   (iv) Suppose now that an economist observes data on a sample of consumers' period-0 and period-1 choices and hunger states. Explain intuitively how she could test for projection bias in her data.

   (v) How does your answer to part (iv) relate to Conlin et al. (2007)'s findings on projection bias in cold-weather clothing orders?

Source: Reproduced from a 3rd year Behavioural Economics exam at LSE

is almost amusing in its banality: someone ordering themselves snacks for a later date.

It is worth asking whether this extended mathematical elaboration gives us any more insight than the simple observation it is supposed to represent. The question refers to 'projection bias', which is how people's current situation affects their predictions about their future needs. It is not difficult to describe projection bias verbally: if someone is hungry, they are more likely to purchase food they do not need. Since the qualitative prediction can be made without mathematics, the only way the mathematics would add something would be if it made a *quantitative* prediction that could be tested against the evidence. But because someone's mathematical 'hunger state' is not observable in the real world, the model cannot be applied directly to empirical evidence. Consequently, the brief reference to evidence at the bottom is only stylised, making no use of the quantitative predictions of the model in the question and introducing a scenario that is only *intuitively* similar: how the weather affects people's likelihood of returning catalogue orders.[7] Despite an outward appearance of rigour, the relationship of this example to reality is wobbly and tenuous.

Within our curriculum review, there was one behavioural economics module that required much more independent judgement (at Exeter). Such instances should be applauded for at least requiring economics students to scrutinise the assumptions of neoclassical economics and apply independent judgement. However, behavioural economics retains many of the same methodological features as standard economic theory, and so critical evaluation in modules like the one at Exeter is still limited in scope.

Let us explain. Having modelled 'rational' behaviour mathematically, behavioural economics is an attempt to model 'irrational' behaviour using similar techniques. But this raises two problems. First, documenting each bias in separate, often artificial laboratory situations – both empirically and theoretically – leads to a situation where we have a theory for every possible bias – the LSE exam quoted above has seven different biases in eight questions – but no way of telling which theory to use and when. In other words, the bias-driven approach often does not give us a clearer method for *predicting* consumer behaviour, only one for rationalising it after it has occurred. For this reason it has been argued by multiple authors that behavioural economics simply contains too many models, without clear empirical and logical reasons for choosing one or the other.[8]

Secondly and relatedly, the approach of drawing a line between 'rational' and 'irrational' behaviour – and treating them as separate problems – precludes the possibility of discovering some of the driving forces behind human behaviour *in general*. As evolutionary biologists have emphasised, behaviour that is 'irrational' by the standards of economic theory might be rational in the context of survival and reproduction.[9] Behaviour that has evolved as a rational response to evolution may seem irrational in contemporary times, but simply documenting this as a 'deviation' from rational behaviour fails to understand why a particular decision was made.[10] All in all, behavioural economics as taught and practised does not seem to have made much progress in uncovering the fundamental cognitive processes behind observed human behaviour.

The problems of behavioural economics are similar to the problems that occur generally when neoclassical economics tries to incorporate new ideas. The concerns of critics are said to be addressed when economists find some way of incorporating their critiques into existing frameworks. The result is often a highly stylised version of what the critic had in mind, and may drop the things that are most important while conforming to certain assumptions that the critic may reject. We saw in Chapter 4 that this happened with Keynes; we saw it above with behavioural economics; a final example is a recent paper by Paul Krugman, subtitled 'a Fisher–Minsky–Koo approach' in a clear attempt to incorporate some of the heterodox economic ideas discussed in Chapter 3.[11] However, Krugman's paper relies on equilibrium analysis, explicitly rejected by both Fisher and Minsky, and does not include endogenous money, the financial instability hypothesis, or even a real financial sector (agents simply borrow from each other in the form of riskless bonds), all of which are central to Minsky's theories. The fact that competing ideas have to be adapted into this kind of framework before they are accepted narrows the parameters of debate and the scope for progress. When there are only competing ideas but not competing frameworks, most methodological questions are taken as axiomatic and understanding is necessarily limited.

But what about econometrics?

Thus far, we have reviewed those parts of the curricula which concern economic *theory*. However, econometrics – the statistical wing of economics – is compulsory on virtually every economics course, and also constitutes much of economic research.[12] Econometrics generally seeks to uncover causal relationships between economic variables when all other things are held constant, *ceteris paribus* relationships in economic language. An example would be how an extra year of education impacts someone's wages when holding their age, gender, race and other relevant factors constant.

Due to its empirical nature – as well as a lack of strong assumptions about people's behaviour – it could be argued that econometrics as a whole fits the 'evaluate empirical evidence' category of our original curriculum review. However, we believe that such a conclusion would be misleading, as the criteria used in our review cannot describe econometrics in sufficient detail.

We have therefore devised a separate set of criteria to evaluate the 28 econometrics modules at our disposal in the hope of giving a more accurate portrayal of econometrics. We believe this mini-review shows that although econometrics focuses on empirical evidence more than most economic theory, it does not necessarily entail critical empirical evaluation. This is because empirical examples are often stylised, with most of the statistical leg work already done for the student, and the evidence presented is rarely used to test economic theory. Furthermore, econometrics classes universally fail to explore the underlying assumptions of econometrics, or to discuss alternative methods of empirical and statistical evaluation. Neither do they deal substantially with fundamental issues surrounding data collection, sampling and inference. Consequently, despite a surface appearance of empiricism, econometrics classes often have a narrow, theoretical focus.

Our review demonstrates that econometrics is overwhelmingly focused on the application of a particular statistical method known as 'linear regression': 26 out of 28 of the econometrics modules in our curriculum review had more than two-thirds of their teaching devoted to this technique. Every chapter of the popular textbook *Introductory Econometrics* by Jeffrey Wooldridge focuses on linear regression.[13] The result is that the technical details of this method – which can become quite complex – push out a focus on raw data, or broader methods that seek to make general statements about statistical populations. In fact, about a third of the available exam marks in econometrics were purely theoretical, not mentioning data at all. Of those exam questions that were not theoretical, less than 10 per cent could be considered an independent approach to an open problem, while over 90 per cent simply asked for the application of a suggested econometric method, or interpreted the results using a given econometric method (generally linear regression).

One might think that open problems are best dealt with outside the exam hall, but less than a fifth of the total marks in these modules were given for independent projects, with the average for core (compulsory) modules at only 14 per cent. What's more, this average was pushed upward by universities such as Sheffield and Exeter, which had averages of about 30 per cent, while higher ranked universities such as Manchester and LSE devoted 8 per cent and 0 per cent of marks, respectively, to independent projects. This seems to suggest that as universities have made their degrees more technically demanding, they have ejected coursework and independent work.

A worrying 11 out of 28 modules in our review had no independent projects whatsoever, and only 6 out of 28 devoted more than a third of their marks to projects. To put this in perspective through comparison with other disciplines, the average proportion of marks given for independent work in the ten 'Social Statistics' modules at the University of Manchester is 47 per cent, including a number of modules where projects and coursework make up 100 per cent of the course.[14]

It could be argued that economics has its own unique methods and approaches when compared to other social sciences, but the similarities – such as a first-hand understanding of data – are fundamental. Economic data must be gathered from people, either directly or indirectly, and social data has well-known limitations: people fail to show up in records, or drop out of repeated surveys, or samples may not be representative of the broader population. Surveys are a particularly important area in social statistics, since respondents may answer dishonestly/inaccurately, be pushed towards certain answers by the question, or simply not know the answer.

Other social sciences are well aware of these issues and devote a lot of time to them. For example, the course outlines for some of the above 'Social Statistics' modules at the University of Manchester contain aims such as 'to introduce students to the principles of collecting data, summarizing data, and interpreting data', or to 'introduce the practical issues involved in the planning and management of surveys and basic analysis of survey data', or to 'explain how the design of a sample determines whether the survey can be used to make generalizations'. In contrast, only one out of our 28 econometrics modules contains any mention of gathering, processing and interpreting social data. Yet surveys are important in economics, since they are used to calculate key statistics such as GDP.[15] According to our interview with economist David Hendry, in the past economics students studied the national accounts in detail in order to better understand macroeconomic data; these days, Nobel Laureate Robert Shiller has stated that 'there's an attitude in the profession that collecting data is for lesser people'.[16]

One positive characteristic of econometrics classes is that students are often asked to state which assumptions they are using for a particular method and how these may be inapplicable in certain situations, as did over 90 per cent of the modules in our curriculum review. However, despite being an improvement over many economic theory classes – where the list of assumptions is far longer and more obscure – the level of critical engagement here is limited.

Questions that ask students to discuss why there is a problem with the basic linear regression model and how it could be overcome typically aim to find a way to 'rescue' the model by using it in a slightly altered form,[17] and little to no discussion is devoted to when linear regression is simply inapplicable. Although linear regression is useful in many contexts, it may not be in others. The political scientist Christopher Achen has demonstrated that even slight deviations from the linear world can wildly disrupt the results of the linear regression.[18] However, there is little discussion of when linear regression is and is not applicable in econometrics classes.

Our review found that *no* econometrics classes discussed what could be called the 'underlying' assumptions of econometrics, which are separate to the more specific assumptions used for particular econometric models. One such assumption is that data can be thought of as generated by unchanging processes that can be easily characterised using probabilities. But the characteristics of data – again, especially in macroeconomics – tend to exhibit large 'shifts' through different time periods, so that the nature of something like unemployment is different from era to era, and this cannot be captured by models that impose an unchanging form upon the variables of interest.[19]

A similar problem was famously noted by Robert Lucas, who – as we saw in Chapter 4 in a slightly different context – argued that empirical estimates of econometric relationships cannot necessarily be relied upon in the future, since people will adapt their behaviour over time to changes in policy, or simply if the (loose) knowledge of the relationship becomes public.[20] Recall that Lucas used this type of reasoning to argue that workers would adapt to inflation, increasing their wage demands and therefore rendering the statistically observed inverse relationship between unemployment and inflation erroneous. Both of these problems can invalidate the type of simple, mechanistic relationships that are often estimated in econometrics.

The problem is that econometrics classes tend to assume the data satisfies the central assumptions of econometrics without exploring the empirical, practical questions of where it came from, its limitations or its general properties beforehand. The famous statistician David Freedman cautioned against this kind of unquestioned application of statistical models as a substitute for an understanding of the particular problem under investigation.[21] A contrasting approach would be to ensure that the student understood how the data had been collected and what problems this might create; then to let the data 'speak for itself', using various tests to see what type of data it is, which processes might be generating it, different subgroups and so forth, before going on to apply one of many potential methods to the problem, one of which may be linear regression.[22]

It's not that abstract theory has no place in econometrics – any branch of mathematics or statistics is fundamentally built on abstract theory. Hence we can understand optional, advanced classes named 'Econometric Theory' (LSE) for being 100 per cent theoretical. However, is it justified that another class at LSE called 'Principles of Econometrics' – which is compulsory for economics students – is 70 per cent theoretical, with no independent projects? Students who come out of this class have clearly not been given a sufficient understanding of when and why econometric techniques should be used, or how to collect and process data – and they won't necessarily get any further exposure to econometrics.

The final issue with econometrics is that, as the empirical wing of economics, it is often assumed to constitute the bulk of the empirical exposure economics students need, even though it fails at this task from a scientific standpoint. Other empirical methods such as economic history, case study methods, social network analysis, surveys and experiments typically fail to appear on curricula, and where they do they are not compulsory like econometrics. This might be understood, if not condoned, if econometrics entailed rigorous empirical testing of economic theory, but this is not the case. 70 per cent of the econometrics modules we reviewed did not contain *any* testing of economic theory, and those that did were largely concentrated in specific universities such as Sheffield and Cardiff, but missing from universities such as Manchester and LSE. Core modules fell especially short in this area, with only 1 out of 8 compulsory modules containing any testing of economic theory. This lack of any quest for empirical falsification perhaps explains the remarkable staying power of some of the economic theories on the curriculum.

Notes

1 Introducing graph theory, useful for network analysis, would also be a positive step forward.
2 See Steve Keen, *Debunking Economics: The Naked Emperor Dethroned?*, London: Zed Books, 2011, 31, for more detail
3 For an introduction to ABM, see Leigh Tesfatsion, 'Agent-based computational economics', *Scholarpedia* 2(2) (2007): 1970.
4 Steve Keen's Minsky model, the kinds of simulations suggested by evolutionary and complexity theory, and Stock Flow-Consistent models, in

the vein of Godley and Lavoie. See Steve Keen, 'Finance and economic breakdown: modeling Minsky's "Financial Instability Hypothesis"', *Journal of Post Keynesian Economics* 17(4) (1995): 607–35; Matheus Grasselli and Marcello Costa Lima, 'An analysis of the Keen model for credit expansion, asset price bubbles and financial fragility', *Mathematics and Financial Economics* 6(3) (2012): 191–210; Jason Potts, *The New Evolutionary Microeconomics: Complexity, Competence, and Adaptive Behaviour*, Cheltenham: Edward Elgar, 2000, 111–31; Wynne Godley and Marc Lavoie, *Monetary Economics: An Integrated Approach to Credit, Money, Income, Production and Wealth*, Basingstoke: Palgrave Macmillan, 2007.

5 See Joshua D. Angrist and Stephen Pischke, 'The credibility revolution in empirical economics: how better research design is taking the con out of econometrics', *Journal of Economic Perspectives* 24(2) (2010): 3–30; and Joshua D. Angrist and Stephen Pischke, *Mostly Harmless Econometrics: An Empiricist's Companion*, Princeton, NJ: Princeton University Press, 2009.

6 George Loewenstein and Peter Ubel, 'Economics behaving badly', *New York Times*, 14 July 2010. Available at: http://www.nytimes.com/2010/07/15/opinion/15loewenstein.html (accessed 21 April 2016).

7 Michael Conlin, Ted O'Donoghue and Timothy J. Vogelsang, 'Projection bias in catalog orders', *American Economic Review* 97(4) (2007): 1217–49.

8 See Drew Fudenberg, 'Advancing beyond advances in behavioral economics', *Journal of Economic Literature* 44(3) (2006): 694–711; and Jason Collins, 'Please, not another bias! The problem with behavioral economics' , *Evonomics*, 2015. Available at http://evonomics.com/please-not-another-bias-the-problem-with-behavioral-economics/ (accessed 21 April 2016).

9 David S. Wilson and John M. Gowdy, 'Evolution as a general theoretical framework for economics and public policy', *Journal of Economic Behavior & Organization* 90, Supplement (June 2013): S3–S10.

10 See Owen D. Jones, 'Time-shifted rationality and the law of law's leverage: behavioral economics meets behavioral biology', *Northwestern University Law Review* 95 (2001): 1141–206.

11 Gauti B. Eggertsson and Paul Krugman, 'Debt, deleveraging, and the liquidity trap: a Fisher–Minsky–Koo approach', *The Quarterly Journal of Economics* 127(3) (2012): 1469–513.

12 Daniel S. Hamermesh, 'Six decades of top economics publishing: who and how?', *Journal of Economic Literature* 51(1) (2013): 162–72.

13 Jeffrey M. Wooldridge, *Introductory Econometrics: A Modern Approach*, Australia: South-Western College Publishers, 2003.

14 Details available on the University of Manchester website: http://courseunits.humanities.manchester.ac.uk/Undergraduate/Social-Sciences/Social-Statistics.

15 See the ONS website for details on how GDP is calculated, http://webarchive.nationalarchives.gov.uk/20160105160709/http://www.ons.gov.uk/ons/rel/elmr/explaining-economic-statistics/understanding-gdp-and-how-it-is-measured/sty-understanding-gdp.html.

16 Jeff Sommer, 'Robert Shiller: a skeptic and a Nobel winner', *New York Times*, 19 October 2013. Available at: http://www.nytimes.com/2013/10/20/business/robert-shiller-a-skeptic-and-a-nobel-winner.html (accessed 21 April 2016).

17 Consider two-stage least squares (ultimately just two linear regressions), robust standard errors (to use the same hypothesis testing procedure) or fixed effects estimation (assuming unobservables are linear then using panel data to eliminate them from the estimated regression). A similar point was made by Aris Spanos, 'Theory testing in economics and the error-statistical perspective', in Deborah G. Mayo and Aris Spanos (eds), *Error and Inference: Recent Exchanges on Experimental Reasoning, Reliability, and the Objectivity and Rationality of Science*, Cambridge: Cambridge University Press, 202–46.

18 Christopher Achen, 'Let's put garbage-can regressions and garbage-can probits where they belong', *Conflict Management and Peace Science* 22(4) (2005): 327–39.

19 David F. Hendry and Graham E. Mizon, 'Unpredictability in economic analysis, econometric modeling and forecasting', *Journal of Econometrics* 182(1) (2014): 186–95.

20 This does not mean that we agree with Lucas's argument that this means only models with microfoundations in economics should be valued. See Robert Lucas, 'Econometric policy evaluation: a critique', in Karl Brunner and Allan Meltzer (eds), *The Phillips Curve and Labor Markets*, New York: North Holland, 1976, 19–46.

21 For a critique of an approach too centred on statistical modelling, see: David A. Freedman, 'Statistical models and shoe leather', *Sociological Methodology* 21 (1991): 291–313. See also Leo Breiman, 'Statistical modeling: the two cultures (with comments and a rejoinder by the author)', *Statistical Science* 16(3) (2001): 199–231.

22 For an example of this, see the following which investigates food security and climate change using 11 different statistical techniques, including linear regression, and tests their predictive accuracy against one another to determine which one(s) are the most appropriate. Julie E. Shortridge, Stefanie M. Falconi, Benjamin F. Zaitchik and Seth D. Guikema, 'Climate, agriculture, and hunger: statistical prediction of undernourishment using nonlinear regression and data-mining techniques', *Journal of Applied Statistics* 42(11) (2015): 2367–90.

Appendix 2

Curriculum review methodology

Overview

The curriculum review analysed 174 economics modules at seven Russell Group universities: Cambridge University, University of Sheffield, Queen's University Belfast, University of Manchester, London School of Economics, University of Glasgow and University of Exeter. It drew on two sources – module course outlines and past exam papers – in an attempt to identify empirically the content and style of undergraduate economics education in the United Kingdom.

The bulk of the research for the curriculum review was carried out in the 2014/15 academic year. We approached 16 universities to ask if they would share their course outlines and past papers with us. Most said no, with only Queen's University Belfast, Oxford and Cardiff saying yes (the last two were not included in the review since we received them too far into the process). This meant that most of the materials for the curriculum review were gathered by supportive students who were studying economics at the universities analysed and the whole process was significantly more time consuming than we had expected. As a result, our sample consists of universities for which we could obtain data, rather than a random sample or representative sample. If, as we argue in this book, the state of academic economics is of public interest then there should be more openness and transparency around what economics students are taught in publicly funded universities in the UK today, and universities should make many of these materials publicly available.

All course outlines in our sample were for the 2014/15 academic year. Exams in our sample were predominantly made up of final examinations for the 2013/14 academic year or sample papers provided to students. In very few instances papers from earlier years were used, as far back as the 2008/09 academic year. However, such papers had always been provided to students for exam practice, suggesting that they were still broadly similar to the final examinations that students would take. For logistical reasons, we generally could not gather mid-terms and coursework in a systematic way. In the few instances when mid-terms could be obtained but final examinations could not, the mid-terms were used as a proxy for the final exams.

Course outlines

While the nature and comprehensiveness of course outlines varied considerably between universities, we used them to collate our data on which textbooks were used, which theories and models were taught and whether non-neoclassical perspectives were mentioned. We also used the course outlines to identify how much of each module's assessment was made up of the final exam so that we could identify how much we were missing by not analysing mid-terms and coursework.

Exam past papers

Of the 174 modules we studied we were able to analyse past papers for 156. This is because some courses are 100 per cent coursework-based, but also because others could not be obtained. There is no reason to believe that the exams we could not collect would have had a particular effect on our results. While an academic from outside economics might assume that if coursework and mid-term exams were added to our results they would improve significantly, our analysis of course outlines and anecdotal evidence from economics students across the UK suggests that these parts of assessment are dominated by multiple choice and assessed problem sets that leave much to be desired. Furthermore, on average at the universities studied, final exams constitute 81 per cent of all assessment and so we are analysing the vast bulk of assessment.

We devised a methodology to understand what knowledge and skills economics education requires students to have in order to graduate and become a qualified economist. We are fully aware that, as with almost any research exercise, judgement is involved in selecting what to measure and carrying out the analysis, and we do not try to hide that. No doubt somebody else could design a curriculum review that arrived at different numbers (though we doubt anyone would conclude that economics education is highly critical and empirical). Our aim here is to state transparently the judgements and assumptions we made, demonstrate why they are reasonable and point out the limitations of our research.

We developed four categories so that we could allocate each exam question into a category and come up with a total for each module, particular groups of modules like macro and micro, universities and the whole sample. These four categories are:

1) **Operate a model:** Operate a model questions ask students to focus on a particular economic model and to perform some task with it. It entails no evaluation of whether the model is appropriate nor its strengths or weaknesses. Such questions can be graphical, mathematical (game theory, constrained optimisation) or even, in some instances, descriptive. Different kind of operate a model questions include:

   a) State and explain a model's assumptions (no indication that this should be done critically, otherwise marked as evaluative).
   b) Derive and describe a model – draw graphs, solve equations, explain the theory, e.g. 'In the Diamond-Dybvig model, explain whether the same outcomes for consumption can be achieved by replacing banks with financial markets in which investment projects can be traded.'
   c) Manipulate a model: once derived, show how something works within the model, e.g. 'Suppose there is VAT i.e. t>0. Show that the results you have derived in part (d) might not hold here. Explain your answer.'
   d) Operate a model to explain a real-world event – a question that asks students to relate the model to the real world, e.g. 'How can the IS/LM model explain the 2008 financial crisis?'
   e) Mathematical computation: questions that were purely mathematical were also classified as operate a model. Sometimes mathematical questions are not related directly to a model; however, the key criterion in operate a model questions is that the student simply works through maths without evaluating it, which also applies to mathematical questions.

2) **Describe questions:** Describe questions simply ask students to write down something from memory. Crucially, describe questions require no form of independent judgement. Describe questions can ask students to describe:

   a) A policy, institution or event, e.g. 'What happened to stock prices during December 2008?', 'What is a fully funded social security system?'
   b) An argument, e.g. 'Describe Larry Summer's theory of secular stagnation', 'Give three reasons why a higher labour income tax may lead to a lower level of GDP growth?'

c) A theory, e.g. 'What is the Friedman rule?', 'Explain the Marshall Lemer Conditions', 'Explain the characteristics of an optimal currency area.'

d) A methodology: common in economic policy analysis module questions, these simply ask students to describe the processes needed to get a particular finding, e.g. 'How did David Card's paper "The impact of the Mariel Boatlift on the Miami Labour Market" go about showing the effects of immigration on wages?'

3) **Evaluative questions:** Evaluation requires some form of independent judgement. For a student to make an independent judgement there must be more than one possible answer or at the very least not a strictly defined 'right' answer. Evaluation questions can include:

a) Evaluate a policy or event, e.g. 'What were the key causes of the 2008 financial crisis?'

b) Evaluate a theory or model, e.g. 'How useful is the Solow Growth Model in understanding long-term economic growth in the United Kingdom?'

c) Evaluate an argument, e.g. 'For the two and a half decades since 1980, unemployment has been systematically higher in Europe than the United States because Europe has continued to have stronger employment protection and more generous unemployment insurance than the United States. Discuss.'

d) Evaluate one theory or model against another, e.g. 'Which better explains the nature of the 2008 financial crisis, Real Business Cycle Theory or New Keynesian models?'

e) Evaluate methodology, e.g. 'How useful do you think regression discontinuity designs have been in investigating the effect of education on wages?'

4) **Multiple choice:** This kind of question is self-explanatory and easy to identify.

Weighting

Each exam question was assessed in turn to see which of our categories it best fitted into. If exam questions seemed to fit multiple categories, the marks were split evenly between these categories. An example of a half-description, half-evaluation question from the review is 'Describe how a researcher would carry out the contingent valuation method in the context of a proposed woodland restoration project. Provide examples of the types of valuation questions used and discuss their advantages/disadvantages in your answer.'

If the questions were clearly designated as having more marks for one part than the other then it was split ¾ to ¼ e.g. 'Derive the Solow growth model and briefly comment on its applicability.'

Aggregating and reporting results

For individual exams, the percentage of each category was calculated by seeing what proportion of *total marks within the exam paper* were assigned to that category. For example, if a paper had section A worth 50 per cent of the paper with one 50-mark question, and section B was worth 50 per cent and had two questions that students had to choose between, each worth 50 marks, then the total marks for that paper would have been out of 150. If question A was fully 'operate a model' and both question Bs were fully 'evaluative', then the score for that exam would be 1/3 operate a model, 2/3 evaluation.

To get aggregated scores for each university, the results for each individual module were multiplied by a weight relating to the credits (or percentage of the year) that they were worth. To aggregate results for all universities combined, each university's scores for each category were summed and then divided by the number of universities.

In Chapter 2 we presented the results for all exams and core micro and macro modules. Core macro and micro exams were classified as microeconomic and macroeconomic exams that were compulsory for the universities' single honours economics course (BSc, or if this was not available BA). So for example, Advanced Macro at Glasgow in Year 3 was not included because not every student has to take it. In most cases, such categorisation was self-explanatory; courses are typically called Microeconomic I, Macroeconomics II etc. In some instances, discretion was used to determine that a module was actually a core macro/micro exam. For example, at Sheffield, in the first year students take the modules Economic Policy 1 and 2, the content of which is clearly the same as macroeconomic and microeconomic courses at other universities. In the instance of QUB, where modules focus on more specific topics (e.g. Economic Growth Theory, Game Theory with Economic Applications) it was decided there was not a clear core/macro syllabus and so they were not included in these figures.

Challenges

The major challenge of the curriculum review lay in the fact that without the mark schemes we (like the students sitting the exams) had to go with what the question asked and this meant that the boundaries between different categories were not always clear. However, in some cases fuzziness was more problematic than others. For example, the boundaries between 'describe a theory' and 'operate a model' can overlap, but this is less relevant to our overall findings because both test technical knowledge and the skills of memorisation and regurgitation of that knowledge rather than independent or critical judgement.

More importantly, it was sometimes hard to tell whether a question was asking the student to evaluate something by making an independent judgement or they were just being asked to reel off something from the lecture notes/slides. Likewise, it is difficult to tell whether the student is actually able to argue a point and come to an independent judgement or whether the question has a single right answer that precludes the possibility of independent judgement. For example, in the exam we analysed for the third year course International Trade at Sheffield (where a mark scheme was included), Question 1C read 'Use your knowledge about trade policy to evaluate the following statement: "tariffs have a more negative effect on welfare in large countries than in small countries."' This question seems a perfect example of critical evaluation, but in the mark scheme it actually says that the answer is categorically 'False', with a set answer required that simply used standard neoclassical models.

Our response to such ambiguity was to give the benefit of the doubt if a question seemed as if it could possibly be evaluative. This includes questions that form the final sub-part of an 'operate a model'-style question and raise queries such as 'name one drawback of the model' for very few marks. From the experience of the authors, our peers and students throughout the movement it is likely that these questions are asking students to remember a one-line answer from the lecture notes and that the marks given do not allow real independent judgement. However, we have defined them as evaluative regardless.

We gathered all the data for the percentage of 'operate a model' questions that made a link to the real world and found that the results were very low, supporting our claim that economics education is abstract and disconnected. Again there was a challenge in defining what constitutes the 'real world'. Does an operate a model question relate to the real world if it simply mentions income, tax or the NHS? What about if it uses real-world data or reports real-world empirical trends? Or does it only count if the student is required to demonstrate substantive knowledge of the real world (and if that was the case how would we know that was a requirement)? Our criterion was that the question had to indicate that it required some kind of real-world knowledge in order to be answered. On this criterion a model that uses data from the real world doesn't count because it doesn't require the student to know anything, while using a model to explain or evaluate some real-world event or trend does count because the student has to bring in their own knowledge to answer the question.

Criticisms of this review could focus either on how the categories have been defined (e.g. that the evaluate criterion is too demanding or weak) or the challenges of applying them consistently and rigorously. We fully acknowledge that there are reasonable arguments for defining categories differently that would give different results. The more interesting question regards the issue of application. Throughout this process we have been aware of the role of judgement in the review and have taken steps to ensure that our process is rigorous while recognising that it isn't objective. In our experience, the process was not so precise that different people would find exactly the same result every time. However, the curriculum review was always conducted by one member of the team and then again by another, to make sure that results were within 5 per cent. We therefore want to be clear that the process was precise enough to support the inferences we have drawn.

We would welcome further research on economics education from any interested parties and would be happy to discuss the pros and cons of our methodology further.

Econometrics review

The econometrics curriculum review was carried out based on different criteria to the other economics modules, simply because the original criteria did not fit. It included econometrics modules from the original sample of seven universities plus two econometrics modules from Cardiff University which were available because the econometrics review was done at a later date. Exam questions were split into three categories:

1. Independent approach to a problem. Questions that give students an issue to investigate or some raw data and then ask them how

they would analyse it and why. E.g. 'You have data on tuition fees and the number of UCAS university applicants from 1990–2010. You wish to understand how the rise in tuition fees has affected the number of applicants. Which method do you use and why?'

2. Abstract/theoretical econometrics. Questions where no actual data or problem is mentioned, but a student is either asked mathematical questions about statistical/probability theory, or asked to manipulate regression models and test statistics at a purely abstract level.

3. Interpreting a given result or applying a suggested approach. Questions where a student is given a particular set of results or econometric method and asked to apply, interpret or evaluate it. Examples would be performing hypothesis tests from a given regression, or discussing omitted variable bias (either in general or for a specific case).

Furthermore, where possible we recorded the percentage of the marks for the *entire module*, as opposed to just the final exam (given by the course outline), that were given for an independent statistical report or project done outside the exam room.

Finally, a series of yes/no questions were asked about each module, with both course outlines and exams used to come to a conclusion. These included 'is the course mostly linear regression (more than two-thirds)?' and 'is there critical discussion of data, data sources, etc.?'

References

Aashish, Velkar. 'Review of CORE eBook', 2016. Available at: http://www.post-crasheconomics.com/review-of-core-ebook/ (accessed 27 April 2016).

Achen, Christopher. 'Let's put garbage-can regressions and garbage-can probits where they belong', *Conflict Management and Peace Science* 22(4) (2005): 327–39.

Ackerman, Frank, and Stanton, Elizabeth A. *Climate Economics: The State of the Art*. Report. Stockholm Environment Institute-US Center, 2011.

Akam, Simon. 'The British umpire: how the IFS became the most influential voice in the economic debate', *The Guardian*, 15 March 2016. Available at: http://www.theguardian.com/business/2016/mar/15/british-umpire-how-institute-fiscal-studies-became-most-influential-voice-in-uk-economic-debate (accessed 24 April 2016).

Aldred, Jonathan. 'Ethics and climate change cost–benefit analysis: Stern and after', Environmental Economy and Policy Research Discussion Paper Series, 2009.

Aldred, Jonathan. *The Skeptical Economist: Revealing the Ethics Inside Economics*. London: Earthscan, 2009.

Allgood, Sam, Bosshardt, William, van der Klaauw, Wilbert, and Watts, Michael. 'Is economics coursework, or majoring in economics, associated with different civic behaviors?', *The Journal of Economics Education* 43(3) (2012): 248–68.

Anderson, Robert. *British Universities Past and Present*. London: Hambledon Continuum, 2006.

Angrist, Joshua D., and Pischke, Stephen. 'The credibility revolution in empirical economics: how better research design is taking the con out of econometrics', *Journal of Economic Perspectives* 24(2) (2010): 3–30.

Angrist, Joshua D., and Pischke, Stephen. *Mostly Harmless Econometrics: An Empiricist's Companion*. Princeton, NJ: Princeton University Press, 2009.

Aristotle. *The Politics*. London: Penguin, 1992.

Association of American Schools and Colleges. 'What is a 21st century liberal education?' Available at: https://www.aacu.org/leap/what-is-a-liberal-education (accessed 22 April 16).

Association of Heterodox Economists. 'Submission from the Association of Heterodox Economics to the consultation on the QAA Benchmark Statement on Economics', 2016. Available at: https://www.business.unsw.edu.au/research-site/societyofhetero doxeconomists-site/Documents/QAA Benchmark.pdf (accessed 27 April 2016).

Atkinson, Tony. *Inequality: What Can Be Done*. Cambridge, MA: Harvard University Press, 2015.

Backhouse, Roger E. *The Penguin History of Economics*. London: Penguin, 2002.

Backhouse, Roger E. *The Puzzle of Modern Economics: Science or Ideology?* Cambridge: Cambridge University Press, 2011.

Ball, Laurence, and Mankiw, Gregory N. 'The NAIRU in theory and practice', *Journal of Economic Perspectives* 16(4) (2002): 115–36.

Barr, Nicholas. 'Income-contingent student loans: an idea whose time has come', in G. K. Shaw (ed.), *Economics, Culture and Education – Essays in Honour of Mark Blaug*. Aldershot: Edward Elgar, 1991, 155–70.

Barria, Carlos. 'PM Cameron says Britain should stand up for Hong Kong rights', *Reuters*, 15 October 2014. Available at: http://in.reuters.com/article/hongkong-china-britain-idINKCN0I 41WF20141015 (accessed 24 April 2016).

Barro, Robert, and Gordon, David. 'Rules, discretion and reputation in a model of monetary policy', *Journal of Monetary Economics* 12(1) (1983): 101–21.

Bateman, Victoria. 'Is economics a sexist science?', *Times Higher Education*, 15 September 2015. Available at: https://www.timeshighereducation.com/blog/is-economics-a-sexist-science (accessed 25 April 2016).

BBC. 'Barack Obama says Brexit would leave UK at the "back of the queue" on trade', 22 April 2016. Available at: http://www.bbc.co.uk/news/uk-36115138 (accessed 27 April 2016).

BBC. 'UK economy records fastest growth since 2007', 27 January 2015. Available at: http://www.bbc.co.uk/news/business-30999206 (accessed 24 April 2016).

Becker, Gary S. *A Treatise on the Family*. Cambridge, MA: Harvard University Press, 1981.

Beckett, Margaret. *Learning the Lessons from Defeat Taskforce Report.* Report. Labour Party, 2015.

Bernanke, Ben. 'Deflation: making sure it doesn't happen again'. Speech, National Economists Club, Washington DC, 2002. Available at: http://www.federalreserve.gov/boarddocs/speeches/2002/200211 21/default.htm (accessed 24 April 2016).

Bernstein, Michael. 'American economics and the national security state, 1941–1953', *Radical History Review* 63 (Fall 1995): 9–26.

Bernstein, Michael A. *A Perilous Progress: Economists and Public Purpose in Twentieth-Century America.* Princeton, NJ: Princeton University Press, 2001.

Bezemer, Dirk. *No One Saw This Coming. Understanding Financial Crisis through Accounting Models.* University of Groningen, Research Institute SOM (Systems, Organisations and Management), 2009.

Blanchard, Olivier. 'The state of macro'. *NBER Working Paper* no. 14259, 2008.

Blanco, Laura, and Mumford, Karen. *Royal Economic Society Women's Committee Survey on the Gender and Ethnic Balance of Academic Economics 2010.* Report. Royal Economics Society, October 2010. Available at: http://www.res.org.uk/ SpringboardWebApp/userfiles/res/file/Womens%20Committee/ Biennial%20Report/Womens%20Committee%202010%20sur vey%20report%202010.pdf (accessed 25 April 2016).

Blaug, Mark. 'The formalist revolution of the 1950s', *Journal of History of Economic Thought* 25(2) (2003): 145–56.

Bourne, Ryan, and Knox, Tim. *A Distorted Debate: The Need for Clarity on Debt, Deficit and Coalition Aims.* Report. Centre for Policy Studies, 2012.

Brady, Phelim. 'Mind the supervision gap', *Varsity*, 10 March 2013. Available at: http://www.varsity.co.uk/news/5787 (accessed 22 April 2016).

Breiman, Leo. 'Statistical modeling: the two cultures (with comments and a rejoinder by the author)', *Statistical Science* 16(3) (2001): 199–231.

Briefing 43: The Poorest Regions of the UK are the Poorest in North-West Europe. Inequality Briefing, 2016. Available at: http://inequalitybriefing.org/brief/briefing-43-the-poorest-regions-of-the-uk-are-the-poorest-in-northern- (accessed 24 April 2016).

British Association of Social Workers. 'The Code of Ethics for Social Work Statement of Principles', 2012. Available at: https://www. basw.co.uk/codeofethics/ (accessed 22 April 2016).

British Economic Association. 'The British Economic Association', *The Economic Journal* 1(1) (1891): 1–14.

Britton, Jack, Dearden, Lorraine, Shephard, Neil, and Vignoles, Anna. *How English Domiciled Graduate Earnings Vary with Gender, Institution Attended, Subject and Socioeconomic Background*. Report. Institute for Fiscal Studies, 2016.

Buchanan, Mark. 'Economists are blind to the limits of growth', *Bloomberg View*, 5 October 2014. Available at: http://www. bloombergview.com/articles/2014-10-05/economists-are-blind-to-the-limits-of-growth (accessed 24 April 2016).

Callon, Michel. 'The democratization of democracy', in Michel Callon, Pierre Lascoumbes and Yannick Barthe, *Acting in an Uncertain World: An Essay on Technical Democracy*. Cambridge, MA: MIT Press, 2009.

Cambridge Society of Economic Pluralism. *CSEP Survey of Economics Students: Is it Time for Change at Cambridge?* Report. Cambridge Society of Economic Pluralism, June 2014.

Cameron, David. 'Transforming the British economy: coalition strategy for economic growth'. Speech given in Shipley, 2010. Available at: http://www.britishpoliticalspeech.org/speech-arch ive.htm?speech=351 (accessed 24 April 2016).

Carlin, Wendy. 'Economics explains our world – but economics degrees don't', *Financial Times*, 17 November 2013. Available at: http:// www.ft.com/cms/s/0/74cd0b94-4de6-11e3-8fa5-00144feabdc0. html#axzz46qYfHtC0 (accessed 27 April 2016).

Carrick-Hagenbath, Jessica, and Epstein, Gerald. 'Dangerous inter-connectedness: economists' conflicts of interest, ideology and financial crisis', *Cambridge Journal of Economics* 36 (January 2012): 43–63.

Chang, Ha-Joon. *23 Things They Don't Tell You About Capitalism*. New York: Bloomsbury, 2011.

Chang, Ha-Joon. *Economics: A Users Guide*. London: Penguin, 2014.

Chetty, Raj. 'Yes, economics is a science', *New York Times*, 20 October 2013. Available at: http://www.nytimes.com/2013/ 10/21/opinion/yes-economics-is-a-science.html (accessed 21 April 2016).

Chwieroth, Jeffrey M., *Capital Ideas: The IMF and the Rise of Financial Liberalization*. Princeton, NJ: Princeton University Press, 2010.

Coase, Ronald. 'Opening speech to ISNIE 1999'. Available at: https://coase.org/coasespeech.htm (accessed 25 April 2016).

Cogley, Timothy, and Sargent, Thomas J. 'The market price of risk and the equity premium: a legacy of the Great Depression?', *Journal of Monetary Economics* 55(3) (2008): 454–76.

Collins, Jason. 'Please, not another bias! The problem with behavioral economics', *Evonomics*, 2015. http://evonomics.com/please-not-another-bias-the-problem-with-behavioral-economics/ (accessed 21 April 2016).

Conlin, Michael, O'Donoghue, Ted, and Vogelsang, Timothy J. 'Projection bias in catalog orders', *American Economic Review* 97(4) (2007): 1217–49.

Contribution of the Arts and Culture Industry to the National Economy. Report for Arts Council England. Centre for Economics and Business Research, 2015.

Cooter, Robert, and Rappoport, Peter. 'Were the Ordinalists wrong about welfare economics?', *Journal of Economic Literature* 22(2) (1984): 507–30.

Coyle, Diane, and Wren-Lewis, Simon. 'A note from Diane Coyle and Simon Wren-Lewis', *Royal Economic Society Newsletter* 169 (April 2015): 15.

Crafts, Nick. '"Post-neoclassical Endogenous Growth Theory": what are its policy implications?', *Oxford Review of Economic Policy* 12(2) (1996): 30–47.

Daly, Herman E. *Ecological Economics and the Ecology of Economics: Essays in Criticism*. Northampton, MA: Edward Elgar, 1999.

Day, Peter. 'Changing how economics is taught', BBC, 3 March 2016. Available at: http://www.bbc.co.uk/news/business-35686623 (accessed 27 April 2016).

Dearing, Ronald. *The Dearing Report: Higher Education in the Learning Society*. Report. London: Her Majesty's Stationery Office, 1997. Available at: http://www.educationengland.org.uk/documents/dearing1997/dearing1997.html (accessed 24 April 2016).

Department for Business, Innovation & Skills. *Participation Rates in Higher Education: Academic Years 2006/2007–2013/2014 (Provisional)*. Report. September 2015.

Diamond, Arthur. 'The core journals of economics', *Current Contents* 21 (January 1989): 4–11.

Dinmore, Guy. 'Monti gets approval for labour reforms', *Financial Times*, 27 June 2012. Available at: https://next.ft.com/content/8d2cf956-c070-11e1-9372-00144feabdc0 (accessed 25 April 2016).

Dinmore, Guy, Sanderson, Rachel, and Spiegel, Peter. 'Straight-talking Monti boosts Italy's hopes', *Financial Times*, 10 November 2011. Available at: https://next.ft.com/content/48461414-0bb5-11e1-9a61-00144feabdc0 (accessed 25 April 2016).

Dinmore, Guy, and Segreti, Guilia. 'Italy races to install Monti government', *Financial Times*, 13 November 2011. Available at: https://next.ft.com/content/f8106b1a-0e21-11e1-91e5-00144feab dc0 (accessed 25 May 2016).

The Distributional Effects of Asset Purchases. Report. Bank of England: Quarterly Bulletin Q3, 2012.

Donelly, Sue. 'William Beveridge's advice for new students', London School of Economics History, 7 October 2014. Available at: http://blogs.lse.ac.uk/lsehistory/2014/10/07/william-beveridges-advice-for-new-students/ (accessed 22 April 2016).

Dow, Sheila, 'Codes of ethics for economists: a pluralist view', *Economic Thought* 2(1) (2013): 20–9.

Dubner, Stephen J., and Steven D. Levitt. *Superfreakonomics: Global Cooling, Patriotic Prostitutes and Why Suicide Bombers Should Buy Life Insurance*. London: Penguin, 2010.

Economics, Education and Unlearning: Economics Education at the University of Manchester. Report. Post-Crash Economics Society, 2014. Available at: http://www.post-crasheconomics.com/economics-education-and-unlearning/ (accessed 27 April 2016).

The Economics Network. 'Economics employers' survey 2014–15'. Available at: https://www.economicsnetwork.ac.uk/projects/sur veys/employers14-15 (accessed 22 April 2016).

Eggertsson, Gauti B., and Krugman, Paul. 'Debt, deleveraging, and the liquidity trap: a Fisher–Minsky–Koo approach', *The Quarterly Journal of Economics* 127(3) (2012): 1469–513.

Emmison, Mike. '"The economy": its emergence in media discourse', in Howard Davis and Paul Walton (eds), *Language, Image, Media*. Oxford: Blackwell, 1983.

Equality in Higher Education: Statistical Report 2013 Part 2: Students. Report. Equality Challenge Unit, November 2013.

The Equality Trust. 'How has inequality changed?', 2016. Available at: https://www.equalitytrust.org.uk/how-has-inequality-changed (accessed 24 April 2016).

Evans, Robert. *Macroeconomic Forecasting: A Sociological Perspective*. London: Routledge, 1999.

Evans-Pritchard, Ambrose. 'Jeremy Corbyn's QE for the people is exactly what the world may soon need', *The Telegraph*, 16 September 2015. Available at: http://www.telegraph.co.uk/

finance/economics/11869701/Jeremy-Corbyns-QE-for-the-people-is-exactly-what-the-world-may-soon-need.html (accessed 24 April 2016).

Farmer, Roger. 'Teaching economics', 23 April 2014. Available at: http://rogerfarmerblog.blogspot.co.uk/2014/04/teaching-economics.html (accessed 25 April 2016).

Ferguson, Charles. 'Heist of the century: university corruption and the financial crisis', *The Guardian*, 21 May 2012. Available at: http://www.theguardian.com/education/2012/may/21/heist-cen tury-university-corruption (accessed 21 April 16).

Ferrari-Filho, Fernando, and Conceicao, Octavio. 'The concept of uncertainty in post-Keynesian theory and in institutional economics', *Journal of Economic Issues* 39(3) (2005): 579–94.

Fine, Ben, and Milonakis, Dimitris. *From Economics Imperialism to Freakonomics: The Shifting Boundaries between Economics and Other Social Sciences*. London: Routledge, 2009.

Flitter, Emily, Cook, Christina, and Da Costa, Pedro. 'Special report: for some professors, disclosure is academic', *Reuters*, 20 December 2010. Available at: http://www.reuters.com/article/2010/12/20/us-academics-conflicts-idUSTRE6BJ3LF20101220 (accessed 21 April 2016).

Foundation for European Economic Development. 'Plea for a pluralistic and rigorous economics', *American Economic Review* 82(2) (1992).

Fourcade, Marion. *Economists and Societies: Discipline and Profession in the United States, Britain, and France, 1890s to 1990s*. Princeton, NJ: Princeton University Press, 2009.

Fourcade, Marion, Ollion, Etienne, and Algan, Yann. 'The superiority of economists', *Journal of Economic Perspectives* 21(1) (2015): 89–114.

Freedman, David A. 'Statistical models and shoe leather', *Sociological Methodology* 21 (1991): 291–313.

Freeman, Alan. 'The economists of tomorrow: the case for a pluralist subject benchmark statement for economics', *International Review of Economics Education* 8(2) (2009): 23–40.

Freire, Paulo. *Education: The Practice of Freedom*. London: Writers and Readers Publishing Cooperative, 1976.

Friedman, Milton. *Optimum Quantity of Money*. Chicago: Aldine, 1969.

Friedman, Milton. 'The role of government in education', in Robert A. Solo (ed.), *Economics and the Public Interest*. New Brunswick, NJ: Rutgers University Press, 1955, 123–44.

Fudenberg, Drew. 'Advancing beyond advances in behavioral economics', *Journal of Economic Literature* 44(3) (2006): 694–711.

Fullbrook, Edward. 'To observe or not to observe: complementary pluralism in physics and economics', *Real-World Economics Review* 62(4) (2012): 20–8.

Furedi, Frank. 'Satisfaction and its discontents', *Times Higher Education*, 8 March 2012. Available at: https://www.timeshigher education.com/features/satisfaction-and-its-discontents/419238. article (accessed 22 April 2016).

Galbraith, James K. 'Who are these economists, anyway?', *The NEA Higher Education Journal* (Fall 2009).

Galbraith, John Kenneth. *The New Industrial State*. Boston: Houghton Mifflin, 1967.

Gapper, John. 'Capitalism: in search of balance – FT.Com', *Financial Times*, 23 December 2013. Available at: http://www.ft.com/ cms/s/0/4a0b8168-6bc0-11e3-a216-00144feabdc0.html#axzz4 6k4tODTg (accessed 24 April 2016).

Giles, Chris. 'A formula for teaching economics', *Financial Times*, 11 November 2013. Available at: http://www.ft.com/cms/ s/0/12e558da-4adc-11e3-8c4c-00144feabdc0.html#axzz46qDSI-Etb (accessed 27 April 2016).

Giles, Chris. 'Team McDonnell: meet Labour's seven economic advisers', *Financial Times*, 28 September 2015. Available at: http:// www.ft.com/cms/s/0/96534d2e-65c1-11e5-a28b-50226830d644. html#axzz46LyM6emQ (accessed 25 April 2016).

Giles, Chris. 'Treasury's Brexit analysis: what it says – and what it doesn't', *Financial Times*, 18 April 2016. Available at: https:// next.ft.com/content/c15cd060-0550-11e6-96e5-f85cb08b0730 (accessed 27 April 2016).

Godley, Wynne, and Lavoie, Marc. *Monetary Economics: An Integrated Approach to Credit, Money, Income, Production and Wealth*. Basingstoke: Palgrave Macmillan, 2007.

Gombrich, Carl. 'Liberal education for a complex world: the challenge of remaining open'. Available at: http://www.carlgombrich.org/ liberal-education-for-a-complex-world/ (accessed 22 April 2016).

Gorgoni, Sara. 'University of Greenwich revises its economics programmes to enhance pluralism and real world economics', Rethinking Economics blog, 14 December 2014. Available at: http://rethinkingeconomics.blogspot.co.uk/2014/12/university-of-greenwich-revises-its.html (accessed 22 April 2016).

Grasselli, Matheus, and Costa Lima, Marcello. 'An analysis of the Keen model for credit expansion, asset price bubbles and financial fragility', *Mathematics and Financial Economics* 6(3) (2012): 191–210.

Guglielmo, Mark. 'The contribution of economists to military intelligence during World War II', *Journal of Economic History* 68(1) (2008): 109–50.

Haldane, Andrew. 'The revolution in economics', foreword to the Post-Crash Economics Society Report, *Economics, Education and Unlearning: Economics Education at the University of Manchester*, April 2015, 3–6. Available at: http://www.post-crasheconomics. com/economics-education-and-unlearning/ (accessed 22 April 2016).

Hamermesh, Daniel S. 'Six decades of top economics publishing: who and how?', *Journal of Economic Literature* 51(1) (2013): 162–72.

Harford, Tim. 'Black-Scholes: the maths formula linked to the financial crash', BBC, 2012. Available at: http://www.bbc.co.uk/news/ magazine-17866646 (accessed 24 April 2016).

Hart, Keith, and Hann, Chris. 'Introduction: learning from Polanyi 1', in Chris Hann and Keith Hart (eds), *Market and Society The Great Transformation Today*. Cambridge: Cambridge University Press, 2011.

Hayek, Friedrich A. 'The use of knowledge in society', *American Economic Review* 35(4) (1945): 519–30.

Hendry, David F., and Mizon, Graham E. 'Unpredictability in economic analysis, econometric modeling and forecasting', *Journal of Econometrics* 182(1) (2014): 186–95.

Hepburn, Cameron. 'Incomplete climate models lead to complacency', *Financial Times*, 1 April 2014. Available at: https://next. ft.com/__anon-opt-in/cms/s/0/d54c0de6-b8e2-11e3-835e-00144 feabdc0.html (accessed 27 April 2016).

Hicks, John R. '"IS-LM": an explanation', *Journal of Post Keynesian Economics* 3(2) (1980–81): 139–54.

Hicks, John R. 'Mr. Keynes and the 'classics': a suggested interpretation', *Econometrica* 5(2) (1937): 147–59.

Higher Education Funding Council England. *Guide to Funding 2015–16: How HEFCE Allocates its Funds*. Report, March 2015.

Higher Education Statistics Authority. 'Income and expenditure of UK higher education providers 2014/15'. Available at: https:// www.hesa.ac.uk/stats-finance (accessed 25 April 2016).

Hirschman, Daniel, and Berman, Elizabeth. 'Do economists make policies? On the political effects of economics', *Socio-Economic Review* 12(4) (2014): 779–811.

HM Treasury. *The Green Book: Appraisal and Evaluation in Central Government*. Treasury Guidance, July 2011.

Holehouse, Matthew. 'NHS spends £23m a year on translators', *The Telegraph*, 6 February 2012. Available at: http://www.telegraph. co.uk/news/health/news/9063200/NHS-spends-23m-a-year-on-translators.html (accessed 25 April 2016).

Hope, Kerin. 'Papademos named new Greek PM', *Financial Times*, 10 November 2011. Available at: https://next.ft.com/content/8fb2b3c8-0afe-11e1-ae56-00144feabdc0 (accessed 25 April 2016).

Hope, Kerin. 'Wanted – a prime minister', *Financial Times*, 7 November 2011. Available at: https://next.ft.com/content/0cfb4bf6-08ca-11e1-9fe8-00144feabdc0 (accessed 25 April 2016).

How Economics Is Used in Government Decision Making. Report. New Economics Foundation, 2013.

Hussey, Trevor, and Smith, Patrick. *The Trouble with Higher Education: A Critical Examination of our Universities*. Abingdon: Routledge, 2010.

International Monetary Fund. *United Kingdom Selected Issues*. Report. 1 June 2016. Available at: https://www.imf.org/external/pubs/ft/scr/2016/cr16169.pdf (accessed 8 September 2016).

An International Student Call for Pluralism in Economics. International Student Initiative for Pluralism in Economics, 5 May 2014. Available at: http://www.isipe.net/open-letter/ (accessed 27 April 2016).

Jevons, William S. *The Theory of Political Economy*. London: Macmillan, 2nd edn, 1879.

Johnes, Geraint. 'Education and economic growth', *Lancaster University Management School Working Paper* 19, 2006. Available at: http://www.lancaster.ac.uk/media/lancaster-university/content-assets/documents/lums/economics/working-papers/EducationEconomicGrowth.pdf (accessed 22 April 2016).

Johnson, Paul. 'We economists must face the plain truth that the referendum showed our failings', *The Times*, 28 June 2016. Available at: http://www.thetimes.co.uk/article/paul-johnson-s5pnw9rn0 (accessed 8 September).

Johnston, James, and Reeves, Alan. 'Economics is becoming an elite subject for elite UK universities', Politics and Policy blog, London School of Economics, 11 November 2014. Available at: http://blogs.lse.ac.uk/politicsandpolicy/the-growth-of-elitism-in-the-uks-higher-education-system-the-case-of-economics/ (accessed 22 April 2016).

Johnston, James, Reeves, Alan, and Talbot, Steven. 'Has economics become an elite subject for elite UK universities?', *Oxford Review of Education* 40(5) (2014): 591–2.

Johnston, Ron, Jones, Kelvyn and Manley, David. 'Predicting the Brexit vote: getting the geography right (more or less)', LSE British Politics and Policy blog, 2 July 2016. Available at: http://blogs.lse.ac.uk/politicsandpolicy/the-brexit-vote-getting-the-geography-more-or-less-right/ (accessed 8 September 2016).

Jones, Owen D. 'Time-shifted rationality and the law of law's leverage: behavioral economics meets behavioral biology', *Northwestern University Law Review* 95 (2001): 1141–206.

Joseph Rowntree Foundation. *Brexit vote explained: poverty, low skills and lack of opportunities*, 31 August 2016. Available at: https://www.jrf.org.uk/brexit-vote-explained-poverty-low-skills-and-lack-opportunities (accessed 8 September 2016).

Josse, Josef. 'Merkel's good politics and bad economics', *Financial Times*, 4 September 2012. Available at: https://next.ft.com/content/89c270d6-f5ed-11e1-a6c2-00144feabdc0 (accessed 24 April 2016).

Kaldor, Nicholas. *The Scourge of Monetarism*. Oxford: Oxford University Press, 1982.

Kay, John. 'We can reform the economics curriculum without creating new disciplines', 15 April 2015. Available at: http://www.johnkay.com/2015/04/15/we-can-reform-the-economics-curriculum-without-creating-new-disciplines (accessed 18 July 2016).

Keen, Steve. *Debunking Economics: The Naked Emperor Dethroned?*. London: Zed Books, 2011.

Keen, Steve. 'Finance and economic breakdown: modeling Minsky's "Financial Instability Hypothesis"', *Journal of Post Keynesian Economics* 17(4) (1995): 607–35.

Keen, Steve. 'For a pluralist education, come to Kingston', *Steve Keen's Debtwatch*, 8 May 2014. Available at: http://www.debtdeflation.com/blogs/2014/05/08/for-a-pluralist-education-come-to-kingston/ (accessed 22 April 2016).

Keen, Steve. 'Why Krugman needs a new school of thought', *The Australian*, 28 April 2014. Available at http://www.theaustralian.com.au/business/business-spectator/why-krugman-needs-a-new-school-of-thought/news-story/7e36b530ca7bb990a1258596e49a8214 (accessed 25 April 2016).

Keynes, John M. 'Alfred Marshall, 1842–1924', *The Economic Journal* 34(135) (1924): 311–72.

Keynes, John M. *The General Theory of Employment, Interest and Money*. New York: Harcourt, Brace & World, 1936.

Klein, Daniel B., and Stern, Charlotta. 'Is there a free-market economist in the house? The policy views of American Economic Association members', *American Journal of Economics and Sociology* 66(2) (2007): 309–34.

Krueger, Anne. 'Report of the Commission on Graduate Education in Economics', *Journal of Economic Literature* 29(3) (1991): 1035–53.

Krugman, Paul. 'Economists and inequality', *New York Times*, 8 January 2016. Available at: http://krugman.blogs.nytimes.com/2016/01/08/economists-and-inequality/ (accessed 24 April 2016).

Krugman, Paul. 'Frustrations of the heterodox', *New York Times*, 25 April 2014. Available at: http://krugman.blogs.nytimes.com/2014/04/25/frustrations-of-the-heterodox (accessed 25 April 2016).

Krugman, Paul. 'How did economists get it so wrong?', *New York Times*, 2 September 2009. Available at: http://www.nytimes.com/2009/09/06/magazine/06Economic-t.html?pagewanted=print&_r=0 (accessed 27 April 2016).

Krugman, Paul. 'Why weren't alarm bells ringing?', *The New York Review of Books*, 23 October 2014. Available at: http://www.nybooks.com/articles/2014/10/23/why-werent-alarm-bells-ringing/ (accessed 21 April 2016).

L'avenir des sciences économiques à l'Université en France. Report. Government of France, 5 June 2014. Available at: http://cache.media.enseignementsup-recherche.gouv.fr/file/Formations_et_diplomes/05/1/Rapport_Hautcoeur2014_328051.pdf (accessed 25 May 2016).

Lanchester, John. *How to Speak Money*. London: Faber & Faber, 2015.

Lanchester, John. *Whoops! Why Everyone Owes Everyone and No One Can Pay*. London: Allen Lane, 2010.

Lavoie, Marc. 'A primer on endogenous credit-money', in Louis-Philippe Rochon and Sergio Rossi, *Modern Theories of Money: The Nature and Role of Money in Capitalist Economies*. Cheltenham: Edward Elgar, 2003, 506–43.

Lazonick, William. *Business Organization and the Myth of the Market Economy*. Cambridge: Cambridge University Press, 1991.

Lee, Frederic S., Pham, Xuan, and Gu, Gyun. 'The UK Research Assessment Exercise and the narrowing of UK economics', *Cambridge Journal of Economics* 37(4) (2013): 693–717.

Lee, Frederic S., and Harley, Sandra. 'Peer review, the Research

Assessment Exercise and the demise of non-mainstream economics', *Capital and Class* 66 (1998): 23–51.

Levitt, Steven D., and Dubner, Stephen J. *Freakonomics: A Rogue Economist Explores the Hidden Side of Everything.* London: Penguin, 2007.

Linning, Stephanie. 'Who said crime doesn't pay? Counting prostitution and drugs in the GDP figure has seen the UK's economy overtake France as fifth largest in the world', *Mail Online*, 27 December 2014. Available at: http://www.dailymail.co.uk/news/article-2888416/Who-said-crime-doesn-t-pay-Counting-prostitution-drugs-GDP-figure-seen-UK-s-economy-overtake-France-fifth-largest-world.html (accessed 24 April 2016).

Loewenstein, George, and Ubel, Peter. 'Economics behaving badly', *New York Times*, 14 July 2010. Available at: http://www.nytimes.com/2010/07/15/opinion/15loewenstein.html (accessed 21 April 2016).

Logan, Robert A. 'Science mass communication its conceptual history', *Science Communication* 23(2) (2001): 135–63.

Lucas, Robert E. '2003 annual report essay – the Industrial Revolution: past and future' *Federal Reserve Bank of Minneapolis*, 2003.

Lucas, Robert E. 'Econometric policy evaluation: a critique', in Karl Brunner and Allan Meltzer (eds), *The Phillips Curve and Labor Markets*. New York: North Holland, 1976, 19–46.

Lucas, Robert E. 'Macroeconomic priorities', *American Economic Review* 93(1) (2003): 1–14.

MacKenzie, Donald, and Millo, Yuval. 'Constructing a market-performing theory: the historical sociology of a financial derivatives exchange', *American Journal of Sociology* 109(1) (2003): 107–45.

Mance, Henry. 'Britain has had enough of experts, says Gove', *Financial Times*, 3 June 2016. Available at: http://www.ft.com/cms/s/0/3be49734-29cb-11e6-83e4-abc22d5d108c.html#axzz4JZbdCmwx (accessed 8 September 2016)

Mankiw, Gregory. *Principles of Economics.* Fort Worth, TX: Dryden Press, 1998.

Manson, Allan, McCallum, Pamela, and Halven, Larry. *Report of the Ad Hoc Investigatory Committee into the Department of Economics at the University of Manitoba.* Report. Canadian Association of University Teachers, 2015.

Marsh, Alex. 'Economics budo', 26 April 2014. Available at: http://www.alexsarchives.org/2014/04/economics-budo/ (accessed 25 April 2016).

Martyn, Rafe. 'Beyond the economic: the true value of Europe', The

Disraeli Room, Respublica, 23 March 2016. Available at: http://www.respublica.org.uk/disraeli-room-post/2016/03/23/beyond-economic-true-value-europe/ (accessed 25 April 2016).

Marx, Karl. *Capital Vol. I – Chapter Twenty-Five*, 1867 [online]. Available at: https://www.marxists.org/archive/marx/works/1867-c1/ch25.htm#S3. (accessed 24 April 2016).

McDonnell, Duncan. 'The rise of governments led by technocrats in Europe illustrates the failure of mainstream political parties', London School of Economic's European Politics and Policy blog, 11 June 2013. Available at: http://blogs.lse.ac.uk/europpblog/2013/06/11/the-rise-of-governments-led-by-technocrats-in-europe-illustrates-the-failure-of-mainstream-political-parties/ (accessed 25 April 2016).

McGettigan, Andrew. *The Great University Gamble: Money, Markets and the Future of Higher Education*. London: Pluto Press, 2013.

McLeay, Michael, Radia, Amar, and Ryland, Thomas. 'Money creation in the modern economy', *Bank of England Quarterly Bullet, Q1 2014*. Available at: http://www.bankofengland.co.uk/publications/documents/quarterlybulletin/2014/qb14q1prereleasemoneycreation.pdf (accessed 24 April 2016).

Measuring Our Value. Report. British Library, 2013.

Media Coverage of the 2015 Campaign. Report. Loughborough University Communication Research Centre, 2015.

Mental Health and Work: United Kingdom. Report. OECD Publishing, 2014.

Mikesell, Raymond F. *The Bretton Woods Debates: A Memoir*. Princeton, NJ: International Finance Section, Dept. of Economics, Princeton University, 1994.

Mill, John, S. *Inaugural Address Delivered to the University of St Andrews*. London: Longmans, Green, Reader, and Dyer, 1867. Available at: https://archive.org/details/inauguraladdres00millgoog (accessed 22 April 2016).

Minsky, Hyman P. 'The Financial Instability Hypothesis', Levy Economics Institute Working Paper No. 74, 1992.

Mitchell, Timothy. 'Fixing the economy', *Cultural Studies* 12(1) (1998): 82–101.

Moran, Mick. *The Regulatory State: High Modernism and Hyper-Innovation*. Oxford: Oxford University Press, 2003.

Morley, Louise. *Theorising Quality in Higher Education*. London: Institute of Education, 2014.

Mount, Ian. 'Spain gets a questionable GDP boost, thanks to drugs and prostitution', *Fortune*, 8 October 2014. Available at: http://

fortune.com/2014/10/08/spain-gdp-drugs-prostitution/ (accessed 24 April 2016).

MSNBC. 'Thomas Piketty, Paul Krugman and Joseph Stiglitz: the genius of economics', YouTube, March 2015. Available at: https://www.youtube.com/watch?v=Si4iyyJDa7c (accessed 21 April 2016).

Nik-Khan, Edward. 'A tale of two auctions', *Journal of Institutional Economics* 4(1) (2008): 73–97.

Nussbaum, Martha. *Not for Profit: Why Democracy Needs the Humanities*. Princeton, NJ: Princeton University Press, 2012.

O'Connor, Sarah. 'Drugs and prostitution add £10bn to UK economy – FT.Com', 29 May 2014. Available at: http://www.ft.com/cms/s/2/65704ba0-e730-11e3-88be-00144feabdc0.html#axzz46k4tODTg (accessed 24 April 2016).

Oreskes, Naomi. 'Beyond the ivory tower: the scientific consensus on climate change', *Science* 306(5702) (2004).

Perman, Roger, Ma, Yue, and McGilvray, James. *Natural Resource and Environmental Economics*. London: Longman, 1996.

Pickering, Will. 'Zero-hours contracts: a UCU briefing', University and College Union, March 2014.

Piketty, Thomas. *Capital in the Twenty-First Century*. Cambridge, MA: Harvard University Press, 2014.

Post-Autistic Economics Network. 'Opening up economics: a proposal by Cambridge students', 14 June 2001. Available at: http://www.paecon.net/petitions/Camproposal.htm. (accessed 27 April 2016).

Post-Autistic Economics Network. 'Open letter from economics students to professors and others responsible for the teaching of this discipline', 2000. Available at: http://www.paecon.net/PAEtexts/ae-petition.htm (accessed 27 April 2016).

Post-Crash Economics Society. 'How should economics change? With Steve Keen, Diane Coyle and George Cooper'. Available at: https://www.youtube.com/watch?v=shZJNG1F6MM (accessed 27 April 2016).

Potts, Jason. *The New Evolutionary Microeconomics: Complexity, Competence, and Adaptive Behaviour*. Cheltenham: Edward Elgar, 2000.

Power, Heather. 'How valuable is the Queen to our economy?', *Business Life*, 31 May 2012. Available at: http://businesslife.ba.com/Ideas/Features/how-valuable-is-the-Queen-to-our-economy.html (accessed 24 April 2016).

Read on Get on: How Reading Can Help Children Escape Poverty. Report. Save the Children, 2014.

Read, Richard. 'A $280 college textbook busts budgets, but Harvard author Gregory Mankiw defends royalties', *The Oregonian*, 12 February 2015. Available at: http://www.oregonlive.com/education/index.ssf/2015/02/a_280_college_textbook_busts_b.html (accessed 22 April 2016).

Reay, Michael. 'The flexible unity of economics', *American Journal of Sociology* 118(1) (2012): 45–87.

Riley-Smith, Ben, and Wilkinson, Michael. 'Michael Gove compares experts warning against Brexit to Nazis who smeared Albert Einstein's work as he threatens to quit David Cameron's Cabinet', The Telegraph, 21 June 2016. Available at: http://www.telegraph.co.uk/news/2016/06/21/michael-gove-compares-experts-warning-against-brexit-to-nazis-wh/ (accessed 8 September 2016).

Robbins, Lionel. *An Essay on the Nature and Significance of Economic Science.* London: Macmillan, 2nd edn, 1935.

Robinson, Joan. *Collected Economic Papers Volume II.* Oxford: Blackwell, 1951.

Robinson, Joan. *Marx, Marshall and Keynes.* Delhi: University of Delhi, 1955.

Rodrik, Dani. *Economics Rules: The Rights and Wrongs of the Dismal Science.* New York: W. W. Norton, 2015.

Rolnick, Art, 'Interview with Thomas Sargent', Federal Reserve Bank of Minneapolis, 2010. Available at: https://minneapolisfed.org/publications/the-region/interview-with-thomas-sargent (accessed 25 April 2016).

Ross, Andrew. 'Message to applicants from Deputy Director GES', The Government Economic Service, undated. Available at: https://www.jiscmail.ac.uk/cgi-bin/webadmin?A3=ind1209&L=CHUDE&E=base64&P=4477856&B=--_003_799B56EC23F30340810F2D7B762611FD10F92CMBXP09dsmanacuk_&T=application%2Fmsword;%20name=%22Message%20to%20Applicants%20from%20Deputy%20Director%20GES.doc%22&N=Message%20to%20Applicants%20from%20Deputy%20Director%20GES.doc&attachment=q. (accessed 25 April 2016).

Rutter, Tamsin. 'The rise of nudge – the unit helping politicians to fathom human behaviour', The Guardian, 23 July 2015. Available at: http://www.theguardian.com/public-leaders-network/2015/jul/23/rise-nudge-unit-politicians-human-behaviour (accessed 24 April 2016).

Said, Edward. *Representations of the Intellectual: The 1993 Reith Lectures.* London: Vintage, 1994.

Samuelson, Paul A. 'Foreword', in Phillip Saunders and William Walstad (eds), *The Principles of Economics Course: A Handbook for Instructors*. New York: McGraw-Hill Publishing, 1990.

Samuelson, Paul. 'Unemployment ahead: a warning to the Washington expert', *The New Republic*, 11 September 1944: 297–9.

Schumpeter, Joseph. *Capitalism, Socialism and Democracy*. New York: Harper & Brothers, 1942.

Scott, James, C. *Seeing Like a State: How Certain Schemes to Improve the Human Condition Have Failed*. New Haven, CT: Yale University Press, 1999.

'Scottish independence: poll reveals who voted, how and why', *The Guardian*, 20 September 2014. Available at: http://www.theguardian.com/politics/2014/sep/20/scottish-independence-lord-ashcroft-poll (accessed 25 April 2016).

Securing a Sustainable Future for Higher Education. Report. Independent Review of Higher Education Funding & Student Finance, October 2010.

Self, Peter. *Econocrats and the Policy Process*. London: Macmillan, 1975.

Sen, Amartya, and Foster, James E. *On Economic Inequality*. Oxford: Clarendon Press, 1997.

Shattock, Michael. *Making Policy in British Higher Education 1945–2011*. Maidenhead: Open University Press, 2012.

Shortridge, Julie E., Falconi, Stefanie M., Zaitchik, Benjamin F., and Guikema, Seth D. 'Climate, agriculture, and hunger: statistical prediction of undernourishment using nonlinear regression and data-mining techniques', *Journal of Applied Statistics* 42(11) (2015): 2367–90.

Skidelsky, Robert. 'Reforming economics', 19 December 2014. Available at: Http://www.skidelskyr.com/site/article/reforming-economics/ (accessed 27 April 2016).

Sloman, John, and Wride, Alison. *Economics*. Harlow: Pearson, 7th edn, 2009.

Smith, Adam. *An Inquiry into the Nature and Causes of the Wealth of Nations*. London: Methuen, 1904.

Smith, Adam. *The Theory of Moral Sentiments*. Cambridge: Cambridge University Press 1790.

Smith, Yves. *ECONned: How Unenlightened Self Interest Damaged Democracy and Corrupted Capitalism*. New York: Palgrave Macmillan, 2010.

Solow, Robert. 'Dumb and dumber in macroeconomics', address

at Joe Stiglitz's 60th birthday conference, 25 October 2013. Available at: http://textlab.io/doc/927882/dumb-and-dumber-in-macroeconomics-robert-m.-solow-so (accessed 27 April 2016).

Sommer, Jeff. 'Robert Shiller: a skeptic and a Nobel winner', *The New York Times*, 19 October 2013. Available at: http://www.nytimes.com/2013/10/20/business/robert-shiller-a-skeptic-and-a-nobel-winner.html (accessed 21 April 2016).

Spanos, Aris. 'Theory testing in economics and the error-statistical perspective', in Deborah G. Mayo and Aris Spanos (eds), *Error and Inference: Recent Exchanges on Experimental Reasoning, Reliability, and the Objectivity and Rationality of Science*. Cambridge: Cambridge University Press, 202–46.

Spulber, Daniel F. *Famous Fables of Economics*. Malden, MA: Blackwell, 2002.

Stern, Nicholas. 'Economics: current climate models are grossly misleading', *Nature* 530(7591) (2016): 407–9.

Stern, Nicholas. *Stern Review: Report on the Economics of Climate Change*. Report. HM Treasury, 2006.

Stille, Alexander. 'Grounded by an income gap', *New York Times*, 15 December 2001. Available at: http://www.nytimes.com/2001/12/15/arts/15GAP.html?pagewanted=all (accessed 24 April 2016).

Stratton, Allegra. 'David Cameron aims to make happiness the new GDP', *The Guardian*, 14 November 2010. Available at: http://www.theguardian.com/politics/2010/nov/14/david-cameron-wellbeing-inquiry (accessed 25 April 2016).

Taylor, Matthew. 'The human welfare economy', Chief Executive's Lecture, RSA, July 2015. Available at: https://www.thersa.org/action-and-research/arc-news/chief-executives-lecture-2015-news/ (accessed 25 April 2016).

The Teaching Excellence Framework: Assessing Quality in Higher Education. Business Innovation and Skills Committee, Third Report of Session 2015–16. London: The Stationery Office, February 2016.

Tesfatsion, Leigh. 'Agent-based computational economics', *Scholarpedia* 2(2) (2007).

Tett, Gillian. 'Economists' tribal thinking', *The Atlantic*, 1 September 2015. Available at: http://www.theatlantic.com/business/archive/2015/09/economists-tribal-thinking/403075/ (accessed 24 April 2016).

'The thinking behind feminist economics', *The Economist*, 20 October 2015. Available at: http://www.economist.com/blogs/

economist-explains/2015/10/economist-explains-17 (accessed 27 April 2016).

Tirole, Jean. 'Market power and regulation', *Economic Sciences Prize Committee of the Royal Swedish Academy of Sciences* (2014): 1–54.

Tol, Richard. 'Bogus prophecies of doom will not fix the climate', *Financial Times*, 31 March 2014. Available at https://next.ft.com/content/e8d011fa-b8b5-11e3-835e-00144feabdc0. (accessed 21 April 2016).

Turner, Adair. *Between Debt and the Devil*. Oxford: Princeton University Press, 2015.

Turner, Adair. 'Preface', in Cambridge Society for Economic Pluralism, *CSEP Survey of Economics Students: Is it Time for Change at Cambridge?* Report. Cambridge Society of Economic Pluralism, June 2014.

Universities and College Union. 'The impact of student satisfaction surveys on staff in HE and FE institutions', October 2010. Available at: https://www.ucu.org.uk/brief_satissurveys (accessed 25 April 2016).

University of Glasgow. 'University of Glasgow graduate attributes'. Available at: http://www.gla.ac.uk/media/media_183776_en.pdf (accessed 22 April 2016).

University of Manchester Archives. 'Faculty of Economic and Social Studies – School of Economic Studies – Report of Council to the University Court 1996 Volume IA', 1996.

University of Manchester Archives. 'Faculty of Economic and Social Studies – Whole Faculty Overview – Report of Council to the University Court 1992', 1992.

University of Manchester. 'The purposes of a Manchester undergraduate education'. Available at: http://documents.manchester.ac.uk/display.aspx?DocID=9804 (accessed 22 April 2016).

Varoufakis, Yanis, and Arnsperger, Christian. 'What is neoclassical economics?', *Post-Autistic Economics Review* 38 (2006): 2–13.

Von Neumann, John, and Morgenstern, Oskar. *The Theory of Games and Economic Behaviour*. Princeton, NJ: Princeton University Press, 1944.

Waring, Marilyn. *If Women Counted: A New Feminist Economics*. San Francisco: Harper & Row, 1988.

Watt, Holly, and Dominiczak, Peter. 'Ed Miliband: school funding to rise under Labour', *The Telegraph*, 12 February 2015. Available at:

http://www.telegraph.co.uk/news/politics/ed-miliband/11408627/
Ed-Miliband-School-funding-to-rise-under-Labour.html (accessed
25 April 2016).

Weigold, Michael, F. 'Communicating science: a review of the literature', *Science Communication* 23(2) (2001): 164–93.

Wilson, David S., and Gowdy, John M. 'Evolution as a general theo-
retical framework for economics and public policy', *Journal of
Economic Behavior & Organization* 90, Supplement (June 2013):
S3–S10.

Wisman, John D. 'What drives inequality?', Working Papers,
American University, Department of Economics, 2015.

Wolf, Martin. 'Bring our elites closer to the people', *Financial
Times*, 2 February 2016. Available at: http://www.ft.com/cms/s/0/
94176826-c8fc-11e5-be0b-b7ece4e953a0.html#axzz46Sy5Kodx
(accessed 24 April 2016).

Wolf, Martin. 'The case for helicopter money', *Financial Times*,
12 February 2013. Available at: http://www.ft.com/cms/s/0/9bcf0
eea-6f98-11e2-b906-00144feab49a.html#axzz46V5sxFR8 (accessed 24 April 2016).

Wolf, Martin. *The Shifts and the Shocks: What We've Learned—and
Have Still to Learn—from the Financial Crisis*. London: Penguin,
2014.

Wood, Diana. 'Problem based learning', *British Medical Journal*,
8 February 2003. Available at: http://www.bmj.com/content/
326/7384/328 (accessed 22 April 2016).

Woodford, Neil. 'Good politics, bad economics', Woodford Funds,
14 January 2015. Available at https://woodfordfunds.com/good-
politics-bad-economics/ (accessed 24 April 2016).

Wooldridge, Jeffrey M. *Introductory Econometrics: A Modern
Approach*. Australia: South-Western College Publishing, 2003.

Wren-Lewis, Simon. 'When economics students rebel', 24 April
2014. Available at: http://mainlymacro.blogspot.co.uk/2014/04/
when-economics-students-rebel.html (accessed 25 April 2016).

Yang, Yuan, and Repapis, Costas. 'Pluralism & real-world economics: a new curriculum at Goldsmiths', Rethinking Economics blog,
16 October 2016. Available at: http://www.rethinkeconomics.org/
news/2015/10/pluralism-real-world-economics-a-new-curriculum-
at-goldsmiths/ (accessed 22 April 2016).

Young, Toby. 'A classical liberal education', *The Telegraph*, 19 April
2013. Available at: http://blogs.telegraph.co.uk/news/tobyyoung/
100213007/a-classical-liberal-education/ (accessed 8 June 2015).